D1712983

Lake Erie Stories

Struggle and Survival on a Freshwater Ocean

Lake Erie Stories

Struggle and Survival
on a Freshwater Ocean

CHAD FRASER

DUNDURN PRESS
TORONTO

Editor: Tony Hawke
Copy-editor: Shannon Whibbs
Design: Jennifer Scott
Printer: Webcom

Library and Archives Canada Cataloguing in Publication

Fraser, Chad
    Lake Erie stories : struggle and survival on a freshwater ocean / Chad Fraser.

ISBN 978-1-55002-782-2

    1. Erie, Lake--History. 2. Erie, Lake, Region--History.
I. Title.

F555.F73 2008   971.3'3   C2008-900389-6

1 2 3 4 5   12   11   10   09   08

Conseil des Arts Canada Council   ONTARIO ARTS COUNCIL
du Canada   for the Arts   CONSEIL DES ARTS DE L'ONTARIO

We acknowledge the support of the **Canada Council for the Arts** and the **Ontario Arts Council** for our publishing program. We also acknowledge the financial support of the **Government of Canada** through the **Book Publishing Industry Development Program** and **The Association for the Export of Canadian Books**, and the **Government of Ontario** through the **Ontario Book Publishers Tax Credit** program, and the **Ontario Media Development Corporation**.

Care has been taken to trace the ownership of copyright material used in this book. The author and the publisher welcome any information enabling them to rectify any references or credits in subsequent editions.

J. Kirk Howard, President

Printed and bound in Canada.
Printed on recycled paper.

www.dundurn.com

Dundurn Press
3 Church Street, Suite 500
Toronto, Ontario, Canada
M5E 1M2

Gazelle Book Services Limited
White Cross Mills
High Town, Lancaster, England
LA1 4XS

Dundurn Press
2250 Military Road
Tonawanda, NY
U.S.A. 14150

For Amy, who always keeps my bow turned into the wind.

Table of Contents

Introduction

Lake Erie is not a peaceful inland sea. Even a seaman who has seen the worst that the world's oceans could throw at a ship quickly learns to respect her unpredictable waters.

Captain Alexander McNeilledge, who created the first sailing chart of the north shore of Lake Erie in 1848, had this bit of advice for the captains who sailed the lake in his day:

> When you are anxious to have a good lookout kept, *you must keep it yourself* [author's emphasis]. Running for the land, or being anxious to make a light in stormy, hazy, or thick weather, let your officers be never so good, *be at the head of it yourself*, and of course you will pay more attention, having it on your mind and being the responsible man.

McNeilledge's book and chart are a revealing look at the life of a sailor on Lake Erie in the early days of settlement. It was a time when small communities, including Port Dover, where the old captain ended up settling down, were just beginning to emerge from untracked wilderness. The end of the War of 1812 — the last great conflict between Canada and the emerging industrial powerhouse to its south — had brought a lasting peace to the region, and cleared the way for the towns and cities that today line the shore to take root.

Captain Alexander McNeilledge, author of the first sailing charts of Lake Erie's north shore, was well known in Port Dover.

McNeilledge, who was born in Greenock, Scotland, in 1791, had spent much of his career on the ocean. His exploits are the stuff of seafaring legend: he first went to sea as a cabin boy at the age of eight, was shipwrecked on Long Island in 1807, saw the Duke of Wellington in Lisbon, and even caught a glimpse of Napoleon Bonaparte, the deposed emperor of France, in exile on the island of St. Helena in 1817. Even what he might have considered to be the more humdrum aspects of his time at sea are thrilling by modern standards. The captain covered huge swaths of the globe, sailing to ports as far afield as China, and running a naval blockade off Buenos Aires. And, for good measure, he endured robbery and plunder at the hands of pirates on the storied Spanish Main.

It is not hard to imagine, then, why McNeilledge was drawn to the quiet Canadian hinterland after such a frenetic career at sea. He first came to Port Dover in 1832, largely at the request of his brother, who had rebuilt an old mill in the town where, he hoped, Alexander could help him by serving as clerk and bookkeeper. Some time later, McNeilledge decided to expand his repertoire by dabbling in farming, as well.

But the life of a landlubber, predictably, could not hold the attention of the old captain for very long, and soon enough he heard the call of the freshwater ocean that now lay in his backyard. And, try as he might, McNeilledge couldn't resist. Soon he was back out on the water, sailing along both the north and south shores of Lake Erie on numerous ships and making a name for himself among the lake's growing fraternity of captains. Back on dry land, McNeilledge was a colourful figure in tiny Port Dover, where he produced a number of mementos, including drawings of ships, ports, and other images of marine life. During his spare time, he could usually be found down at the harbour, overseeing the comings and goings of the many sailing vessels and sharing tall tales of the sea with his fellow captains.

Still, even though he had experienced much during his long saltwater career, McNeilledge knew not to underestimate Lake Erie. Even in these early days of settlement, its temperamental nature was well known to those who sailed the lake or lived along its shores. The very existence of his chart and narrative about the many hazards of sailing the waters off the north shore speaks to the fact that the old captain spent a good deal of time worrying about his fellow sailors out on the lake. And he had good reason. Since the Welland Canal had opened in 1829, more and more ships were clogging Lake Erie, their holds stuffed with the food, stone, and lumber that were desperately needed to fuel the construction boom.

Not surprisingly, the increased traffic brought with it more and more shipwrecks — and a higher toll in human lives. Of his chart, McNeilledge says simply: "The courses and distances will be found to be pretty correct for any stranger to go by, and will often ease the mind of the man having the charge."

The Shallow Sea

Lake Erie is the second smallest of the five Great Lakes by surface area (only Lake Ontario is smaller), and the smallest by volume. Its southerly location gives it a climate that is downright tropical in the summertime, prompting tourists from around the world to flock to places like Point Pelee, Long Point, and the Lake Erie islands, to bask in Erie's warm waters and soak up the sun on some of the finest beaches in North America. Not as well recognized is the fact that Lake Erie is along the same latitude as northern California and Rome, giving the fertile farmland surrounding it a long and relatively moderate growing season. The rich soil produces bountiful harvests of a staggering variety of fruits and vegetables, not the least of which is grapes, the key to the region's growing winemaking industry.

Fishing has always been a cornerstone of life on Lake Erie. While recreational angling now dominates along the southern shore, the Canadian side is home to one of the largest commercial freshwater fisheries in the world. But it has always been a difficult way to make a living. From time immemorial, fishermen have dealt with Erie's notoriously brutal weather and extremely perilous working conditions as they toil, often fully exposed to the elements, on their cramped boats, or "tugs" as they're commonly known. Worse, as industrialization took hold in the region, overfishing and pollution bedevilled the industry, putting a strain on the already narrow profit margins of many small fisheries.

Eileen Lowe, whose husband, Andy, operated the fish tug *M & K* out of Port Dover, notes just one of these calamities in her journal entry of April 1, 1970: "Disaster for fishermen — ban on export of perch, pike from Lake Erie — today … Mercury poisoned fish must be drawn down here from Lake St. Clair … News very dark for fishing industry." At other times, the sheer cost of running one of these sophisticated machines threatened to bankrupt fishermen, as Lowe notes in her January 22, 1968 entry: "*M & K* had trouble with engine … Cost $4,000 … We have to raise $2,000 collateral … Always something."

The Doretta L, *a typical Lake Erie fish tug, in harbour at Wheatley, Ontario.*

Despite all these difficulties, commercial fishing remains vital to Lake Erie, and a visit to the harbour towns along the north shore will likely reveal an impressive array of fishing boats in port.

Part of the explanation for Lake Erie's famed dark side can be found in its geological makeup. With an average depth of only nineteen metres, Erie is the shallowest of the Great Lakes. This very lack of depth makes for waves of legendary ferocity when high winds and storms hit, which they do very frequently, particularly in the spring and autumn months. Another reason is simple location; its southerly position puts Lake Erie on what could be called a fault line of weather, a place where both warm southern air masses and cooler air seeping down from the arctic move through quickly, and frequently collide. The result of these actions can be swift and deadly as gale-force winds and even waterspouts seem to rise out of nowhere. Even those lucky enough to be on shore have reason for concern, as the howling wind can literally push the water clear across the lake, causing low water levels at one end and massive increases at the other. (The record difference between the eastern and western end of the lake during one of these phenomena is 4.88 metres.)

Watching one of these storms blow ashore is like having a front-row seat for an awesome spectacle, as the crests of the waves, pushed high by the rising bottom as they approach the beach, are literally blown into a hissing spray by the high winds. It is at these times that I have said a silent prayer of thanks that I wasn't out there, fighting for my life on a ship that has found itself in the grip of Lake Erie's fury. But, as we shall see, the lake's past is littered with the stories of those who haven't been so lucky.

The Cat Nation

Little is known about the people from whom Lake Erie takes its name. No Europeans are known to have had direct contact with the Erie nation. The information we have comes mainly from comparisons to their neighbours, specifically the Huron, who occupied a small area around Lake Simcoe and Georgian Bay, and the Huron's bitter enemies, the tribes of the Iroquois Confederacy, whose territory included much of New York State (and who were actually made up of five different nations: the Mohawk, Oneida, Seneca, Onondaga, and Cayuga). The *Jesuit Relation*, field reports filed by French missionaries working in the wilds of North America, also give an account of the Erie, but the *Relation* speaks mainly of their extermination at the hands of the Iroquois in a war that seems to have escalated around the middle of the seventeenth century.

The priests, for their part, don't seem to have witnessed any of this conflict firsthand. What they knew of it undoubtedly came from the Iroquois, as the *Jesuit Relation* for 1653–54 notes: "We, however, are left in peace, and Father Simon le Moine, who has recently returned from the upper Iroquois, assures us that they were arming themselves to set out from that quarter, to the number of eighteen hundred men."

The Erie lived along the south shore of Lake Erie, roughly from present-day Buffalo as far west as Sandusky, Ohio. The origin of the name is unclear, but the *Relation* for 1653–54 notes that the Iroquois referred to the Erie as "Ehriehronnons" or "people of the panther," a supposed reference to the large number of wild cats living in their territory at the time. The French, understandably, paraphrased this into "*Nation du Chat*" or "Cat Nation." In the end the label was appropriate, both for the Erie and for the lake on which their territory bordered.

Like the big cats, the Erie, whose numbers are thought to have peaked at around fourteen thousand, had a reputation for being both gentle farmers and excellent warriors whose intensity and fearsomeness terrified their enemies. They were certainly no easy opponent for the Iroquois, as the *Relation* for 1653–54 states:

> Two thousand men are reckoned upon, well skilled in war, although they have no firearms. Notwithstanding this, they fight like Frenchmen, bravely sustaining the first discharge of the Iroquois, who are armed with our muskets, and then falling upon them with a hailstorm of

poisoned arrows, which they discharge eight or ten times
before a musket can be reloaded.

According to the French, the Erie spoke a language similar to the Huron
and were by no means wanderers. Well settled in many small villages along
the shores of the lake and farther inland, the Erie lived a largely sedentary
life. That is, until the skirmishes with the Iroquois became more frequent.
The final battle between the two nations was started, according to the
Jesuits, very much by accident. The Erie had sent thirty representatives
to the Seneca for peace negotiations when, according to the *Relation* for
1655–56, one of the Erie representatives killed a Seneca "by some unexpected
accident." The enraged Seneca, in turn, immediately ordered the massacre
of the rest of the Erie party. Only five of the delegation managed to escape
their captors and inform their brethren of the frightening new war that was
now upon them.

During the hostilities that followed, each side waged a bloody guerilla-
style campaign and, in the words of the *Relation*, "tried to capture and burn
more prisoners than its opponent." The climax reportedly came in 1654,
when a force of roughly 1,200 Iroquois cornered 3,000 Erie warriors in one
of their villages, which was surrounded by a high palisade. The chiefs of
the attacking force first approached the bulwarks, "showing themselves in
French costume in order to frighten their opponents by the novelty of this
attire." After the Erie firmly rebuffed their demands for quick surrender,
the mayhem began in earnest. The Iroquois first tried to scale the palisades,
but as the arrows rained down on their heads, "they were killed as fast
as they advanced." After several hours of enduring these heavy losses, the
Iroquois regrouped and settled on a final strategy to break the stalemate.
They carried their canoes toward the fort, using them first as shields and
then, in a novel approach, turning them on their ends and employing them
as ladders with which to climb the walls that protected the besieged Erie.
It was enough to turn the tide, and as their attackers began to overwhelm
them, the Erie's resolve suddenly softened, and many attempted to flee.
This was when, according to the *Relation*, the Iroquois took full control
of the village and "there wrought so much carnage among the women and
children that blood was knee deep in certain places."

Even though they had prevailed, the losses the Iroquois had suffered
at the hands of the Erie were so heavy that the invaders were forced to
"remain two months in the enemy's territory, burying their dead and caring
for their wounded."

Nonetheless, the defeat marked a fatal blow for the Erie. Now reduced to a shred of their former strength, the remnants of the nation were either scattered, killed, or absorbed into the tribes of their Iroquois vanquishers. An empty silence fell on Lake Erie's southern shore, as nature began to reclaim the longhouses and villages of the former occupants. Along the north shore, a similar scene had played out three years earlier, in 1651, when the Neutral nation fell before the Iroquois' arrows. This tribe was so named by the French because they were neutral in the bitter long-standing feud between the Huron and the Iroquois. They were also said to be largely agrarian and similar in many ways to the Huron, who knew the Neutrals as "Attawandaron," which meant, simply, that the Neutral spoke a different language. In the end, their neutrality was not enough to save them from the encroaching Iroquois, and they, too, vanished.

This was largely the state that French traders and missionaries found the region in when they began to pass through over a decade later. Over the following two centuries, this trickle of new European arrivals would become a torrent, and they would transform Erie's shores. Through it all, the lake sustained them, her waters providing huge catches of fish, and her forests yielding the raw materials necessary for building the cities, towns, and farms that would go on to form the foundation of the area's economy.

Even so, none of it came easily.

Chapter 1

"The Earthly Paradise of Canada": French Adventurers on Lake Erie

On Christmas Day in 1678, eighteen frightened and exhausted French carpenters shivered in a drafty log cabin on the bank of the Niagara River, thirty-five kilometres above Lake Erie.

The men, led by a former French soldier named La Motte de Lucière, had sailed over a month earlier from Fort Frontenac, at the eastern end of Lake Ontario. Their small, two-masted brigantine was literally bursting with wood, rigging, and all the materials they would need to build a second, larger vessel, or barque, which they intended to sail across Lake Erie in order to open up trade with the Native tribes living in the vast interior of North America.

The first phase of the project, the construction of the barque, was extremely ambitious. Once the men sailed across Lake Ontario and into the Niagara River, they faced a back-breaking hike through the dense forest and around the mighty Niagara Falls with the ship's cargo strapped to their backs. From there, they would select a site near Lake Erie and build a small shipyard. Only then could they get on with the business of actually building the barque.

The voyage had not started out well; La Motte's crew had sailed from Fort Frontenac perilously late in the season, and the fierce autumn gales howled throughout the sailing, pushing the brigantine to the brink of capsize many times. Father Louis Hennepin, a missionary of the Récollet order, who travelled with the expedition, describes the sailing in his 1698 account, *A new discovery of a vast country in America:*

> The winds and the cold of autumn were then very violent, insomuch that our crew was afraid to go in so little a vessel. This obliged us and the Sieur de la Motte, our commander, to keep our course on the north side of the lake, to shelter ourselves under the coast against the northwest wind, which otherwise would have forced us upon the southern coast … This voyage proved very difficult, because of the unseasonable time of year, winter being near at hand.

Farther west, while seeking shelter from the raging wind and high seas in the mouth of the Humber River, the men awoke to find the brigantine frozen in by the advancing ice. The tiny ship would certainly have been crushed to pieces if not for the crew's desperate, and ultimately successful, bid to cut it out with axes.

Finally, on December 5, the crew's fortunes turned for the better. The day dawned calm and clear, and the wind turned favourable for sailing. The brigantine made steady progress across the lake, arriving at the mouth of the Niagara River and making its way as far as present-day Lewiston, New York, by December 18. It was here that the crew found themselves on that miserable Christmas morning, unable to proceed any farther.

The expedition had come to a crossroads. The harsher-than-expected weather and the onset of winter had made any attempt to unload the brigantine and carry its contents around Niagara Falls impossible. So, the men decided to put their tradesmen's skills to work; chopping down some surrounding trees, they built the small cabin, along with a surrounding palisade for defense, to wait out the weather. But even this was not done without great difficulty, as the ground was already so frozen that they had to throw boiling water on it several times just to drive in the stakes for the palisade.

As crippling as they seemed, the torments of cold and labour were the least of the men's worries. For in the farthest reaches of New France, far from the safety of their settlements along the St. Lawrence, these early

French adventurers were far from the masters of their own fate. That depended entirely on the local First Nations, whose intimate knowledge of the land was essential to all European exploration and trade. And this particular expedition had far from good relations with the local Iroquois nation — actually members of the Seneca tribe, affiliated with the wider Five Nations of Iroquois — who saw the shipbuilding effort on Lake Erie as an incursion into their territory. The Frenchmen were keenly aware of this, as Father Hennepin notes "… this new enterprise of building a fort and houses on the river Niagara … was like to give jealousy to the Iroquois, and even to the English, who live in this neighbourhood and have a great commerce with them …"

Iroquois warriors had kept a constant watch on the men from the time their vessel entered the mouth of the Niagara, sometimes hidden by the dense forest and at other times in plain view, their fearsome war clubs and tomahawks held at the ready. They would not let the beleaguered Frenchmen go any farther, and La Motte's crew worried that it was only a matter of time before the warriors lost their patience entirely and gave in to their most violent aims.

Their commander had no illusions about the precariousness of his position, either. Hunched around the fire on that frigid, miserable Christmas Day, La Motte came to the conclusion that the only way for the project to move forward was to negotiate an agreement with the Iroquois. So, on December 26, he set out for the nearest village on snowshoes, bringing with him seven armed men and Hennepin, because the father was said to have a working knowledge of the Iroquois' language. After five days' travel, they arrived at the village of Tagarondies, where they met with the chief in council.

But the negotiations, which dragged on for three full days, did not break the logjam as La Motte had hoped. In a gesture of goodwill, he offered the Iroquois the traditional gifts of cloth, beads, and tools, including hatchets and knives. In return for their endorsement, La Motte promised the Iroquois two things: blacksmith services at the new fort once it was constructed and, a bit more flimsily, reduced prices on trade goods as a result of the healthy business he expected to find in the North American heartland. It wasn't much, but it was all that La Motte had.

The chief was not impressed. He argued that the presence of a French fort in the area would certainly obstruct the route his people normally used to travel to the nearby English and Dutch colonies to trade. Why would he jeopardize these lucrative relationships for such negligible gains? In the end, the Iroquois' response was vague; while not a definite no, the Natives certainly withheld their approval; if the French wished to continue with this foolhardy venture, they would have to do so at their own risk.

To make matters worse, just as the crestfallen La Motte and his party were preparing to depart, a war party returned to the village with two prisoners from another tribe. The life of one was spared, but the other was put to death with what Hennepin calls, "such exquisite torments that Nero, Domitian, and Maximilian never intended the like …" After viewing the day-long agony of the captive at the Iroquois' insistence (during which parts of the poor soul's body were reportedly cut off and fed back to him, as well as to some of the village children), the horrified Frenchmen returned to their miserable cabin at Lewiston in utter despair. To La Motte, putting a sailing ship on Lake Erie now seemed a near impossible goal. His men would be lucky enough to come through the winter with their lives.

Priest or Pathfinder?

Mired in what was undoubtedly the worst Christmas of his life, La Motte had no way of knowing that, back at Fort Frontenac, a plan to rescue his men and the project was hurriedly coming together. The man responsible for it was the same one who had charged La Motte with his mission in the first place — René-Robert, Cavelier de La Salle.

On that very Christmas, despite the fact that winter had arrived in full fury on Lake Ontario, La Salle boarded a small brigantine and made sail toward the Niagara River. His vessel was stuffed with the supplies La Motte's men desperately needed to get through the winter and, more importantly, with further gifts to placate the hostile Iroquois.

It was the first step on a journey that would take La Salle to the very heart of the North American continent, turning him into one of the world's most renowned and controversial explorers, and inextricably linking his name with Lake Erie.

La Salle's early childhood gives no hint of the destiny that awaited him in the backwoods of North America. Quite the contrary; he was born into a well-to-do bourgeois family in Rouen on November 21, 1643. His father, Jean Cavelier, was a successful wholesale haberdasher, and the title de la Salle, which young Robert took, was the name of the family's estate near Rouen.

Robert received his early education at the Jesuit college in his hometown, which his father, convinced that Robert was brighter than his older brother, had insisted he attend. There, under the strict discipline of the Jesuit fathers, Robert excelled, particularly in mathematics and sciences. He was so successful, in fact, that the fathers encouraged him to take his vows, which he did at the age of fifteen, and joined the Jesuits' powerful Society of Jesus in Paris. But there is evidence that La Salle's motives in becoming an ordained priest may have gone further than religious conviction, as Professor Paul Chesnel, in his 1901 work, *History of Cavelier de la Salle*, explains:

> … he afterwards entered the Society of Jesus as a novice, undoubtedly expecting to be sent as a missionary to remote countries; thus he did reconcile filial obedience with an inherent desire for voyage and adventure. But being possessed of a proud nature, he soon realized that he lacked the docility essential to the making of a good priest …

Despite his independent streak, La Salle would spend the next seven years in the Society teaching math and sciences. But his imagination was captivated by the vast wilderness of North America. This was undoubtedly fuelled, at least in part, by reading the Jesuit *Relations*, which were published between 1632 and 1673. These were regular reports filed by missionaries in the field, and they were very popular reading in France. The missionaries' tales of mighty forests, thundering waters, and savage Native warriors would certainly have made an impression on the young La Salle. He made several requests to be sent to North America, but each was declined; under the rigorous discipline of the Jesuit order, one did not request reassignment, one was told where to go. In light of La Salle's ongoing struggles to leave the comfortable confines of Paris, it is not hard to imagine how it must

Illustration courtesy of National Archives of Canada C-007802

René-Robert, Cavelier de La Salle. The controversial explorer sought to vastly expand the boundaries of New France.

have rankled when his older and supposedly less intelligent brother, Jean, a priest of the Sulpician order, was sent to Quebec as an abbé.

Finally, in 1665, after years of struggling to reconcile his religious calling with his thirst for adventure and exploration, the latter won out, and La Salle tendered his resignation to the fathers, claiming he had to be released from his vows due to his "moral frailties." On March 28, 1667, he left the convent for good.

Suddenly penniless (he had taken an oath of poverty as part of his vows, which denied him access to the Cavelier family fortune), La Salle quickly came to the realization that there was no future for him in France. In early 1667, he boarded a ship bound for Canada, taking with him several grand ideas, honed over many years, for expanding the size and scope of King Louis XIV's holdings in North America, possibly linking them to a lucrative trade route through the Great Lakes to Asia. It was the first inkling of the vast trading network the lakes were set to become.

A Route to the Southern Sea

Quebec in 1667 was still a relatively new settlement, living in a precarious peace with the neighbouring First Nations. Samuel de Champlain had founded it in 1608 and, though the colony had grown, it still counted less than 10,000 souls as permanent inhabitants, with a large number of these arriving only two years before as soldiers sent by Louis XIV to take the offensive against the Iroquois. That campaign had led to the peace and the soldiers, rewarded with free land, had begun to play a major role in the colony's growth.

But farming and fishing were not profitable enough on their own to attract the infusion of enterprising young blood that New France so desperately needed; that honour went to the fur trade. This displeased the king's powerful colonial minister, Jean-Baptiste Colbert. Believing that a thriving New France would give the mother country a considerable advantage over colonial rivals like England and Spain, he was frustrated by reports of the number of young men who had fled their settlements and headed west to immerse themselves into Native society and the fur trade. With many of these coureurs de bois gone, Quebec lacked the labour force necessary to promote the growth of a settled population and increase its standard of living.

Looming over all of this, of course, was the powerful Catholic Church. In Quebec, it took the form of several different orders, the most dominant being the Jesuits. The church was a major landholder in the colony, and was deeply embedded in the lives of the colonists in many ways: providing labour and funding, helping them to clear their land, and establishing colleges and other institutions. But the church's main goal was to establish a society based on moral, and by modern standards puritanical, grounds in New France, and key to this was its self-proclaimed mission to bring the continent's Native people into God's flock. The church actively pursued this goal by sending missionaries throughout the present provinces of Quebec and Ontario, as well as into upper New York State, with a major missionary effort focusing on the Huron people, known as Sainte-Marie or Huronia, near southern Georgian Bay.

Although the missionary orders were very much rivals, one thing that united them was their dislike of the colony's fur traders, especially the coureurs de bois, who lived among the Natives and therefore outside the church's long grasp. What irked them even more was that many traders engaged in the destructive practice of trading liquor for furs, exposing Native people to the destructive effects of alcohol, including debilitating long-term addiction. This issue divided Quebec's citizens perhaps more than any other, and made the missionaries' already difficult job nearly impossible.

It was into this confused and politically charged world that La Salle stepped when he landed at Quebec City sometime between June and November of 1667. Almost immediately, the outspoken young man from Rouen drew the ire of both the fur traders and the missionaries: to the traders, he was a child of privilege who had managed to quickly corral the favour of the colony's governor, Daniel de Rémy de Courcelle. Mostly, however, they feared that La Salle's schemes to expand the colony's wealth would cut into their outlandish profits.

To the Jesuits, La Salle was an enigma. Who was this man who had so easily abandoned the missionary life? they wondered. Above all, the fathers were curious about La Salle's motives. Did he still possess the zeal for Catholicism that he had shown as a boy, or was he no better than the traders, interested only in profits? La Salle drew the suspicion of just about everyone in New France.

But to the Sulpician order, seen as a lesser religious force than the Jesuits in New France, La Salle represented an opportunity. Sensing this energetic young former Jesuit's potential as a useful ally, they decided to grant him several thousand hectares of land outside Montreal, which was at this time a crude village that had been founded some thirty years earlier and had a meagre population of only a few hundred residents.

A frontier town mainly populated by traders, coureurs de bois, and their Native allies, Montreal was a far cry from Quebec City's relative cleanliness and almost European charm. Militarily, it was a disaster waiting to happen: with few fortifications, the settlement was largely indefensible. Its residents lived in constant fear of the surrounding Native tribes, who were often openly hostile to their very presence in the area. They could, and often did, attack colonists who dared to wander outside Montreal's palisades.

None of this appeared to trouble La Salle. Working through the fall and winter of 1667, he managed to make his land arable, clearing the dense forest and planting crops. Along with his tenant farmers, he made his farm, or seigneury, a modest success — before long, it began turning a small profit.

But, just as he had in France, La Salle was looking for a way to turn his back on a quiet life in the countryside. Throughout his first two years in Canada, he tried to think of plans for financing and undertaking his voyages of discovery. In the winter of 1669, two Iroquois who had camped on La Salle's land fired his imagination even further: they told him of a river to the south of Lake Erie called the Ohio. It took nine months, they said, to follow the river down to its mouth. There, it opened onto a large sea. Listening to the men's vivid descriptions of this river, La Salle became convinced that the time to act on his plans was at hand. He decided he had to set out for the Ohio as soon as possible "in order," he wrote, "not to leave to another the honour of finding the way to the Southern Sea, and thereby the route to China."

Among the Iroquois

As La Salle was well aware, the main stumbling block to an expedition as ambitious as the one he was planning was finding enough money to get it off the ground. To that end, La Salle, working diligently over the previous two years to develop his property, found himself with a valuable asset. He decided to sell most of the land back to the Sulpicians, keeping only his house, which he intended to use as a fur-trading factory. The sale netted him the considerable sum of 3,000 livres. But that was the easy part; more difficult would be convincing Governor Courcelle to allow him to undertake the voyage at all. La Salle set off for Quebec by canoe to make his case.

Courcelle listened carefully as La Salle, whose eloquence was by this time well known, put forward his plans. Courcelle approved of the young explorer's ambition and desire to explore the Ohio but, mindful of Colbert's orders that the colony not spread itself too thin, was reluctant to allow La Salle to strike out on his own. What if, after all, the young man was to follow so many others into the life of a simple coureur de bois? It would be a great loss.

So, Courcelle proposed a compromise; he would grant La Salle permission to conduct his expedition. But the governor requested that he couple his efforts with those of a Sulpician missionary, François Dollier de Casson, who was journeying to the same area to explore the possibility of converting Native people living in the Ohio Valley to Christianity.

The Sulpicians' superior, Abbé de Queylus, was at first cool to Courcelle's idea, writing of his fear that La Salle's temper, "which was known to be somewhat volatile, might lead him to quit [the expedition] at the first whim." So de Queylus assigned a second Sulpician, René de Bréhant de Galinée, to accompany La Salle and Dollier. According to Galinée's own modest description of his skills: "I had already some smattering of mathematics, enough to construct a map in a sort of a fashion …"

La Salle begrudgingly accepted Courcelle's terms, but he must have been seething inside. The independent-minded young man had left the ultra-conservative Society of Jesus so he could explore and trade on his own and now here he was, forced to embark on the adventure of a lifetime with two priests in tow.

But he needn't have worried about his travelling companions. Dollier was more than qualified for what lay ahead; a giant of a man and a former soldier in the French army, he was said to be so strong he could carry two men sitting in his hands. He had been in New France since 1666, and had served as an army chaplain during the offensives against the Iroquois before venturing to Fort Sainte-Anne on Lake George to serve as a missionary. Here, he played a role in saving the garrison from a bout of scurvy.

Galinée, a Sulpician priest all his life, had studied mathematics and astronomy at the Sorbonne before arriving in New France in 1668. He was said to have at least a working knowledge of Native languages, and it was to be his job to create a written record of the expedition's travels, which he did brilliantly, proving that he was also a talented writer. The journal he left behind is a highly detailed and historically important document without which we would know precious little about the earliest European explorations of Lake Erie.

The expedition, consisting of seven canoes, each carrying three men, set off on July 6, 1669, guided by two Iroquois canoes. Aboard were the same men who had camped at La Salle's seigneury the previous winter and had told him about the Ohio River. Galinée provides an excellent description of the versatile craft that carried the men on their way:

These are little birchbark canoes, about twenty feet long and two feet wide, strengthened inside with cedar floors and gunwales, very thin, so that one man carries it with ease, although the boat is capable of carrying four men and eight or nine hundred pounds weight in baggage ... This style of canoe affords the most convenient and commonest mode of navigation in this country, although it is a true saying that when a person is in one of these vessels he is always, not a finger's breadth, but the thickness of five or six sheets of paper, from death.

The Frenchmen, many still unaccustomed to living outdoors in the backwoods of New France, also found the Native diet quite disagreeable by European standards. According to Galinée:

The ordinary diet is Indian corn, called in France Turkey wheat, which is ground between two stones and boiled in water; the seasoning is with meat or fish, when you have any. This way of living seemed to us all so extraordinary that we felt the effects of it. Not one of us was exempt from some sort of illness ...

Fortunately for the French members of the party, fish were abundant, and one "had only to throw a line in to catch forty or fifty of the kind here called *barbue* [catfish]." Hunting was also promising, with the men feasting on moose on two occasions during the paddle down the St. Lawrence River.

The canoeists entered Lake Ontario and made their way along the south shore, entering Irondequoit Bay, at the site of present-day Rochester, New York, on August 11. The voyage continued to be hard on the French, particularly Dollier, who was felled by a fever that Galinée thought would certainly kill his plucky travelling companion. But here is where the venerable Dollier's innate toughness shone through: as he lay suffering, the stricken father was heard to murmur, "I would rather die in the midst of this forest in the order of the will of God, as I believe I am, than amongst all my brethren at the Seminary of Saint Sulpice."

They had no sooner paddled into Irondequoit Bay when the men were immediately greeted by a group of Iroquois bearing gifts. Hoping to win the confidence of these Natives, and thereby make their journey through the area much safer, they reciprocated by offering tools, mainly knives and needles, as well as glass beads and coloured pieces of cloth, which the Iroquois deemed valuable. This prompted the Native party to invite the Frenchmen to accompany them to their nearby village. La Salle, thinking, perhaps, that this could only be a good opportunity to improve relations with these Iroquois, decided to take them up on their offer. So, with Galinée and eight other Frenchmen in tow, he left the canoes with Dollier, now on the mend from his illness, and departed into the forest on foot.

It was at this village, two days' hike from the shore, that the Frenchmen saw firsthand the destructive effect the fur traders' alcohol was having on Native people. After eight days of feasting and meeting with the village elders in council, a shipment of brandy arrived from the Dutch colonies in New York State. Quickly falling under the influence, the Iroquois threatened, according to Galinée, to "break our heads" in retribution for the murder of one of their relations at the hands of a French colonist in Montreal. Then, in this atmosphere of heightened tension, La Salle got a taste of what La Motte would experience ten years later: a young prisoner was brought into the village square and slowly burned with hot irons over the course of six hours while La Salle's men tried helplessly to intervene (although Galinée's report indicates that some of the French wished to witness the entire torture from beginning to end). To make matters worse, the Dutch interpreter, whom they had brought with them from Montreal, astonishingly, knew very little French, rendering him utterly useless, particularly in such an extreme situation. The terrified men finally decided to abandon the village when, in Galinée's words, "everybody assembled in the square with a small stick in his hand, with which they began to beat the cabins on all sides with a very great clatter, to drive away, as they said, the dead man's soul, which might have hidden itself in some corner to do them harm."

La Salle's party slipped back through the woods to where Dollier and the rest were waiting with the canoes. As they loaded their supplies and took up their paddles, they no doubt hoped that the past few days were not a harbinger of what awaited them as they plunged ahead toward Lake Erie — and the unknown.

A Fateful Meeting

September 24, 1669, found the expedition in the small Iroquois village of Tinawatawa, which was located near present-day Hamilton, Ontario. Here, the uneasy cooperation between La Salle and the Sulpicians, which had held up relatively well so far, finally began to unravel.

Two days earlier, the expedition's Iroquois guides had received word that two Frenchmen had arrived at Tinawatawa. Unaware of anyone else dispatched this way, La Salle and the Sulpicians decided to send two men ahead to investigate, with the rest following behind to arrive a day or two later.

One of the two Frenchmen, it turned out, was the French explorer Adrien Jolliet, who had left Montreal a few months before La Salle and the priests to determine the existence of a rumoured copper mine in the Lake Superior region. In the end, Jolliet told La Salle, Dollier, and Galinée that he did not have time to visit the site of the rumoured mine. However, while he was preparing to return to Montreal, the local Ottawa tribe had given him an Iroquois prisoner to take back to the southern lakes as a token of the peace the Ottawa wished to establish with the Iroquois. It was this prisoner who convinced Jolliet to return to Montreal not by the northern route through Georgian Bay and the Ottawa River, but farther south, traversing Lake Huron and Lake St. Clair, passing down the Detroit River, and then paddling east on Lake Erie. In the process of doing so, Jolliet had become the first European known to have set eyes on Lake Erie.

While Jolliet related the details of his journey, he slipped in the detail that there was at present no mission to many of the tribes who were residing in the area of Lake Superior. This had an immediate and profound impact on Galinée and Dollier, who saw their chance encounter with Jolliet as nothing less than a sign from God. They quickly decided to abandon their Ohio Valley objective and reverse Jolliet's route to Lake Superior. Jolliet told the two priests that he had left a canoe on the shores of Lake Erie, near present-day Port Stanley, which he invited them to take if the local Native people had not discovered it first. Jolliet had abandoned the craft at the behest of his Iroquois companion, who thought it would be safer for Jolliet to walk along what is now the Grand River and proceed to Tinawatawa on foot instead of paddling any farther on Lake Erie.

The meeting cannot have been a pleasant one for La Salle, who viewed Jolliet much differently than the Sulpicians did. The competitive, controlling young man from Rouen would certainly have envied Jolliet his successful — and largely solo — journey of discovery. Indeed, La Salle had undertaken his entire quest for the Ohio and the route to China, risking everything in the process, for the express purpose of being the first one to find it. To La Salle, Jolliet was a rival to be bested, and nothing more.

But in all of this there was a silver lining that La Salle certainly recognized, and later seized: if the expedition were to split up, and Dollier and Galinée were to go their own way, it would absolve La Salle of his responsibility to Courcelle and de Queylus to accompany the Sulpicians any further. He would be free to find and explore the Ohio River on his own.

Coincidentally, Galinée reports, La Salle had come down with a fever while he had been out hunting, a few days before the encounter with Jolliet. But, as with many things involving La Salle, the authenticity of his sickness was found to be less than convincing by some of the men, including Galinée, who notes wryly that "Some say it was at the sight of three large rattlesnakes he found in his path whilst climbing a rock that the fever seized him."

Whether real or imagined, the illness certainly played into La Salle's desire to strike out on his own. Galinée writes: "M. de la Salle's illness was beginning to take away from him the inclination to push farther on, and the desire to see Montreal was beginning to press him. He had not spoken of it to us, but we have clearly perceived it."

When the matter was brought up, then, La Salle "begged us [Dollier and Galinée] to excuse him if he abandoned us to return to Montreal, and added that he could not make up his mind to winter in the woods with his men, where their lack of skill and experience might make them die of starvation."

With that, the decision was taken to divide the expedition. Again, according to Galinée: "The last day of September M. Dollier said Holy Mass for the second time in this village, where most of us, on M. de la Salle's side as on ours, received the Sacrament in order to unite in our Lord at a time when we saw ourselves on the point of separating."

The next day, Dollier and Galinée paddled toward the Grand River with three canoes, while their Dutch interpreter and two Iroquois warriors made out on foot in a bid to procure Jolliet's abandoned canoe at Port Stanley before the winter closed in.

Meanwhile, La Salle kept his own counsel and set off on a very different course than the one ascribed to him by the two priests. Historians still debate the range of La Salle's travels after his parting with Dollier and Galinée, but some historians believe that La Salle, with roughly four canoes and twelve men, wintered in the Niagara area before setting off for the Ohio River in the spring. They likely would have made it to the Ohio sometime either in the late winter of 1669 or the spring of 1670 (deprived of the meticulous journal-keeping of Galinée, La Salle's men left no documentary evidence of their explorations), following it as far as present-day Louisville, Kentucky. But the river had not been what La Salle had expected. Full of vegetation, shoals, and countless other obstacles, the mighty Ohio was not navigable to sailing ships. Worse, without the Sulpicians to temper La Salle's authoritarian leadership style, his men had come to bitterly resent him, and made no effort to hide their growing disdain. This would prove to be his undoing: one night, after the party made camp on the riverbank and La Salle had fallen into a deep sleep, they took the decision to desert. Quietly, they gathered all the supplies they could and disappeared into the forest. The next morning, La Salle awoke to find the camp ransacked and only one loyal Iroquois guide remaining. Angry and bitter, he came to the conclusion that he could go no farther. He dejectedly retreated to Montreal, arriving there late in 1670.

Ironically, it would be the two Sulpicians who would do the bulk of the exploring in the Lake Erie region over the next year. With the help of a map Galinée had made of Jolliet's journey from Lake Superior, the priests, along with seven other men from the original expedition, arrived at Lake Erie's shores in the middle of October. The lake's sheer expanse overwhelmed the Frenchmen, as Galinée proclaims: "At last we arrived ... at the shore of Lake Erie, which appeared to us like a great sea because there was a great south wind blowing at the time. There is perhaps no lake in the country in which the waves rise so high, because of its great depth and extent."

In hopes of finding the Dutch interpreter and the men sent ahead to find Jolliet's canoe, which Dollier hoped could replace his worn-out vessel, the party paddled along the Canadian shore, getting as far as Port Dover before the autumn winds made it impossible to go any farther. So here, near the mouth of the Lynn River and with no word from the canoe party, they built a small homestead to wait out the winter, becoming the first Europeans ever to do so on Lake Erie. Galinée was so moved by the beauty of the spot, it inspired him to write of that winter:

> I leave you to imagine whether we suffered in the midst of this abundance in the *earthly Paradise of Canada* [author's emphasis]; I call it so because there is assuredly no more beautiful region in all of Canada. The woods are open, interspersed with beautiful meadows, watered by rivers and rivulets filled with fish and beaver, an abundance of fruits, and what is important, so full of game that we saw there at one time more than a hundred roebucks in a single band, herds of fifty or sixty hinds, and bears fatter and of better flavour than the most savory pigs of France. In short, we

Photo by author

A view from the wintering place of Dollier and Galinée near Port Dover.

may say that we passed the winter more comfortably than we should have done in Montreal.

Astonishingly, Galinée even foretells Lake Erie's prosperous wine industry, which wouldn't seriously take root for another two hundred years, when he writes:

> … the vine grows here only in sand, on banks of lakes and rivers but although it has no cultivation it does not fail to produce grapes in great quantities as large and as sweet as the finest of France. We even made wine of them, with which M. Dollier said Holy Mass all winter …

Here, in two small cabins, the Sulpicians passed five months and eleven days of one of the harshest winters yet experienced by the French in Canada. In one cabin, they built a small altar, where they said Mass three times a week. As the temperature dropped and the snow flew outside of their snug abode, no one else ventured past for three whole months, until one day late in the winter, the fathers encountered a number of Iroquois who had come to the area to hunt beaver. According to Galinée: "They used to visit us and found us in a very good cabin whose construction they admired, and afterward they brought every Indian who passed that way to see it."

Photo by author

A monument marking where René de Bréhant de Galinée and François Dollier de Casson spent the winter of 1669–70. They were the first Europeans to winter on Lake Erie.

On March 23, 1670, three days before setting out again, the missionaries claimed the "earthly paradise" in the name of King Louis XIV. On a hill overlooking the lake, they erected a large cross, along with an inscription outlining not only the land claim, but the fact that the party had been the first Europeans ever to winter in the area.

Unfortunately for the Sulpicians, however, Lake Erie did not awake from her winter slumber in a cheerful mood. On the second day out of Port Dover, near what is now called Turkey Point, the wind caught Galinée's empty canoe while the party was windbound on shore and blew it out into the open water. Two men attempted to save it, but after nearly drowning themselves in the freezing water, finally decided to let it go. With only two canoes remaining, the party again split up; supplies were shifted into the remaining boats and five men went ahead on foot, with four paddling the canoes. The two groups met sporadically on the way down the coast, including a strenuous portage over Long Point, before finally finding Jolliet's canoe hidden between two trees at Kettle Creek in Port Stanley. Strangely, though, there was no sign of the Dutchman and the two Iroquois.

And there never would be. Over the centuries since the Dollier and Galinée expedition, no trace of these men has ever been found. It was among the first of many mysteries that now colour Lake Erie's long and storied history.

With everyone now embarked in the canoes, the party made much quicker progress than it did when over half of the men had to struggle through the dense, untracked forests of southern Ontario. But still, by the time they reached Point Pelee, weeks later, they were exhausted and completely out of provisions. The saving grace had been that game had proven abundant during this leg of the journey, especially in the area of present-day Rondeau Provincial Park.

But this would be the only good news for the party. For it was here, on Canada's southernmost mainland point, that Lake Erie finally lost her patience with the Sulpicians and struck their expedition with what would amount to a fatal blow. Galinée describes:

> We landed there on a beautiful sand beach on the east side of the point. We had made that day nearly twenty leagues, so we were all very much tired. That was the reason why we did not carry all our packs up on the high ground, but left them on the sand and carried our canoes up to the high ground. Night came on and we slept so soundly that a great north-east wind rising had time to agitate the lake with such violence that the water rose six feet where we were, and carried away the packs of M. Dollier's canoe that were nearest the water and would have carried away the rest if one of us had not awoke. Astonished to hear the lake roaring so furiously, he went to the beach to see if the

baggage was safe, and seeing that the water already came as far as the packs that were placed the highest, cried out that all was lost.

The rest of the exhausted men, including Dollier and Galinée, stumbled to the beach to survey the damage. It was worse than they thought, for the altar and sacraments the fathers would need to establish their mission had been washed into the lake and lost. There was now no other choice; returning to Montreal was the only option. But they decided to do so by continuing on to Lake Superior anyway, still reversing Jolliet's original route. They would then head for Montreal via the northern route on the Ottawa River.

As they passed out of Lake Erie, the hunting remained excellent, something that the Sulpicians attributed, at least in part, to an act of faith (or more appropriately, vandalism) that they committed while ascending the Detroit River to Lake St. Clair. Spotting a large rock on shore that was painted in a human likeness and praised by local Natives as a spiritual guardian, the men, still furious that they would be unable to set up their planned mission, disembarked from their canoes and set upon the statue with axes, smashing it to the extent that they carried the largest pieces out to the middle of the river and dropped them into the water. "I leave you to imagine whether we revenged upon this idol, which the Iroquois had strongly recommended us to honor, the loss of our chapel," Galinée writes. "We attributed to it even the dearth of provisions from which we had hitherto suffered." Galinée makes no note of the response of the local Native people, other than to mention in passing that they were camped in the area, but he concludes: "God rewarded us immediately for this good action, for we killed a roebuck and a bear that very day."

Finally, after an uneventful voyage on Lake Huron and through northern Georgian Bay, the Sulpicians arrived at Sault Ste Marie, where they were welcomed by a group of Jesuit missionaries who had established themselves there not long before. No doubt here, in the hostile backwoods of North America, any rivalry between the orders would have been set aside for the benefit of the rare company of other Frenchmen.

After a stay of only three days, Dollier and Galinée, still anxious to return to Montreal, hired a Native guide and set out on the last leg of their long journey home, finally arriving there after twenty-two days and dozens of back-breaking portages. On June 18, 1670, they entered the

Photo by author

A monument erected by Parks Canada to mark the spot where Dollier and Galinée claimed the Lake Erie region for France.

city. Galinée, sick with fever when they returned, wrote simply of that day: "We were looked upon rather as persons risen from the dead than as common men."

They had been gone 347 days.

Soldiers and Shipwrights

Ten years later, as La Salle rushed to La Motte's aid, his 1669 expedition to Erie's edge with Dollier and Galinée would certainly have been on his mind. Little is known about the years of his life immediately following his expedition to the Ohio. Some historians claim that La Salle set out on another expedition between 1671 and 1673 that culminated in the discoveries of both the Illinois and Mississippi Rivers, but there is no firm evidence of this. What is known is that he turned up in Quebec in late 1670 and, short of money, was back in Montreal again in 1672.

Then, in a pattern that was becoming common in La Salle's story, his luck took a dramatic turn for the better thanks to a new alliance with the aristocracy — this time with New France's powerful new governor, Louis de Buade, Comte de Frontenac.

There were a number of similarities between the two men: both were headstrong leaders who employed an authoritarian style; both were willing to go to great lengths to make money; and, most importantly, both heartily disliked the Jesuits, whom they saw as too entangled in the colony's affairs.

Frontenac, like La Salle, was also a divisive character in New France. He went against Colbert's policy of maintaining a compact, self-sufficient colony. Likely more for personal gain than for any other reason, he frustrated the minister's intentions by establishing Fort Cataraqui well beyond the settled boundaries of New France, on the site of Kingston, Ontario. This action had the predictable effect of inflaming both the Jesuits and the traders. The Jesuits worried about the impact of the fort, and the brandy trade that was sure to follow it, on the surrounding First Nations. The traders, particularly those based in nearby Montreal, were incensed because they saw Fort Cataraqui as a threat to their livelihood, intercepting furs farther up the St. Lawrence River.

La Salle, on Frontenac's recommendation, sailed to France in 1674. Travelling to the court at Versailles, the ambitious explorer successfully petitioned the king to grant him Fort Cataraqui, exclusive trading rights to the land surrounding it, and even letters of nobility for himself and his descendants (La Salle later renamed the fort Frontenac in honour of his wealthy patron). It was during the return voyage that La Salle met Father Hennepin, yet another priest who would play a vital role in the exploration of Lake Erie.

But even in the face of the enormous wealth that his newfound stake in the western fur trade offered, the desire for further exploration did not leave

La Salle. Two years after taking up residence at Fort Frontenac, he was back in France, this time seeking permission to construct two more forts. One would be at the entrance to Lake Erie and the other at the southern end of Lake Michigan, from which he hoped to explore the American Midwest. Though he was by now being derided in France as "fit and ready for the madhouse," his perseverance and oratorical skills won the day again, and he was permitted to carry out his plan to explore the western part of North America.

For La Salle, the pieces were now quickly beginning to come together: after procuring royal permission, he put the wealth he had acquired at Fort Frontenac to work, going on something of a shopping spree in France, hiring shipwrights and purchasing rigging, sails, and iron fixtures that were not yet available in the colony.

His crew was also beginning to take shape. He had convinced the young La Motte de Lucière to come back to New France with him, and had made connections, through the influential Prince de Conti, with Henri de Tonty. A former soldier like La Motte, Tonty's hand had been torn away by a grenade, and his arm was subsequently fitted with an iron prosthesis. But, far from being discouraged, and possessing almost boundless energy, young Tonty was in Paris looking for a new adventure. Conti referred him to La Salle who, according to the *Relation of Henri de Tonty Concerning the Explorations of La Salle from 1678 to 1683*, Tonty's narrative of the La Salle expedition, "received me with his usual civility." In fact, the two men hit it off right away, growing very close during the long voyage back to New France. The packed ship included not only La Salle, Tonty, and La Motte, but thirty shipwrights and carpenters whom La Salle had managed to employ for the expedition. Tonty would go on to become La Salle's chief lieutenant in the odyssey that lay ahead.

Erie's First Shipyard

When La Salle's barque arrived at the Niagara River in early January 1679, he wasted no time in setting off to find out how La Motte and his men were faring. He left the vessel's pilot, a man named Luc, in charge of the ship and strode toward La Motte's cabin at Lewiston on his own, likely on snowshoes, a Native invention that rivalled the canoe in usefulness for travel in Canada.

He walked straight into a scene of disappointment. La Motte, still rattled by his encounter with the Iroquois at Tagarondies, had done little to advance the project further. This, La Salle quickly rectified; on January 22, he marched La Motte and his men around Niagara Falls to what is now known as Cayuga Creek. This, he felt, would be an excellent site for the construction of his vessel, which he had decided to name the *Griffon*, after the mythical winged beast on Governor Frontenac's coat of arms. At the point where the creek empties into the Niagara River, he put La Motte and his men to work building a dock and a number of small cabins. Shortly afterward, La Salle would return to the mouth of the Niagara and, on the site of present-day Fort Niagara, build his own small fort, Conti, a tribute to the prince who had referred the young Tonty to La Salle in Paris.

But just as things were starting to look up for the beleaguered crew, a messenger arrived to inform La Salle that the barque that had carried him to the Niagara, and was loaded with the *Griffon's* sails and outfitting, had been wrecked at its mooring on Lake Ontario. La Salle and a few men rushed to the scene. The official narrative, *Relation of the Discoveries and Voyages of Cavelier de La Salle from 1679 to 1681*, which La Salle may or may not have had a hand in writing, describes the incident: "His vessel, laden with merchandise, suffered shipwreck on the southern shore of the lake [Lake Ontario] … through the fault of the pilot, who, with all the sailors, left it in order to go ashore to sleep."

A late seventeenth-century impression of the building of La Salle's Griffon, *the first ship to sail on Lake Erie.*

La Salle was furious. He had expressly told Luc to beware of the fierce storms that frequently ravage western Lake Ontario. But Luc, newly arrived from France, had not taken the explorer's warnings seriously. The result was the Great Lakes' first-ever shipwreck. There would, unfortunately, be a great many to follow, and Luc would only be the first of many navigators to underestimate the lakes' ferocity.

With the men only able to recover a very small number of the supplies that the barque carried, the expedition was again in serious trouble. In a desperate bid to resupply his men, La Salle decided to set off for Fort Frontenac on foot, leaving Tonty in charge. The trip was a testament to La Salle's physical strength, as the official *Relation* bears out:

> One day when he was in haste to get back to Fort Frontenac, he undertook the journey ... by land and on foot with only a little sack of Indian corn, — even this becoming exhausted while he was still at a distance of two days' journey from the fort where, however, he did not fail to arrive safely.

But, despite the setbacks, in La Salle's absence work carried on at the ramshackle shipyard, which by now consisted only of a few crude outbuildings. Father Hennepin describes them as "cabins made of rinds of trees; and I had one made on purpose to perform Divine Service therein on Sundays, and other occasions."

By January 26, just before La Salle returned to Fort Frontenac, the keel of the *Griffon* was laid. The men continued to labour throughout the winter, which, thankfully, was reasonably mild. But the project continued to push them to their limits. The loss of the barque on Lake Ontario meant that provisions were cut nearly to starvation levels and, even though La Salle and La Motte had both made additional efforts to win the Iroquois' approval, they remained a menace, as Hennepin describes:

> ... they came now and then to our dock, and expressed some discontent at what we were doing. One of them, in particular, feigning himself drunk, attempted to kill our [black]smith, but was vigorously repulsed with a red-hot iron bar, which, along with the reprimand he received from me, obliged him to be gone.

This incident was followed a few days later by a visit from an Iroquois woman who informed the Frenchmen that the men of her tribe had resolved to "burn our ship in the dock, and had certainly done it, had we not always been upon our guard." By spring, incidents like these were beginning to take their toll, along with enduring intense privation and cold. Despite Tonty's best efforts to placate the men, murmurs of desertion began to reverberate more loudly through the tiny camp.

In May, the *Griffon* was finally set afloat in the Niagara. The frightened, exhausted men, eager to be aboard ship, where they were safe from the threat posed by the Iroquois, immediately quit their crude huts and slung up their hammocks below the *Griffon's* main deck. Hennepin, displaying his usual flair for the dramatic, describes the Iroquois' reaction to this turn of events:

> The Iroquois being returned from hunting beavers, were mightily surprised to see our ship afloat ... they could not comprehend how in so short a time we had been able to build so great a ship, though it was but sixty tons. It might have been called a moving fortress; for all the savages inhabiting the banks of those lakes and rivers I have mentioned ... were filled with fear as well as admiration when they saw it.

If the Iroquois were even half as impressed as Hennepin says, it is not hard to imagine the lift that this would have given to the sagging morale of La Salle's shipwrights.

The Fate of the *Griffon*

Back at Fort Frontenac, La Salle was dealing with his own morale problems. His growing band of enemies had been eagerly spreading the word about the struggles of the Lake Erie expedition. This made La Salle's task of re-provisioning his men even more difficult, as the official *Relation* describes:

> Meanwhile, those who were envious of M. de La Salle — seeing that, despite the difficulties attending the transport of the rigging through so many rapids, and despite the opposition of the Iroquois, his vessel was finished — gave out that the undertaking was a rash one, that he would

never come back, and many other like things. By such talk they aroused all M. de La Salle's creditors, who, without awaiting his return and without notifying him, made seizure of all the goods he possessed at Montreal and at Quebec, even to his secretary's bed, having them appraised at their own rates, although Fort Frontenac alone, of which he is the proprietor, would suffice to pay all his debts twice over, should he die in the prosecution of his discoveries.

Needless to say, the official *Relation* must have made fascinating reading for the French minister of marine, to whom it was submitted in the early 1680s.

Despite all this, La Salle, anxious for news of his *Griffon* and "judging that the harm was done, and that his foes had no other aim than to cause him to miss a journey for which he had prepared with so great effort and expense," set off again for Fort Conti, again with a fully loaded vessel, arriving in early August.

What he saw must have utterly astonished him. The *Griffon*, complete, was swinging at anchor on the Niagara River. The tiny ship consisted only of a main deck, with a large aft cabin and space in the hold for extra hammocks. For armament, the *Griffon* carried only seven small iron guns of various types, and was only about eighteen metres long and 4.5 metres at the beam. A plain vessel with very simple sail rigging and little intricate carving, save for a figurehead, the *Griffon* also had little colour to its hull; it had been treated instead with pine tar and coated with varnishes of pine resin.

Tonty had already tried to get her out of the river and onto the lake, but with a steady unfavourable wind, found he could make no progress against the strong current. Here, again, La Salle took control. With the men pulling hard on ropes from shore, the *Griffon* slowly, steadily edged forward, until it finally overcame the current and emerged out onto the open lake. As it did so, the men, thirty-four in all, including Hennepin and two other Récollet missionaries, scrambled aboard.

Lake Erie had her first sailing ship.

Considering the struggles so far, it is perhaps ironic that the first sailing across the lake was rather uneventful, aside from a near collision with Long Point in heavy fog. Again, the *Relation* provides perhaps the best retelling of the trip: "He [La Salle] set out on the 7th of August of the same year, 1679, shaping his course west by south; and his navigation was so fortunate, that on the morning of the 10th ... he reached the mouth of the strait through which Lake Huron pours into Lake Erie [the Detroit River] ..."

Tonty, who had been sent ahead to meet the barque at the Detroit River, was camped near present-day Colchester when he saw the ship, after passing around Point Pelee and through the treacherous Pelee Passage, emerge unscathed: "We were encamped at the entrance to the Detroit, where there was so little ground on account of a marsh laying behind us that, as the wind was blowing fresh from the northeast across the lake, the waves began to dash over us, awakening us earlier than we should have wished. At daybreak, sighting the barque, we made three smoking signal fires, when she put in toward land. We ran out to her in a canoe."

The *Griffon*, following the same route as Dollier and Galinée ten years before, passed up the Detroit River and through Lake St. Clair, the latter of which the three Récollets aboard the ship named as they passed through. The *Griffon* then entered Lake Huron, fighting the wind all the way, along with a fierce storm on August 24 that nearly wrecked the tiny ship. Only the pilot, Luc, managed to keep his head and steer the crew to safety while the rest of the men, huddled together on deck and prayed for their lives. It would be the highlight of Luc's short career on the Great Lakes.

The *Griffon* finally arrived at the Jesuit mission at Michilimackinac, in northern Michigan, at the end of August. The Jesuits, along with their Native charges, were awestruck by the ship, her white sails spread full against the sky as she dropped anchor. After they paddled out to greet the *Griffon* in their canoes, and were welcomed aboard by La Salle's weary crew, the explorer managed to make contact with an advance party he had sent forward to trade for furs. (Some of these men had in fact deserted to the area of Sault Ste Marie, probably thinking La Salle would never make it as far as Michilimackinac. Tonty eventually had to go and bring them back.) The traders had been successful — La Salle loaded more than 12,000 livres worth of furs into the *Griffon*'s hold, more than enough to appease his anxious creditors at Quebec and fetch him a tidy profit in the process.

His men now back aboard and his financial future secured, La Salle decided to use the *Griffon* to speed him even further on his voyage, sailing her onto Lake Michigan as far as present-day Green Bay, Wisconsin. Here, he made a fateful decision that would end the expedition's brief period of peace for good. Left with a small crew of men and four canoes to continue his journey, and convinced that his explorations were back on track, La Salle decided to continue on into the American Midwest, sending Luc and the *Griffon* back to Niagara to unload the furs and ship them back to

Montreal. Once this was done, they were to sail the *Griffon* back to La Salle at Green Bay.

Standing on the shore, La Salle watched his prized vessel, with its small fortune in furs, fade off into the distance, firing a salute from one of her iron cannons as she went.

It would be the last time anyone would see the *Griffon* and her small crew.

In the Name of the King

For La Salle, the disappearance of the *Griffon* would only be the latest in the long line of humiliations that had bedevilled his explorations for more than ten years. In the aftermath, the explorer was convinced that Luc and the *Griffon*'s crew had stolen his furs and then burned the ship. But the fact that neither the men nor the furs were ever seen again points to a far different fate; more likely the *Griffon* met her end in a storm somewhere on Lake Michigan or possibly Lake Huron. In hindsight, it could easily be argued that for the tiny ship to have made the arduous voyage a second time in safety would be nothing short of a miracle; with no suitable marine charts available — and considering Luc's previously demonstrated recklessness in losing the supply barque on Lake Ontario — the odds were certainly stacked against the *Griffon*.

Though archaeologists have not been able to positively identify the wreck of the *Griffon* in the years since, they have uncovered a number of strong candidates. Two potential sites lie near Manitoulin Island in Georgian Bay, an area renowned for its incredible number of submerged rocks and shoals, and on Lake Michigan near Escanaba, just north of where La Salle last saw the ship at Green Bay.

In any case, after the explorer wished the *Griffon*'s crew luck and dispatched them back to Niagara, he continued on foot and by canoe south on Lake Michigan with fourteen men, including Tonty, and built a small fort at the mouth of the St. Joseph River before continuing on as far as present-day Peoria, Illinois. Here, the men laid the groundwork for yet another, more permanent fort, this one named Fort Crèvecoeur, or heartbreak — a tribute to the many troubles the explorer had endured to reach this spot.

But as the months passed and with still no word from the *Griffon*, La Salle began to grow more and more worried. Finally, on March 19, 1680, he decided to retrace his steps in search of his ship and return toward

Lake Erie. He set out with a small number of men, travelling at first by canoe and then mostly on foot, "through woods so thickly intertwined with briars and thorns that in two and a half days his men had their clothes torn to shreds, and their faces so covered with blood and slashed that they were not recognizable."

On April 21, he arrived back at Fort Conti, which he discovered (perhaps not entirely to his surprise) had been burned to the ground by the Iroquois after he had sailed away from it aboard the *Griffon* the previous summer. Despondent that he had not yet been able to find any trace of the ship, he continued on to Montreal, where he knew he would need all of his oratorical skills to placate his ever-anxious creditors, who continued to dog him at every turn. In all, the trip from Lake Michigan was a voyage that the official *Relation,* in perhaps only a mild exaggeration, described as "the most toilsome that ever any Frenchman has ever undertaken in America."

But the stubborn La Salle still refused to be stopped. Over the next two years, while continuing to sink deeper and deeper into debt, he would again reunite with the men he had left at Fort Crèvecoeur. But as if he had not suffered enough, he was in line for further disappointment when he learned that most of these had deserted in the interim, raiding the fort's stores and leaving poor Tonty to rely on the surrounding Native people for his very survival.

And yet, this was still only the beginning of La Salle's troubles.

His mission continued; fighting starvation, thanks to the loss of the supplies he had expected the *Griffon* to bring back, he eventually made his way to the Mississippi River, pursuing it as far as present-day Vernon, Louisiana, near the shores of the Gulf of Mexico. There, in a small and sombre ceremony on April 9, 1682, he claimed the entire territory of Louisiana in the name of King Louis XIV.

It made for a rare scene indeed, especially in the wild backwoods of the South. La Salle appeared in all the regalia of the old country — including a gold-laced red cloak — and, surrounded by his remaining men, erected a cross on the site with a plate buried beneath it that bore a simple inscription: "In the name of Louis XIV, King of France and of Navarre, this ninth of April, 1682."

With this simple act, La Salle had expanded New France's boundaries far beyond anyone's expectations, including, it appeared, the king's. When word of La Salle's Louisiana claim reached the royal court some months later, Louis XIV was heard to exclaim that the explorer's discovery was "very useless."

The main problem was that all of this sudden expansion left the colony spread dangerously thin, leaving the new French claim open to a range of challenges, not the least of which came from the many Native tribes living in the territory.

It seemed that Colbert's warnings about pushing the boundaries of New France too far were already beginning to come true.

Back in France, the royal court had finally run out of patience with La Salle. The explorer had made it back to the mother country early in 1684 with yet another grand plan, this one involving the settlement of a new colony in Louisiana which, he hoped, would form the basis of a massive French presence in the Midwest. But the king was so thoroughly fed up with La Salle by this point that he was no longer welcome at the royal court; he had to propose his idea in a written report.

It was a far cry from the heady days when La Salle could count on having the rapt attention of the most influential members of the French elite.

But La Salle did have one more trick up his sleeve: he had made sure that the maps that were shown to the king were slightly altered, showing the mouth of the Mississippi to be much closer to Spanish holdings in New Mexico. In other words, an ideal base from which to launch an attack on France's colonizing rivals. To further entice the king, La Salle wrote that the river would make an excellent port for an armada, even though the explorer knew this not to be the case. The king also learned that La Salle could command an army of thousands of Native warriors — yet another figment of the explorer's overactive imagination.

Nonetheless, it was on this flimsy basis that La Salle sailed from France on August 1, 1684, with a flotilla of four ships and 288 settlers, including a number of women and La Salle's brother Jean, bound for the Gulf of Mexico. It was a horrible trip: like almost all of La Salle's journeys it was plagued by sickness, lack of drinking water and provisions, and, of course, desertions. The Spanish captured one ship, which contained a large portion of the party's supplies, and another ran aground in the Gulf. In the end, only thirty-six souls, including La Salle, were left to soldier onward.

Here, in the harsh backwoods of the South, La Salle's bad temper and aggressive leadership style finally undid him. In Texas, on the night of March 18, 1687, five settlers crept into the tent of three of his most trusted lieutenants, including his nephew and a Native guide who had been with La Salle for years. While the men slept, the five set upon them with axes, killing all three.

The next day, while a distraught La Salle was angrily questioning his men about the murder of his closest friends, he did not notice Pierre Duhaut, a merchant and one of La Salle's many creditors, lying in wait in the tall grass, his musket at the ready. When La Salle moved close enough, Duhaut seized the opportunity, leaping forward and firing at point-blank range. The bullet found its mark; La Salle slumped over and was immediately dead.

The conspirators then stripped his body naked, taking even his scarlet cloak, which had survived all of the explorer's many shipwrecks, and left his corpse lying out in the open. Just days later, three of the plotters, ostensibly during an argument over trade goods, but by now probably feeling the full weight of what they had done, shot each other to death in a last, desperate bid to avoid justice. The rest of the party, sick and half-starved, slowly made their way to Montreal on foot, arriving there over a year later, on July 13, 1688.

Louis Joutel, a member of the failed expedition, writing in his *Journal of the Last Voyage Performed by Monsieur de La Salle*, provides both an excellent description of La Salle's troubled character and the main reason for the explorer's ultimate demise:

> Such was the unfortunate end of Monsieur de la Salle's life, at a time when he might entertain the greatest hopes, as the reward of his labours. He had the capacity and talent to make his enterprise successful; his constancy and courage and his extraordinary knowledge of arts and sciences, which rendered him fit for anything, together with an indefatigable body, which made him surmount all difficulties, would have procured a glorious issue to his undertaking, had not all those excellent qualities been counterbalanced by too haughty a behaviour, which sometimes made him insupportable, and by a rigidness toward those that were under his command, which at last drew upon him an implacable hatred, and was the occasion of his death.

Despite his troubles, La Salle's explorations of the Mississippi and the Midwest are his greatest legacy. But the construction and sailing of his tiny *Griffon* marked a watershed in the history of the Great Lakes, as well. With this single event, Europeans no longer saw the lakes as vast, undiscovered bodies, but as an integral part of a new and lucrative fur-trading network. To underscore the point, over the next eighty years, more and more voyages would be made upon them, further uniting New France with the continent's rich interior. Lake Erie, with all of its vast potential, was beginning to take its place as the foundation of a new North American empire.

With the charting of the lake, however, came new and unexpected rivalries. French aspirations on the continent would begin to crumble in earnest by the mid-eighteenth century when the British, now hemmed in along the eastern seaboard, began to feel threatened by the giant French claim now stretching across the entire Midwest. More and more, British settlers and traders began to challenge this claim, making an armed confrontation almost inevitable.

In 1754, things came to a head when the first shots of the Seven Years' War (known as the French and Indian War in North America) were fired by a small British detachment under a young lieutenant-colonel, George Washington, in the same Ohio Valley that had so entranced La Salle over eighty years earlier. In a foreshadowing of even greater conflict to come for Washington, he wrote excitedly of his first action in the field against French forces: "I heard the bullets whistle, and, believe me, there is something charming in the sound."

As Colbert had predicted, the French had stretched their boundaries too far, and their army was spread so thin that the British steadily pushed them back to Quebec until, in 1763, the dream of New France died forever when British General James Wolfe forced the capitulation of the city on the Plains of Abraham.

The ensuing peace would be short-lived. Little more than a decade later, a new player would emerge to challenge the British for control of the lakes, this one from a quite unexpected quarter. In 1776, the nascent United States of America declared her independence from Britain, triggering another bloody war that would drag on for seven more years until, under Washington's steady leadership, she would claim her place — ironically, with the help of the French — among the world's free nations.

In the first few years of the nineteenth century, the newborn country, now looking to consolidate its territorial gains, would continue the colonization La Salle had begun and launch a massive campaign of expansion into the Lake Erie region. But this intrusion of new settlers into traditional Native lands would once again stoke the fires of conflict. What ensued was a war that would determine the ultimate fate of not only one lake, but an entire continent.

Chapter 2

"We Have Met the Enemy":
The War of 1812 on Lake Erie

A s the nineteenth century dawned, the land surrounding the western basin of Lake Erie remained mostly untamed wilderness. Passing groups of Native tribesmen hunted and trapped on the Lake Erie islands, but aside from a few adventurers who happened this way, the archipelago remained unsettled.

But change was taking place all along Lake Erie's southern coast. The newly formed United States was expanding steadily westward and settlers, driven by adventure and cheap land on America's frontier, were beginning to arrive in steadily growing numbers. By the summer of 1812, many had carved small farmsteads out of the forests of modern-day Ohio and Pennsylvania. The migration eventually found its way onto the islands in the autumn of 1811, when seven families, led by Seth Done of Ohio, cleared one hundred acres at what would later become the settlement of Put-in-Bay on South Bass Island. The location was perfect, with fertile soil and a deep, well-protected harbour. By the summer of 1812, the colonists had raised a crop of wheat and constructed a number of log cabins and outbuildings at Put-in-Bay.

But there was a dark cloud hanging over all of this seemingly idyllic development; as the settlers pushed north and west into the Great Lakes region from America's eastern seaboard, they forced many Native nations off their traditional lands, creating friction, and sometimes violence, between the two groups. Exacerbating this was the fact that many First Nations already had trade and military ties with the British in Upper Canada, who supplied them with gifts of weapons, tools, and ornaments in order to sustain their loyalty. By 1810, many Ohio Natives had banded together under the Shawnee chief Tecumseh, who was on friendly terms with Major-General Isaac Brock, the commander of all British military operations in Upper Canada.

By early 1812, an atmosphere that can only be described as sheer terror pervaded the small American Lake Erie settlements, fuelled mainly by the horrifying tales of torture and kidnapping at the hands of fierce Native warriors that had quickly spread throughout the communities. As journalist and South Bass Island resident Lydia Ryall put it a century later in her 1913 book, *Sketches and Stories of the Lake Erie Islands*, this was a period "when tomahawk and scalping knife hung constantly over the heads of lake shore and island dwellers, and life for them was one continued round of apprehension." Out of fear, many farmers slept with their muskets close at hand.

The situation came to a boil immediately after America declared war on Great Britain in June 1812. Later that summer, Done's party was ambushed and driven from Put-in-Bay by a band of British scouts and their Native allies. After looting and burning the settlers' cabins and outbuildings, they set fire to the wheat crop, reducing it to smoldering embers. All too aware of their vulnerable situation, the colonists had, just days earlier, tried to save thousands of bushels by rowing them across to the Ohio mainland, but British and Native scouts later found the crop hidden in a decrepit storehouse and burned it as well.

So ended the first attempt to settle the Lake Erie islands, but they would play a key role in the coming struggle for control of the lake, and in the process would bear witness to the bloodiest naval battle ever to occur on the Great Lakes.

Erie in the Crosshairs

When U.S. President James Madison officially declared war, most Americans believed that taking Canada would be, in the oft-quoted words of his predecessor Thomas Jefferson, "a mere matter of marching." But any expectations of an early victory were soon dashed. Isaac Brock knew that it was crucial for the British forces in Upper Canada to strike first if they were to defeat the Americans, who vastly outnumbered them and were largely fighting on their home soil. To that end, he wasted little time going on the attack, gathering a force of 1,300 men, consisting mostly of local Canadian militia and Native warriors, and setting off for Fort Detroit. After a short skirmish on August 16, 1812, Brock promptly surrounded the fort and placed it under siege, trapping American General William Hull and 2,000 soldiers inside. Outnumbered nearly two to one, Brock knew he would not be able to maintain the siege for long. If an upset British victory was to be achieved on this day, a desperate gamble was his only chance.

Keenly aware that the Americans feared the tactics of his Native allies above almost everything else, Brock dispatched one of his aides to the beseiged fort. Once allowed inside the gates, he presented Hull with a letter from Brock demanding Hull's surrender. The letter went on to make specific mention of the Natives, noting that while Brock did not wish to launch a "war of extermination," his Native allies would be "beyond control the moment the contest commences."

As it turned out, Brock's instinct was on the mark. Hull immediately surrendered Fort Detroit and the surrounding Michigan Territory without a shot being fired. The British occupation of Michigan would hold strong for a full year, until it was finally toppled by the Americans in late 1813.

Although Brock's success at Detroit boosted British morale, it reinforced to his commanders back in Kingston, Ontario, and especially to Sir George Prevost, the newly minted governor of British North America, that control of the Great Lakes would be imperative in mounting any kind of defence of the colony. Lake Erie was especially important, as Fort Malden (then known as Fort Amherstburg), in Amherstburg, Ontario, was provisioned almost exclusively through a waterborne supply line stretching to it from Long Point. If the Americans were able to cut that line, it would be only a matter of time before the entire Western District of Upper Canada fell into their hands.

But the optimistic Prevost felt he had an important edge over his opponents in this area. Fifty-five years earlier, during the Seven Years' War, the British had established the Provincial Marine, a permanent armed fleet on the Great Lakes. Back then, this tiny force had been especially effective against the French. But the Marine had faltered badly in the years since 1763, and had been reduced to a sort of glorified water taxi, shuttling troops and supplies from one port to another. It had too few sailors, and most of those who remained had no combat experience. Some of its officers, no doubt enjoying the relative ease and safety of Marine life, stayed in their jobs well into their elderly years.

Many Provincial Marine vessels were also badly in need of repair. On Lake Erie, the Marine boasted only two seaworthy warships of any real strength, with barely enough men to sail them: the *Queen Charlotte*, built in 1809, and the *Lady Prevost*, newly launched in 1811. Both were stationed at Fort Malden. The smaller *General Hunter* was also available, but it was only lightly armed. The rest of the force consisted of two small merchant vessels that Amherstburg's master shipwright, William Bell, had been converting into warships: the *Chippewa* and the *Little Belt*, with only two guns each.

Fortunately for the British, Prevost was a born administrator, and moved quickly to streamline the rickety Marine. He sacked its elderly commodore and two of its captains, and reduced the ranks of many of its officers in light of their meagre battle experience. Prevost also placed responsibility for the Marine where it more properly belonged: under Royal Navy Commodore James Yeo, who was responsible for all Navy operations on the Great Lakes. He also started a shipbuilding program, which on Lake Erie meant adding the construction of the HMS *Detroit* to William Bell's workload. Soon to become the Lake Erie fleet's flagship, the *Detroit* was capable of carrying twenty guns, a powerful vessel for the Great Lakes at the time.

The village of Amherstburg had grown into a bustling community by 1812. The town's inhabitants were mainly shipwrights, carpenters, and other tradesmen serving the Provincial Marine dockyard and Fort Malden.

The fort had been built by the government of Upper Canada in 1796, mainly to defend the southern frontier against the American expansion that had been surging in the wake of the revolutionary war. But, like the flotilla of Provincial Marine vessels moored there, it was also considerably run down by the time the war began. This was a situation that Prevost, his hands already full dealing with myriad political and military problems, was working to rectify as the situation between Great Britain and the United States grew ever more grave. Fort Malden was also the headquarters of the British Indian Department, and British officers and their Native allies could often be seen walking its grounds.

Lieutenant-Colonel Henry Procter was Fort Malden's commander. Known as an energetic, resourceful officer, he had taken command just prior to Brock's victory at Detroit. A surgeon's son, Procter had served briefly near New York during the revolutionary war, and was respected by his men and his superiors; Brock himself once praised Procter's "indefatigable industry," and it was this quality in particular that would soon be put to the test at the notoriously under-provisioned Fort Malden.

An Unlikely Shipyard

Across Lake Erie, the Americans, with no armed ships capable of challenging the British, were racing to get their own fleet on the water. In October 1812, Sailing Master Daniel Dobbins chose Presque Isle Bay, at Erie, Pennsylvania, almost directly across from the British supply depot at Long Point, as the site of the American base on the lake, and quickly got down to the business of turning it into a functioning shipyard. Dobbins had been at Detroit with Hull and, interestingly, had managed to negotiate his release through a British colonel named Nichols, who was an old acquaintance. Such "paroles" were not uncommon during this period, and, upon his release, Dobbins crossed Lake Erie in an open boat along with several of the men from Fort Detroit before finally making his way to Presque Isle.

Dobbins's choice for the site of the U.S. base was not without controversy. At the mouth of the harbour was a sandbar that reduced the water's depth to a mere 2.5 metres, insufficient to allow a fully armed warship to pass over. Dobbins was sharply upbraided by Captain Jesse Elliott, the Navy commander responsible for the region, who wrote to Dobbins that it appeared to him "utterly impossible to build gun boats at Presque Isle. There is not enough water on the bar to get them into the lake. Should there be water, the place is at all times open to the attacks of the enemy … I have no further communication to make on the subject." But Dobbins vigorously defended his choice, responding, "There is a sufficiency of water to let them [the U.S. fleet] into the lake, but not a sufficiency to let heavy armed vessels of the enemy into the bay to destroy them. The bay is large and spacious, and completely landlocked, except at the entrance." It was soon to be a moot point: when Commodore Isaac Chauncey, commander of all U.S. Navy operations on the Great Lakes, arrived to inspect the operation at Erie in January 1813, he approved of Dobbins's work and ordered him to "get out timber, and prepare for the building of two sloops of war." These were in addition to two gunboats that Dobbins was already building at the time. Shortly after his visit, Chauncey sent Dobbins plans for two more warships, bringing the emerging Lake Erie flotilla to a total of six vessels.

Dobbins, as he had in locating the naval base, took on the ships' construction with enthusiasm, and even though the winter of 1813 was brutally cold, he managed to get almost every blacksmith and carpenter on the Ohio frontier involved in the project. Three hundred shipwrights and axemen were working and living in Erie itself, nearly doubling the village's population. Erie's citizens took up the cause as well, ransacking the village for every scrap piece of iron and helping bring lumber, canvas for sails, and every other provision imaginable overland along narrow roads and through untracked forests from as far away as Pittsburgh and even Philadelphia.

In early March, the project got a boost with the arrival of Noah Brown, a shipwright from New York, and twenty-five carpenters. As the warships were only being constructed for one purpose — the annihilation of the British presence on Lake Erie — Brown opted for a no-nonsense approach, eschewing all nonessential features so as to get them on the water as quickly as possible. There would be no ornamental features — not so much as a figurehead. As Brown noted to one of the carpenters: "We want no extras — plain work is all that is required; they will only be wanted for one battle; if we win, that is all that is wanted of them; if the enemy is victorious, the work is good enough to be captured." Chauncey was also putting pressure on Brown, writing him often and urging him to "drive on as fast as possible my dear Sir."

By mid-March, Dobbins and his crew had laid the keels of the four gunboats and were hard at work on all six vessels. These ships, particularly the twenty-gun behemoths *Niagara* and *Lawrence*, would play legendary roles in the coming battle for control of the lake.

Some seven hundred kilometres away, in Newport, Rhode Island, twenty-seven-year-old Oliver Hazard Perry was growing restless. Newly promoted to the rank of master commandant, he had climbed rapidly through the ranks of the fledgling U.S. Navy. The Perry family was well-connected in Navy circles and as a result, when America fell desperately short of sailors upon the eruption of conflict with France in 1799, Oliver's father was called out of retirement to command the frigate *General Greene*. Young Oliver, then only twelve years old, excitedly went along, serving as a midshipman on this, his first assignment at sea. Between 1799 and 1802, the *General Greene* saw relatively little action, but young Perry became thoroughly hooked on life at sea, and by all accounts was a hardworking sailor. His peacetime career path then led him through a series of relatively humdrum tours on four other Navy ships, the most notable being the fabled USS *Constitution*, before he was assigned his own command, the schooner *Revenge*, in early 1810.

At twenty-five, and already steeped in a family tradition of shipboard life, Perry was undoubtedly eager to have the chance to prove himself in a command role. But what should have been a very exciting period in the young captain's life ended up being all too short. During a routine coastal patrol in the summer of 1810, the *Revenge* hit a reef in Block Island Sound and was completely wrecked. No one was injured, and a subsequent inquiry pinned the entire blame for the incident on the *Revenge*'s pilot, leaving Perry free of any responsibility. Absolved, but far from satisfied, Perry returned home to Newport. He was there, commanding a small fleet of gunboats — and yet again far from the action — when war came in June 1812.

With the war came a new lease on life for Perry, and in light of his recent troubles, he was determined to make the most of it. He wrote to Paul Hamilton, then secretary of the navy, requesting to be reassigned to the Great Lakes, which he correctly reasoned would be at the centre of the action in the coming naval war. He kept in touch with Isaac Chauncey as well, a prudent move, as it turned out. Chauncey was so impressed with Perry's diligence and enthusiasm that he urged William Jones, who had replaced Hamilton, to give Perry command of the naval force on Lake Erie, a recommendation Jones took in February 1813.

The assignment was a massive one for such a young officer, but if Perry felt overwhelmed, he certainly didn't show it, immediately dispatching his best officers to Erie before arriving there himself on March 27, 1813.

As a commander, Perry had a number of attributes that would help him considerably in the months ahead, not the least of which being a great deal of charisma, which certainly made a strong impression on his colleagues at Erie. As Usher Parsons, who would later become the surgeon on Perry's flagship, the *Lawrence*, gushed in a speech to the Rhode Island Historical Society, forty years after the Battle of Lake Erie, on February 16, 1852:

> Possessed of high-minded moral feeling, he was above the low dissipation and sensuality that many officers of his day were prone to indulge in. His conversation was remarkably free from profanity and indelicacy, and in his domestic character … he was a model of every domestic virtue and grace…. On the subjects of history and drama he was well read, and had formed opinions that evinced patient thought.

OLIVER H. PERRY.[1]

Oliver Hazard Perry was only twenty-seven years old when he took command of the American fleet on Lake Erie.

Perry also inspired fierce loyalty in his men. In Parsons's words: "Every germ of merit in his officers was sure to be discovered and encouraged by him, and no opportunity was ever lost of advancing those who performed their duty with cheerfulness and fidelity."

Matters of defence were Perry's first priority when he arrived in Erie. Although it had been used as a military post by the French up to 1760, none of those fortifications still stood and, as Daniel Dobbins's son William wrote in his 1875 book, *History of the Battle of Lake Erie*, "… not a single piece of ordinance remained, and the only thing in the shape of a *cannon* was a *small iron boat howitzer*, with which the villagers celebrated the fourth of July." To rectify the situation, Perry met with Major-General David Mead, the local army commander, who promptly called out the local militia. While the militiamen were poorly armed and almost completely lacking in discipline, their presence provided at least some defence from the British, who routinely sailed across the mouth of the harbour to get a look at what was going on inside.

Through the months of April and May, the construction effort went on at a frenetic pace, and by early July all six of the new ships, the *Lawrence* and *Niagara*, as well as the schooners *Ariel*, *Scorpion*, *Porcupine*, and *Tigress*, were afloat on Presque Isle Bay and in the process of being fitted out.

The new ships were soon joined by the brig *Caledonia* and the *Somers*, *Ohio*, and *Amelia*, small, armed merchant vessels that Perry had sailed to Erie after he took part in the capture of Fort George at Niagara-on-the-Lake in the spring of 1813. The journey had been far from easy, plagued the whole way by thick fog. Worse, Perry had to relinquish command of the small flotilla only two days out of port after coming down with a severe fever. He quickly returned however, when according to Usher Parsons: "a small boat with two men appeared under the lakeshore. They brought with them intelligence from Erie that the enemy had just appeared there, and was probably in pursuit of us." To his relief, when Presque Isle came into view there were no British vessels in sight.

In just five short months, Dobbins, Brown, and Perry had managed nothing less than a miracle: they had created a fully armed and functional naval fleet on Lake Erie out of almost nothing. But one challenge remained before they could seriously challenge the British: they needed to get their new warships over Presque Isle's formidable sandbar.

Procter's Challenge

At Fort Malden, meanwhile, Henry Procter was growing more and more worried; dark rumours about the budding American fleet had made their way across the lake, terrifying the people of Amherstburg. Procter believed the Americans' ultimate goal was to combine the strength of their army with that of their new flotilla and launch an amphibious attack on his fort.

Procter's regulars and militiamen had also been severely tested by frequent border skirmishes over the past year, and his supply line from Long Point was proving troublesome. The constant threat of bad weather on unpredictable Lake Erie, along with the constant worry of enemy attack, reduced the flow of food and supplies to a trickle. As a result, conditions often bordered on starvation for the soldiers, townspeople, and their Native allies, and men and materials were often waylaid at Long Point, delaying the construction and rebuilding of the British fleet.

The dire conditions at Amherstburg were especially difficult for the Native warriors, who were beginning to lose faith in their British friends. As Procter noted in a letter to Robert McDouall, Prevost's aide-de-camp, on June 16, 1813: "At present they [the Native warriors] are not half fed, and would leave us if they were not warm to the cause. The want of Meat does operate much against us. As does the want of Indian arms and goods."

In order to have any chance on Lake Erie, Procter, in the spirit of General Brock, firmly believed that the British had to strike hard at the new American shipyard. He wrote to James Yeo, and to Prevost throughout the spring of 1813, practically begging for reinforcements of both land troops and sailors for the fleet. As the spring wore on, with little substantial response to his pleas, Procter's tone grew ever more desperate. "I am surprised they have not appeared on this lake," he wrote of the American fleet in June, "We are well aware of the necessity of dealing the first blow, indeed we owe everything to our having done so." No doubt Procter was relieved to see Royal Navy Commander Robert Heriot Barclay step onto the dock at Amherstburg on June 6, 1813.

The road that led Barclay to Lake Erie stood in stark contrast to that of Perry, though both were highly ambitious officers and dyed-in-the-wool navy men. Barclay, like Perry, went to sea at the tender age of twelve under the sponsorship of a close relative. In Barclay's case, it was his uncle who secured him a place aboard the warship *Anson*. Unlike Perry, however, Barclay's first tour was marked by treacherous combat. The French Revolution had driven Britain to war with Spain and France, and the *Anson* played a significant role, taking many French and Spanish vessels as prizes in a number of fierce firefights.

In 1804, none other than Horatio Nelson, Britain's most celebrated naval commander, assigned Barclay to his own ship, the legendary *Victory*. This would have been a significant feather in the cap of such a young officer. But he was only there for barely a month before being reassigned to HMS *Swiftsure*, a ship-of-the-line. It was aboard the *Swiftsure* that Barclay would take part, on October 21, 1805, in arguably the most significant naval confrontation in Royal Navy history — Trafalgar. The battle, between thirty-three combined Spanish and French vessels, and twenty-seven British ships, was closely fought, but by evening the British had managed to eke out

Image courtesy of Toronto Reference Library T-15259

Young Robert Heriot Barclay was already a seasoned veteran of naval combat when he arrived on Lake Erie.

a victory. The cost in lives was staggering, particularly for the vanquished French/Spanish fleet: twenty-two of their vessels had been sunk or taken, with 4,408 seamen killed, compared to 449 British. Nelson, who had been hit by a sniper concealed in the rigging of a French vessel, died while being treated aboard his flagship. "Thank God I have done my duty," were his reported last words.

If that wasn't enough, a violent storm hit that night, battering the decrepit fleets even further. At one point, Barclay and some of his crewmates were involved in an attempt to rescue their French brethren, managing to pull 170 from the crippled warship *Redoubtable* before her hull finally broke up.

After the horrors of Trafalgar, Barclay briefly returned home to Scotland before seeking a post on another navy ship, which he obtained with relative ease, quickly returning to sea as a second lieutenant aboard the frigate *Diana*.

It was while he was aboard the *Diana*, attacking a French convoy in a small boat, that Barclay suffered a wound that nearly ended his career, and his life, prematurely. In the heat of the fight, a cannonball fired from the bow of a French ship hit Barclay in the left shoulder, smashing the bones in his left arm to pieces. The *Diana*'s surgeon was left with no choice — Barclay's arm had to be amputated at the shoulder.

After the *Diana* returned to Britain in 1809, Barclay again headed home to Scotland to recuperate, but his stay would be a short one: in light of increasing tension between Britain and the United States, young, ambitious officers like Barclay were needed overseas. He was reassigned to Halifax.

Barclay would likely have been elated at this turn of events; being sent to the front lines of a potential war zone surely meant that, after all he had been through, he would finally be rewarded with his own command. It was not to be. There were no suitable ships at Halifax when he arrived, so he instead spent four long, frustrating years on patrol in the Atlantic. He was in Bermuda when he received orders to report to Kingston, Ontario, to take over command of all Royal Navy operations on the Great Lakes. He had only been in the post for ten days, however, when he was abruptly reassigned to Amherstburg. Barclay was not without reservations about his new position at first, noting that "This [Lake Erie] command was offered to Captain [William Howe] Mulcaster, the next in command to Sir James Yeo, who to my personal knowledge declined it in consequence of its ineffectual state and Sir James Yeo refusing to send seamen." Still, Mulcaster's experience did not seem to give Barclay pause. He promptly set off for Long Point, where he boarded the *Lady Prevost* for Amherstburg.

Barclay's early assessment of the situation coincided with Procter's view that immediate action needed to be taken against the American fleet. His opinion was reinforced when he sailed the *Queen Charlotte* to Erie to see for himself how far the Americans had progressed. What he saw shocked him so much that the next day, from the depot at Long Point, he dispatched a letter to Major-General John Vincent, commander of the British forces in the region:

> I reconnoitred Presque'isle yesterday and found two corvettes in a very forward state indeed — they being both launched — and their lower masts in such a force, with the very backward state in which I am sorry to state the *Detroit* is in, must give the enemy a very great superiority on this lake — taking also into consideration the men I have — the badly organization even of those — together with the great want of stores at Amherstburg renders the prospect rather gloomy — nor can anything clear the cloud except an immediate reinforcement of troops to enable General Procter to join me in an attack on Presque'isle and destroy the squadron before they can get quite ready.

Barclay was also frank about the sorry situation at Amherstburg, noting to Prevost in a July 13 letter: "I have to state that there is a general want of stores of every description at this post, but more especially *iron* [author's emphasis] ... all of which have been demanded long ago." The lack of iron posed a major problem for William Bell in outfitting the *Detroit*. Though there was a surplus of lumber, iron was not as easy to acquire in the rural, sparsely populated Western District. Bell managed to finish the job, however, largely by salvaging everything he could from defunct vessels in the dockyard, and on July 29 the *Detroit*, complete, slid into the Detroit River. But, in the words of Barclay, "there is neither a sufficient quantity of ordnance, ammunition or any other stores and not a man to put on her."

Barclay attempted to buy Bell and his shipwrights time by blockading Presque Isle Bay, occasionally trading fire with the militiamen guarding it. But with so few resources, he was unable to remain on station for very long. While Barclay's ships were away from Presque Isle in early August, Dobbins managed to slip his entire fleet over the bar by removing all unnecessary weight and raising the warships on specially designed wooden floats. The operation was not an easy one: it took the Americans an entire night to get the *Lawrence* alone over, unloading all of her guns and supplies onto the beach until she was light enough to pass. The American flagship finally entered the lake at 8 a.m. the next morning.

Henry Procter was furious at this turn of events, seething in a letter to Prevost on August 18: "I now suppose they [the American fleet] are establishing themselves on the Bass Islands which form Put-in-Bay, an excellent harbour, and which I would have occupied if I had had the means." Even worse for the Fort Malden garrison was that the armaments meant for the *Detroit*, including the sixteen twenty-four-pound carronades vital for close combat, had been captured by the Americans when they took Fort York [in present-day Toronto] in July 1813. With the fall of York and the consequent weakening of the supply line to Amherstburg, the prospect of famine now loomed large. Worse, if in light of the dire circumstances Procter's Native warriors decided to abandon him, the Western District would almost certainly be lost. Barclay had no other choice: even though he knew that his was the weaker of the two fleets, the time to take on the Americans for dominance of Lake Erie was drawing near.

On September 6, thirty-nine sailors arrived from Long Point. These men were to form the Royal Navy nucleus of Barclay's crew. The other 410–420 men were comprised mainly of landsmen, most with little or no sailing or combat experience, and a small contingent from the Royal Newfoundland Regiment: useful soldiers capable of serving at sea as well as on land. But even with these late arrivals, Barclay was still drastically short of men. As for the *Detroit*, the warship was now armed and ready, though mostly with long-range cannons that had to be stripped from the ramparts of Fort Malden. It was a true hodgepodge of munitions; when the *Detroit* finally sailed for Put-in-Bay on September 9, she carried a wide variety of guns, and was almost entirely lacking the short-range carronades needed to take on Perry's ships in close quarters.

"Don't Give Up the Ship"

September 10, 1813, dawned clear and cool. As the sun broke over the eastern horizon, a lookout high in the rigging of the *Lawrence* spotted the silhouette of what could only be a sail in the distance, toward the Upper Canadian mainland. "Sail ho!" he cried, repeating the phrase six times, once for each of the approaching British warships. According to Parsons,

Photo by author

A cannon on the grounds of Fort Malden. Artillery had to be stripped from the fort for use on the HMS Detroit.

who was on the deck of the *Lawrence*, then "... the hoarse voice of the boatswain resounded through all the ships, 'all hands up anchor!'" With that, more than five hundred men aboard the American flotilla sprang to life, hauling up anchors, raising sails and preparing the fleet to leave the shelter of Put-in-Bay.

For Perry, the main obstacle to victory was now completely out of his control. The wind had been blowing out of the west-southwest all morning, working in Barclay's favour as his ships drove steadily south toward Put-in-Bay. But after a long summer of waiting, Perry had no intention of passing up a chance to take control of Lake Erie once and for all. He decided that he would fight anyway. It was then, as Perry was planning his battle lines, that the aggressive young commander's luck took a dramatic turn for the better; at 10:00 a.m., with the British fleet closing in on his position, the wind suddenly swung around to the southeast, giving his ships the momentum they needed to clear Put-in-Bay and take on the British in the open water to the west of South Bass Island. Parsons describes the feeling of awe that swept the American crews as they slowly drifted toward the British vessels: "We now discovered the English squadron, hove to in a line about five or six miles to the leeward…. The vessels were freshly painted, their red ensigns gently folding in the breeze, they made a very gallant appearance."

Barclay had arranged his ships in a line with the tiny *Chippewa* leading the flagship *Detroit*. The *General Hunter* was next, followed by the *Queen Charlotte* and *Lady Prevost*. The tiny *Little Belt* brought up the rear.

Perry, in response, chose to go commander against commander, lining his ship, the *Lawrence*, up against Barclay's *Detroit*, with the two gunboats *Ariel* and *Scorpion* ahead in case these fast-sailing schooners were needed to carry orders back to the rest of the fleet. Directly behind came the three-gun *Caledonia* to take on the *General Hunter*, the *Niagara*, twin to Perry's *Lawrence*, to face the *Queen Charlotte*, and the smaller warships *Somers*, *Porcupine*, *Tigress,* and *Trippe,* to take on the *Lady Prevost* and *Little Belt*.

The wind no longer in his favour, Barclay, whose vessels were armed mostly with longer-range guns, attempted to maintain as great a distance from the American fleet as possible. Out of range of their short-range carronades, he planned to strike as hard as he could before they closed the distance. Thus, for over ninety minutes, until 11:45 a.m., the two fleets drifted ever so slowly toward one another while onboard, according to Parsons, "a profound silence reigned for more than one hour…. It was like the stillness that precedes the hurricane."

It was during this excruciating wait that Perry performed the act of bravado for which, at least in the United States, he is perhaps best known. Having gathered the crew of the *Lawrence* together on deck, he took the opportunity to show them his personal battle flag. William Dobbins provides this rather fanciful description of the moment in his *History of the Battle of Lake Erie*:

Perry ... unfolded the flag, and mounting a gun-slide
addressed them: My brave lads, the description on this
flag is the last words of the gallant Captain Lawrence, after
whom this vessel is named: *'Don't Give up the Ship!'* shall I
hoist it? 'Aye, yie, sir!' was the unanimous response...

James Lawrence had been captain of the USS *Chesapeake*, which had
been captured off Boston by the British frigate *Shannon* three months
earlier. Many of her crew were killed or wounded in the bloody battle,
Lawrence among them. As he lay dying on the deck, he shouted out "Don't
give up the ship!" to drive on the few who remained alive.

Suddenly, the silent drift was shattered by a burst from one of the
Detroit's long guns, which splashed into the water short of its target, Perry's
Lawrence. As the Americans drew closer, lining up to return fire, another
shot bellowed forth from the *Detroit*, this time striking the *Lawrence*'s
forecastle, smashing through the deck in a shower of wooden splinters. The
battle was immediately joined when *Ariel* and *Scorpion* opened up with
their bow-mounted cannons. About five minutes later the British replied
with a full-on barrage from all ships, hammering Perry's fleet and focusing
their fire on the *Lawrence*, as the Americans attempted to edge close enough
to strike with their lethal broadside carronades. After a few moments,
Perry ordered the *Lawrence*'s gunners to unleash a volley, but it fell short,
splashing harmlessly into the water. Still, Perry drove the *Lawrence* on, but
she was suffering badly under the fire of the British guns, and the men
who sailed her were being cut down one by one. Usher Parsons, who was
tending to wounded sailors before Perry had even returned the first British
volley, describes the grisly scene unfolding below deck:

> For more than two long hours, little could be heard but
> the deafening thunders of our broad-sides, the crash of
> balls dashing through our timbers, and the shrieks of the
> wounded. These were brought down faster than I could
> attend to them, farther than to stay the bleeding, or
> support the shattered limbs with splints, and pass them
> forward upon the berth deck. Two or three were killed
> near me, after being wounded.

Especially worrying for the crew of the struggling *Lawrence* was the
fact that the *Niagara* had not made sail with the rest of the fleet, but was

instead holding back, firing on the British only with her two bow-mounted cannons, to little real effect.

Finally, around 12:15 p.m., the *Lawrence* was in close enough range to loose a broadside upon the *Detroit*, which she did with devastating results, her cannon ripping into the British flagship's side and shredding her rigging. But the absence of the *Niagara* from the American line stacked the odds against the *Lawrence* even further. Sensing hesitation on the part of Jesse Elliott, the *Niagara*'s captain (and the same officer who had earlier rebuked Daniel Dobbins for his choice of Presque Isle as the American naval base), British Captain Robert Finnis of the *Queen Charlotte* ordered his ship forward, and now it, along with the *Detroit*, was pounding away at Perry's flagship. Perry describes the results in his official account to Navy Secretary Jones:

> Every brace and bowline shot away, she became unman-ageable, notwithstanding the great exertions of the sailing master. In this situation, she sustained the action upwards of two hours, within canister distance until every gun was rendered useless, and the greater part of her crew either killed or wounded…

With the body count on the *Lawrence* mounting and his men falling all around him, Perry realized that to have any chance of winning the day, he would need an even more aggressive strategy. And, in his customary way, he wasted little time in employing one. At 2:15 p.m., he ordered a small open boat brought up and, taking his now lowered battle flag under his arm, descended over the side of the *Lawrence*, leaving Lieutenant John Yarnell in charge and giving him permission to surrender the flagship to the British if he deemed it necessary. Perry, now fully exposed to the British fire, was then rowed across to the *Niagara* as she passed about a kilometre to leeward. As soon as Perry was clear, Yarnell, anxious to stop the terrible bloodbath that had been unfolding aboard his ship for the better part of two hours, ordered the stars and stripes lowered. The American flagship had surrendered.

Unfortunately, the British were in no position to take advantage of this happy turn of events. As the American fleet had drawn closer, its short-range guns had become ever more lethal. The British ships, the *Detroit* in particular, were literally being torn to pieces. The scene aboard the flagship was one of horror, as her sails and rigging were now totally useless, and the barrage of cannonballs and the resulting wooden projectiles flying from the deck had killed and maimed many of her gunners. The Americans had also perched snipers high in their rigging, a tactic reminiscent of Nelson's death at Trafalgar, and as the sails of the British ships fell away, their soldiers and sailors were left with little cover from the snipers' musket fire.

The British had seen Perry depart the *Lawrence* and row toward the unscathed *Niagara*. They had fired on him, but the inaccuracy and unreliability of the muskets of the period made hitting such a small target nearly impossible. As for Barclay, he remained in command of the *Detroit*, but a splinter had torn a large gash in his thigh. Worse, as he was trying to focus on how his warships, their line now in total disarray, might cope with Perry and the *Niagara*, an American cannonball struck him in the back, tearing his right shoulder blade to shreds. With Barclay now totally out of action, command of the fleet, such as it was, fell to Second Lieutenant George Inglis.

Captain Elliott was the first to greet Perry when he climbed aboard the *Niagara*. Anxious, perhaps, to avoid having to explain his apparent reluctance to join the battle to his commander, Elliott offered to take Perry's rowboat and go to the back of the line to bring up the gunboats *Tigress* and *Trippe*,

Image courtesy of National Archives of Canada C-040873

An early twentieth-century painting of Perry's victory over the British fleet in the Battle of Lake Erie.

both of which had fallen behind. Driven only by his desire to rejoin the fray, Perry quickly consented, ran his flag up the *Niagara*'s mainmast, and ordered her turned about and driven directly toward the tattered British line.

The British, for their part, responded with all the fire they could muster, but it was mostly ineffective against the rapidly closing American warship. And just when it seemed things couldn't get any worse, they did: the heavily damaged *Queen Charlotte*, now listing out of control and with her captain, Robert Finnis, killed by an American cannonball earlier in the battle, drifted into the side of the *Detroit* and ran her bowsprit into the flagship's rigging, hopelessly entangling both ships. Seeing the opportunity to land the decisive blow, Perry drove through the hole the *Queen Charlotte* had left in the British line and, in yet another shade of Nelson at Trafalgar, unleashed repeated broadsides into the bows of both helpless ships. After fifteen minutes of this ruthless pounding, a crewman on the *Niagara* spotted a small white flag fluttering above the deck of the shattered *Detroit*. Slightly more than three hours after the battle had started, and with the combined fleets having drifted almost to West Sister Island, it was over. George Inglis described the final minutes as they occurred on the *Detroit*, in his official report to Barclay, written just hours after the surrender:

> … the ship laying completely unmanageable, every brace cut away, the mizzen topmast and gaff down, all other masts badly wounded, not a stay left forward, hull shattered very much, a number of guns disabled, and the enemy's squadron raking both ships, ahead and astern, none of our own in a situation to support us, I was under the painful necessity of answering the enemy to say we had struck, the *Queen Charlotte* having previously done so.

The death toll was staggering: aboard the British ships, forty-one soldiers, officers, and sailors lay dead, the vast majority on the *Detroit* and *Queen Charlotte*. Ninety-four were wounded, and the first and second in command on every ship was either killed or injured. Perry's squadron saw only slightly lighter casualties, with twenty-seven killed and ninety-six wounded. Like the British, most were aboard the flagship, the *Lawrence*, which counted over two-thirds of her crew among the dead or infirm.

Mere moments after the guns fell silent, Perry famously summed up the day's action in a note to General William Henry Harrison. He wrote:

Dear General:

We have met the enemy and they are ours. Two ships, two brigs, one schooner and one sloop. Yours with great respect and esteem,

O.H. Perry

Aboard the *Detroit*, Barclay's condition was grave, with both arms now useless. James Young, the *Detroit*'s surgeon, was keeping watch over him. Young had managed to stabilize his commander, but Barclay still suffered greatly, so much so that he later told Perry that he was afraid he would die if he wasn't soon returned to Upper Canada. Perry did what he could to send Barclay home as quickly as was possible, impressing Barclay so much with his actions that he made the following note in his official account to Yeo: "Captain Perry has behaved in a most humane and attentive manner, not only to myself and officers, but to all the wounded."

A Legacy of Peace

Just before the sun set, a short, sombre ceremony was held that could be heard from all ships, both British and American. At its conclusion, as per longstanding naval tradition, the dead seamen from both fleets were wrapped in individual canvases and sent to their final resting place in Lake Erie's watery depths. William Dobbins provides this poetic description in *History of the Battle of Lake Erie*:

> As the mellow rays of the Autumnal sunset were radiating from the Western horizon, the blue waters of Lake Erie closed over the remains of these gallant sons of Neptune and Mars, whom, but a few hours before, were hurling defiance and death at each other, but now hushed in death and everlasting peace, their spirits in the presence of their God.

The families of these men, particularly those of the dead British sailors, many of whom could probably not even find Lake Erie on a map, would be left with no visible reminder, or gravesite, at which to grieve their losses.

But the slain officers who led them would not be going home, either. Again, as was the naval protocol of the day, they were kept onboard the ships for a land burial that was planned for the following day, when the battered fleet would arrive back at Put-in-Bay. Through the long night, the wounded vessels lay at anchor near West Sister Island. Lake Erie was calm, and the wind silent; all that could be heard echoing between the ships were the moans and shrieks of the wounded and the dying.

The solemn mass funeral for the officers at Put-in-Bay featured the colours of both the United States and Great Britain flying at half-mast, and Barclay, who miraculously managed to leave his bed for the service, leaning on Perry for support as the bodies of six officers, three British and three American, were committed to a mass grave, the only marker of which became known as the "Perry willow" or "lone willow." According to local legend, the hearty tree grew from a shoot planted in the burial mound by one of the surviving seamen. Although the Battle of Lake Erie was a point of nationalistic pride in the United States, the creaking willow, which finally fell to the ground almost a hundred years later, in 1900, was the only marker of this sacred site.

Finally, just two years after the battle's centenary in 1915, the construction of Perry's Victory and International Peace Memorial (known simply as "Perry's Monument" to the locals) was completed on the site. A committee of nine states and the U.S. government funded the ambitious project. At 107 metres, the memorial, a tower composed of a simple single column, stands as a symbol of the peace that has existed between Canada and the United States ever since the War of 1812. To ensure the high human cost of the Battle of Lake Erie is never forgotten, the position of the officers' communal grave, upon which the monument is built, is marked on the floor (the remains were moved to the site from their original resting place). When one enters, the stone marking the spot, bearing an inscription that reads simply, "Beneath this stone lie the remains of three American and three British officers killed in the Battle of Lake Erie, September 10, 1813," is immediately visible.

From the observation deck of Perry's Monument, it is possible to see the mainlands of both the United States and Canada on a clear day. Fittingly, the monument is often visible across much of the western basin of Lake Erie, no matter what side of the border one is on.

For the British, the loss of the Battle of Lake Erie was a devastating blow. In the storied history of the Royal Navy, it marked the first time an entire squadron had been lost in a single battle. Barclay returned to Britain to face

Photo by author

Perry's Victory and International Peace Memorial towers 107 metres over the Bass Islands.

a court martial and was thoroughly exonerated, the Admiralty realizing he had done all he could against a clearly superior foe. He retained only limited use of his right arm, and part of his right thigh was cut away as a result of his wounds. One observer noted that Barclay "tottered before a court martial like a Roman trophy." Though cleared, Barclay's reputation never recovered. He struggled to find another command and died in Scotland in 1837.

The battle also marked the defeat of the British in the Western District. With Lake Erie now under American control, Procter ordered Fort Malden burned and beat a hasty retreat. True to his worst fear, Perry did use his fleet, along with some of the captured British ships to transport a massive force to the Canadian mainland. When the Americans arrived at the village, however, they found no one but a few undoubtedly terrified residents. Shortly afterward, at the Battle of Moraviantown, Procter made a final stand against the invaders, who had chased his weary troops for days along the Thames River. While he managed to escape, Tecumseh was killed, and his Native warriors were left in disarray. Like Barclay, Procter, too, faced a court martial over the Lake Erie campaign, but unlike his Royal Navy comrade, he would find no retribution. He was found partly responsible for the loss of the fleet and of Fort Malden. His career was over. Embittered, he died at Bath on October 31, 1822, at the age of fifty-nine.

Perry was lauded as a hero and promoted to captain, but the Lake Erie campaign proved to be the high-water mark of his naval career. He was given command of the frigate *Java*, then, in 1819, he was transferred to the *John Adams* and sent on a diplomatic mission to Venezuela, where he contracted yellow fever and died less than six years after the Battle of Lake Erie, on August 23, 1819.

The first real commemoration by the American veterans of the battle was held in 1852, at the home of Judge Lockwood, then one of just a handful of buildings at Put-in-Bay. The veterans laughed, told stories of the old days, and remembered their fallen comrades. They returned to Lockwood's home every year until 1868, when those who remained were simply too old and ill to make the trip.

Usher Parsons, who desperately wanted to go but could not because of illness, wrote to a fellow veteran that summer: "The tenth of September is drawing near when we have engaged to commemorate once more the victory on Lake Erie. With failing health, I fear I shall not be able to join you as agreed upon, for life and health are not at our own disposal. I hope that you will go and if I fail to get there, please give my kind regards to such of our friends as retain remembrance of me."

Chapter 3

The Battle of Pelee Island:
The Upper Canadian Rebellion of 1837

American and Canadian settlers continued to pour into the Lake Erie frontier during the twenty years that followed the War of 1812. It was almost as though the conflict, which had wreaked such havoc on the area's settlements and caused many, like Port Dover, Ontario, to be put to the torch, had never happened at all.

On Pelee Island, on the Canadian side of the Lake Erie island chain in the lake's western basin (and today Canada's southernmost community), William McCormick was one of these postwar pioneers. In the spring of 1834, the fifty-year-old county administrator and former member of the Upper Canadian legislature moved his large family, which included eleven children, from their home in Colchester, on the shore of Lake Erie in Essex County, to the remote island. Once established on the island, they began construction of a permanent home, a log homestead at the north end.

McCormick had first taken an interest in Pelee Island in 1815, one year after the end of the war, when Colonel Thomas McKee, a soldier and high-ranking Indian Department official, died suddenly. McKee had originally been granted the lease to the island, on a 999-year term, by several local

Illustration courtesy of National Archives of Canada C-085349

An 1882 portrayal of a Pelee Island vineyard shows the pastoral nature of the early settlement.

Native chiefs in 1788. With his passing, Pelee Island fell to his son and only heir, Alexander. In turn, William McCormick leased it and, with a partner, started a pig farm there.

But apart from McCormick's hog operation, which he ran from Colchester, there was very little settlement on Pelee Island in the immediate postwar years. Even after William bought the island outright in 1823, only a few European and Native tenant farmers lived there. The only industry of any kind was a small sawmill that cut and shipped limited amounts of cedar, some of which was used in the reconstruction of Fort Malden, at Amherstburg, after the British had burned it in order to prevent the fort, which was their headquarters in the Western District of Upper Canada (present-day southwestern Ontario), from falling into the hands of American invaders during the war.

But in a larger context, McCormick's arrival on Pelee Island could not have come at a worse time. Aside from the physical challenges of carving out a settlement in the isolated, unforgiving wilderness, there was political danger in the air; all of Upper Canada, in fact, was crackling with the fear of armed insurrection. What McCormick couldn't have known at the time was that his tiny, remote island haven would soon find itself squarely at the centre of the action.

Trouble had been brewing throughout the first few years of the 1830s, when William Lyon Mackenzie, a fiery publisher and former member of the colonial legislature, had been stirring up resistance to the "Family Compact," the colony's well-connected ruling elite, and their ardent champion, British Lieutenant-Governor Francis Bond Head. A week before his protests turned to open rebellion, Mackenzie had published a multipage broadsheet manifesto calling on all English-Canadian colonists to rise up against the government and assert their independence. Mackenzie backed his argument for rebellion in the manifesto:

> … with governors from England, we will have bribery at elections, corruption, villainy and discord in every township, but independence would give us the means of enjoying our many blessings. Our enemies in Toronto [the colony's capital] are in terror and disarray — they know their wickedness and dread our vengeance.

On the evening of December 5, 1837, Mackenzie moved to turn the anger imbued throughout the manifesto into action. Leading an angry, largely drunken mob armed with muskets and pitchforks, he set off from Montgomery's Tavern, north of Toronto, down Yonge Street toward the colonial legislature. These men, who dubbed themselves the "Patriots," had one simple objective: the armed overthrow of Head's government and the creation of an American-style democracy in the colony.

They had only marched about five kilometres, however, when one of the rebels, spotting an approaching government police patrol, fired his musket. The rest of the group, believing they were under attack, quickly dispersed in terrified confusion. The police responded with a musket volley of their own, and, when the smoke cleared, one rebel lay dead and several others were wounded. The leaders of the uprising were left with few options; unable to return to their homes, many, including Mackenzie, soon fled the city and made for the American border. Almost before it

Illustration courtesy of National Archives of Canada C-085349

Upper Canadian rebellion leader William Lyon Mackenzie.

began, the first major confrontation of the Upper Canadian Rebellion of 1837 was over.

For most English Canadians, the story of the rebellion ends here. But what is not as well known is that Mackenzie's attempted uprising had strong support in the Upper Canadian countryside. This is especially true of the Western District, where hundreds of men from communities like St. Thomas and London, under the command of another former parliamentarian, Charles Duncombe, were on the march toward Toronto to support Mackenzie on the day of the confrontation. When news of Mackenzie's defeat reached them, Duncombe decided to disband this ragtag force, causing many of the rebels to simply melt back into the population and return to their farms. Interestingly, their wily commander eluded capture by sneaking across the border into Michigan disguised as a woman. This was surely no mean feat for the tall, bearded Duncombe.

Sympathy for the rebels in the countryside was given a further boost by the Upper Canadian militia itself. Immediately following the Montgomery's Tavern incident, Head ordered 400 militiamen under the command of Hamilton aristocrat Colonel Allan MacNab to occupy the troublesome western communities and subdue the rebels. The force later ballooned to over 1,900 men, and the occupation caused great hardship for the townsfolk, who were forced to billet MacNab's undisciplined soldiers. Historian Edwin C. Guillet describes the situation in his authoritative 1968 book on the rebellion, *The Lives and Times of the Patriots*: "In many instances the soldiery drove away cattle and sold them cheap to their friends ... wheat was seized in large quantities, and what was not worth stealing was wantonly destroyed; jars of preserves were ruined by the addition of filth, and every other species of villainy [was] practiced by the ultra-loyal gangs."

As a result of such careless and destructive tactics, MacNab's plan to intimidate the rural population failed. Mackenzie and his men found many willing hands to help them make their way to safety in the United States.

Once there, they began to plot their revenge.

Liberators or Invaders?

This was the uncomfortable environment in which the settlers of Pelee Island found themselves in early 1838, a mere twelve kilometres from the Upper Canadian coastline. The McCormick family, having arrived less than four years earlier, had only recently finished construction of their new homestead, which consisted of two log cabins connected by a small apartment at the island's north end.

At this time, Pelee Island was far from the birdwatcher's and wine drinker's paradise that it is today. The island's interior was still heavily forested, and contained a rich diversity of plant life. Scattered throughout the interior on small clearings were a handful of log homes and farmsteads built by the tenant farmers. Dauntingly, the lowlands (about two-thirds of the island) were covered by dense marsh, as Thaddeus Smith, who wrote the first definitive history of Pelee Island, entitled simply *Point au Pelee Island*, in 1899, describes:

> There were three marshes, two small ones, and one over 4,000 acres [1,618 hectares] extending entirely across the island, and it was impossible to pass from north to south except on a narrow, sandy strip thrown up by the waves. This marsh was often overflowed by water running into it from the lake. It was always covered with water from a foot to five feet deep, but was overrun with a heavy growth of aquatic grapes and other vegetation.

The winter of 1837–38 had been harsh, but the settlers had provisioned themselves well and were hunkered down in their small homesteads, anxiously awaiting the spring thaw and the return of the growing season. Across the nearby border with the United States, however, events beyond their control were about to worsen their situation considerably.

The rebels had regrouped in New York State by late December of 1837, and had occupied tiny Navy Island, just inside the Canadian border on the Niagara River. The island's only two inhabitants, a farmer and his wife, had fled before the Patriot advance, and the rebels proceeded to turn their home into a de facto military base. By this time, of course, the Patriot cause had captured the attention of many Americans living along the border, and had aroused considerable sympathy among the men of nearby Buffalo and from settlements all along the southern shore of Lake Erie. Many were only too happy to seize the opportunity to cause trouble for Her Majesty's Canadian subjects, especially in the wake of the War of 1812. St. Catharines resident Robert Marsh, who joined Mackenzie at Navy Island, captures the sentiment in his *Narrative of a Patriot Exile*, published over a decade later: "It was all excitement in Buffalo, Cleveland, Detroit and all along the frontier, as well as Lockport, Rochester, and in fact, the whole country was awake, many and strong were the inducements for young, as well as married men, to engage in so glorious a cause; if they had families, there were plenty that would see them provided for."

No doubt one of the major "inducements" for these men, many of whom were drawn from the lowest classes of the young country's citizenry, was Mackenzie's promise of free land in Upper Canada once it was "liberated." All told, they would swell Mackenzie's invasion force at some points during the occupation of Navy Island to over a thousand men.

Meanwhile, across the river from Navy Island on the Canadian mainland, a force of more than 4,000 British regulars and Upper Canadian militiamen, again commanded by Allan MacNab, had gathered and begun to sporadically bombard the rebels with artillery fire. While at first this had little effect (MacNab was all too aware of the political dangers of firing cannons toward American territory), the sniping between the two groups continued to escalate. On December 29, things reached a boiling point. MacNab sent a small raiding party to storm the rebel steamship *Caroline*, which the rebels used to ferry their supporters between the island and the American mainland. This they quickly accomplished, setting the steamer on fire once they managed to climb aboard. Burning and out of control, the ship drifted lazily downriver, where it beached and broke into pieces just short of tumbling over Niagara Falls (though later authors, for dramatic effect, would claim that the *Caroline* did, in fact, plunge to her untimely end). One rebel, who was an American citizen, was killed in the incident.

THE DESTRUCTION OF The Caroline, STEAMBOAT, BY FIRE, FALLS OF NIAGARA, UPPER CANADA.

A fanciful sketch of the destruction of the steamer Caroline. *In reality, it ran aground before reaching Niagara Falls.*

But even with the Buffalo recruits swelling their numbers, in the end the Patriots proved no match for MacNab's well-trained and well-armed troops. With the *Caroline* destroyed, their link to the American mainland was dramatically weakened, and supplies and men dwindled. On January 13, MacNab unleashed a heavy artillery bombardment on the island and soon had Mackenzie's invaders in full retreat.

Seeing his army on the run, Mackenzie's top "general," Rensselaer Van Rensselaer, quickly convened an emergency session of the revolutionary "government-in-exile" (which by this time had begun calling itself the government of the Republic of Canada). It was quickly decided that it would be futile to continue the fight along the heavily fortified Niagara frontier. Instead, the Patriots hatched a new plan: they would redirect their strength to the more sparsely defended (and arguably more sympathetic) Western District. Loading their wagons with muskets and ammunition they had mostly stolen or borrowed from the Americans, the remaining rebel troops set off along the southern shore of Lake Erie toward Ohio, gathering manpower and weapons from sympathizers along the way.

But, despite their high hopes, the Patriots would fare little better in the western Lake Erie region during the opening weeks of 1838. Their first raids in the region were complete fiascos. The rebels were quickly dispersed, and thoroughly embarrassed, by British regulars and Canadian militia at Fighting Island, and later at Bois Blanc Island, both on the Detroit River near Amherstburg. In February, soldiers from Fort Malden took the Patriots' only ship, the stolen schooner *Anne,* while she drifted off Amherstburg in the Detroit River. After bombarding the *Anne* with artillery and musket fire from shore, members of the Kent and Essex militia waded into the frigid river and clambered aboard. They had little difficulty overrunning the remnants of the defeated crew. Patriot commander Edward Theller describes the taking of his ship in his 1841 account of the rebellion:

> It was no boys' play now. Many of our men were wounded and considerable damage done to the rigging. Captain Davis, who was holding on to the anchor, was shot in the wrist and the groin, of which he afterwards died, and away went the anchor. The enemy aimed with fatal precision at the helmsman, and he fled below, leaving the boat to her own will, and as the down-hauls had been cut away by the shot, the sails could not be managed. Unskilled as mariners, confusion reigned among us; and the schooner

drifting with the ice, we were a few moments aground on the main shore, presenting an inclined front to the irritated and triumphant marksmen of the enemy.

Captain Davis, unfortunately, wasn't the only one to lose his life in that night's action. As Theller goes on to report: "A little boy, a Canadian refugee engaged in bringing us loaded muskets, was killed in the act, fell overboard, and his body found on shore the next morning."

To make matters worse for the rebels, U.S. President Martin Van Buren had been growing increasingly concerned about Patriot incursions pulling his country into yet another costly war with Great Britain, which was something that the U.S. army, which consisted of a mere 7,000 regulars at this point in its history, was in no way prepared for. In an attempt to cool things down on America's northern border, Van Buren dispatched Major-General Winfield Scott, a hero of the War of 1812, to try to put a kink in the Patriots' plans.

In the face of mounting U.S. pressure and dwindling food and ammunition, Patriot commander Donald McLeod was sent out from Buffalo to Conneaut, Ohio, where he hastily convened a war council with the top western Patriot commanders. There, a strategy was decided upon: one force, comprising 450 rebels, would cross the ice from Sandusky and invade Pelee Island while another, smaller, force would attempt to take Fort Malden. Once the two armies prevailed, the plan went, they would meet on the Canadian mainland where, with the supposed help of the citizens of the Western District, they would push the British forces and Canadian militia back toward Toronto. The council also appointed three men to head up the Pelee invasion and designated them ranks in the rebel army. They were "Colonel" H.C. Seward, "Captain" George Van Rensselaer (a nephew of "General" Van Rensselaer), and "Major" Lester Hoadley.

Why the Patriots opted to concentrate their strength on the sparsely populated Pelee Island and not the headquarters of the British army in the Western District is unclear, but such a decision shows a stunning lack of military strategy among the rebellion's top commanders. It was a shortcoming that would cost them dearly.

A Sixth Sense

On the evening of February 25, 1838, the Pelee Island invasion force gathered at Sandusky Bay and prepared for the long march across the frozen surface of Lake Erie. The makeup of the party reflected the large degree to which the rebellion was now dependent on American manpower to keep it going. Of the 450 men gathered on that cold February night, only two could later be confirmed as British subjects — one Stevenson, who ended up staying behind due to an illness, and McGally, the raiding party's drill sergeant.

The severity of the winter also favoured the invasion force. The ice covering Lake Erie was estimated to be in excess of thirty-eight centimetres thick from shore to shore, more than suitable for the planned march.

To the residents of Sandusky, the Patriots must have appeared a rather curious sight, indeed. Dressed in tattered overcoats and worn-out boots and arranged in a single column, some carried muskets, but most were forced to make do with pitchforks and swords. They brought no field artillery with them; instead, they towed wooden sledges loaded with ammunition for their muskets and pistols. At the head of the column, a young flagbearer wielded the Patriot banner: a red, white, and blue flag bearing the word "Liberty" set below two white stars set on a blue bar; the two stars representing Upper and Lower Canada (presently Ontario and Quebec, respectively). McGally would likely have called out the time as they marched.

In addition to their scarcity of firearms, the force was also very poorly provisioned, carrying almost no food at all. Hoadley, Seward, and "Captain" Van Rensselaer, rightly counting on the islanders to be well-stocked for the winter, opted to increase the force's mobility by travelling as light as possible. Plunder would be the order of the day.

Once the party left the shelter of Sandusky Bay, however, they found the ice of the open lake to be thicker and more jagged than they expected, which slowed them down considerably. The raiders had hoped to land under the cover of the early morning darkness, but dawn had long since broken by the time they landed at the south end of the island near Fish Point. From there, they formed up again and plodded northward through Pelee's thickly forested, snow-covered interior, ransacking the small cabins and farmsteads, and taking prisoners as they went.

What became evident early on to the invaders, however, was that the majority of the island's residents had already fled. Exactly how the islanders had been alerted to the approaching invaders is unclear, though it is likely they were aware long before that something dreadful was in the offing. Frightening rumours had swirled throughout the Western District throughout the winter of 1837. Vast numbers of Patriots and their bloodthirsty American allies, it was said, were gathering along the shores of Ohio, Pennsylvania, and

Michigan, preparing to strike. The rebel raids of January 1838 at Fighting Island and Bois Blanc Island, and the capture of the *Anne* only added to the tension. As the rebellion had spilled westward and transformed into a largely American enterprise, many citizens previously sympathetic to Mackenzie's cause began to change their minds. Instead of hoping for more political freedoms, these supporters, along with the rest of the population, now began to fear what now appeared to be a looming American invasion. Memories of the War of 1812 still lingered in the minds of many of the colonists. In the streets of many of the small border communities, women and children were afraid to go out alone.

William McCormick would have been no less aware of the troubling political situation. Having served in the Upper Canadian parliament from 1812–24, he would have been familiar with Mackenzie, Duncombe, and the other Patriot leaders. It would also have been clear to McCormick that his own political leanings — his wife was of United Empire Loyalist stock and he was a staunch ally of the government — would have made his vulnerable island settlement a tempting target for Patriot rebels bent on revenge.

In any case, when the rebels reached the McCormick homestead, they found that it, too, had been deserted. But it was not lost on them that the property made an excellent defensive position, overlooking Scudder Bay and offering a clear view of the Canadian mainland, from which any effort to reclaim the island would have to be launched. The homestead was also surrounded by dense forest, making it relatively easy to defend against a landing party. As they had done with the farmhouse on Navy Island, the rebel commanders chose to make the McCormick home their headquarters for as long as they chose to remain on the island.

During the ensuing days, groups of rebels came and went from the shore, at some points swelling the invaders' numbers to over a thousand men. And they cared little about the damage they caused, freely helping themselves to the settlers' property and nearly destroying many of the settlements. As Thaddeus Smith writes: "When the rebels raided Pelee Island they wrought great damage not alone to the McCormicks, but to others of its inhabitants. The cabin owned by the father of Peter and Simon Fox — who later became residents of North Bass [Island] — was made a place of rendezvous. The raiders ate up all the potatoes and other supplies that the family had stored away, leaving them destitute of provisions."

The invaders also shot and ate much of the settlers' livestock. And whatever they did not immediately need, they sent back to the Ohio shore with the constantly arriving and departing Patriot soldiers. In effect, Pelee Island was now American territory.

Blood on the Ice

William McCormick was nothing if not tough-minded, and he was not about to give up on the island community he had worked so hard to build without a fight. Shortly before the invaders had arrived at his homestead, he had bundled up his large family, including the seventy-four-year-old matriarch, Elizabeth Turner, and set off across the frozen lake toward the Canadian mainland. A few hours after he arrived, a party of Pelee landowners, including three or four members of the local Essex militia, who were wintering near Leamington, crossed to Pelee in an attempt to reclaim their property, but were promptly fired upon by the rebels, who took some prisoner and forced the rest to turn back. It is not known whether William McCormick participated in this early effort at resistance, but two days later, a party of these men, led by McCormick, arrived at Fort Malden, fifty-six kilometres away, to inform the garrison's commander, Colonel John Maitland, of the rebels' presence on the island and of their apparent determination to stay.

Maitland, a gifted tactician and a thirty-year veteran of the British army, had seen action in Spain and Portugal with the Duke of Wellington's army before taking command of the 32nd Regiment of Foot, based at Fort Malden, in 1818. By all accounts, he was greatly admired by those under his command — a soldier's soldier who valued his men's well-being above all else. He was also decisive, and wasted no time going on the attack. Early on March 1, he dispatched Captain Glasgow of the Royal Artillery to see if the ice covering Lake Erie would support the weight of fully equipped troops and artillery. By noon, Glasgow had returned and informed Maitland that it was indeed strong enough for such a mission. The colonel then set to organizing his force, which consisted of one company of the 32nd Regiment of Foot, one company of the 83rd Regiment of Foot, one company of the Essex Volunteer Militia, thirty members of the St. Thomas and Sandwich Volunteer Cavalry, and a small party of Native warriors — nearly 500 men in all. They were well-armed and well-provisioned, and towed behind them two six-pound brass cannons. Maitland took command of the strike force himself.

That same evening, the column set off from Amherstburg, with Maitland riding at its head, to repel the invaders. With a few of the Pelee men accompanying them, they marched along the lakeshore through the night as far as Colchester, arriving there at two o'clock in the morning. After resting their horses (and themselves) at the town's small tavern, they stepped off the shore. After Maitland satisfied himself that the ice was indeed sound, he marched the force on toward Pelee Island, arriving about two kilometres off the north shore near dawn.

Here, on the frozen ice north of Scudder Bay, Maitland began to set his plan to retake Pelee Island into motion. He ordered Captain George Browne, a veteran of the 1815 Waterloo campaign against Napoleonic France, and two companies of regulars and militia, along with about twenty-five volunteers from the Sandwich and St. Thomas Volunteer Cavalry (approximately 100 men in all) to wheel around to the south end of the island. Gambling that his main force could outgun the rebels encamped at the McCormick homestead, Maitland knew they would have no choice but to fall back to the south and attempt to cross back into the United States. When they did, Browne would be waiting to pounce.

With Browne's men on their way, Maitland and his remaining troops marched head-on toward the Patriot encampment on Scudder Bay. But when they reached the shore they were greeted not by the fierce resistance they had been expecting, but instead by a ghostly silence. The rebels, apparently, had already left the McCormick residence and run off into the woods. One soldier with Maitland's force observed that the rebels had fled in such haste that potatoes had been left boiling on the fire. After making sure the homestead was secure, Maitland and his men set off in pursuit of the rebels, but, as Maitland describes in his after-action report: "The troops moved on in extended order, but as the wood was thick, and the snow extremely deep and heavy, the men were much retarded in their progress."

Meanwhile, Browne's force had completed its march to the south end of the island and found the spot where the rebels had landed days earlier. Even though they had made relatively good time, the march had been challenging, as the ice along the shore was heavily buckled. Browne ordered a halt, and while the exhausted men ate breakfast he sent two Native scouts into the woods to bring back information on the Patriots' movements. One of the scouts returned shortly after, informing an alarmed Browne that the main rebel column of between 300 and 400 men was, in fact, quickly bearing down on his position. He also reported that he had neither seen nor heard anything of Maitland's force, but assumed that they were in hot pursuit of these "fellows."

James Ermatinger, who had accompanied Browne and commanded the St. Thomas Cavalry, attempted to send a Native scout through to Maitland with a message to send reinforcements as fast as possible, but the commander, still trailing far behind the rebels and bogged down in the deep snow, could not be reached. Browne, meanwhile, chose to believe the enemy numbers were exaggerated and ordered his men to form a skirmishing line across the escape route with their muskets held at the ready. Abandoning their breakfast, the soldiers took up their positions, aimed into the heavy forest — and waited. Trooper Samuel Williams, riding up on the rebels' right side with the Sandwich and St. Thomas Volunteer Cavalry, describes what happened next in his account of the battle, which was published years later in Charles Oakes Ermatinger's book, *The Talbot Regime*:

> [Browne's men] were strung out in a long line across the ice like fence posts. The enemy were approaching them at a quick march. We could not see them just at first. They approached Captain Browne's force in solid column, and then spread out in a line about the same length as that of the British infantry. There were about 500 of the enemy. Captain Browne had ninety and our troop [the Sandwich and St. Thomas Volunteer Cavalry] numbered but twenty-one. Both sides fired simultaneously. We got none of this volley. We were approaching at a gallop. We heard the enemy call out, "There comes the cavalry! Fire on them!" They did so and the bullets whistled around us. We were coming on their flank. We halted and fired. The infantry charged with fixed bayonets at that moment, in the face of a heavy fire from the enemy. When the infantry were within about six rods [thirty metres] of the enemy the latter retreated in disorder, running like wild turkeys every way, leaving five killed; while we had one soldier and one trooper, Thomas Parish, slain on the spot.

Rebel leaders Hoadley, Rensselaer, and Seward, expecting that the British might try to cut off their escape, had decided to take Browne's force head-on. Barging out of the forest and forming a skirmishing line on the ice, the rebels drove straight toward Browne's men, unleashing a heavy musket volley as they went. Very quickly, British casualties began to mount.

Browne, clearly taken off guard by the deadly effectiveness of the rebel assault, ordered a return volley, but this did little to halt the rebel advance. Running out of options, Browne, in desperation, ordered his men to fix their bayonets and charge into the rebel ranks. It was a last-ditch move that, in the end, would prove decisive.

For the rebels, faced with the possibility of horrific bloodshed at the end of the British bayonets, shades of the failures of Montgomery's Tavern and Navy Island began to re-emerge. With the roaring British regulars striding toward them, their shimmering bayonets aimed straight at the rebels' chests, panic quickly set in. Having now witnessed death firsthand, these idealistic, but totally amateur, soldiers could stand no more. They quickly broke ranks and fled in complete disorganization. Worse, all three of the rebel commanders, Rensselaer, Hoadley, and Seward, lay dead on the ice, slain in the initial exchange of musket fire.

Sensing a rout in the making, a relieved Browne now shifted tactics; instead of desperately trying to salvage as much of his force as he could from the strong Patriot advance, he went on offense, ordering Captain Ermatinger and the cavalry to run down the fleeing rebels. Ermatinger, "flourishing his sword," according to Trooper Williams, led his horsemen in hot pursuit of the Patriots, chasing them away from shore and out onto thinner ice. When his horse's hoof began to crack through, however,

The Battle of Pelee Island, as depicted by C.H. Forster. At least a dozen men died in the clash.

Illustration courtesy of Parks Canada Agency – Fort Malden NHSC

Ermatinger deemed the risk too great and wheeled back toward the island. The rebels, eager to escape the well-armed horsemen, continued to surge ahead. Some accounts mention rebels falling through the ice and drowning as they tried to flee, but if this is so, the historical record is unclear as to exactly how many; Thaddeus Smith cites an unnamed soldier who claimed that about a hundred died this way, but this account has been contradicted by numerous others, including that of Trooper Williams, who noticed only five rebels killed in the entire exchange. Edwin C. Guillet mentions in *The Lives and Times of the Patriots* that one witness later claimed that fourteen rebels were buried at Fish Point. Again, if this is true, the exact whereabouts of these graves is unknown. It is generally accepted that around eleven Patriots met their end on that bloody day.

A Grim Homecoming

Maitland and the main British force finally emerged out of the forest and arrived on the scene about three hours after the battle had ended, having known nothing of its occurrence. His troops, following the rebels through the deep snow and dense forest of the island's interior, had not heard the musket volleys. Maitland, in his official report, counted that eleven rebel prisoners, some of them badly wounded, were taken, as well as forty muskets and a "large tri-coloured flag with two stars and the word 'Liberty' worked upon it."

For the British, the price of liberating Pelee Island from the Patriots had been high. From Maitland's official after-action report:

> I regret to say that the taking of this island has not been gained without considerable loss on our part, and I have to request that you report, for His Excellency's information, that thirty soldiers of the 32nd Regiment fell in this affair, two of whom were killed, the others, some dangerously, some seriously wounded [two more would later die of their injuries, along with Thomas Parish of the Sandwich and St. Thomas Volunteer Cavalry]. I sincerely regret the loss of so many brave soldiers, and feel it the more, when I reflect they did not fall before an honourable enemy, but under the fire of a desperate gang of murderers and marauders.

Maitland goes on to describe the solemn return to Amherstburg that same day:

> Having secured the woods, and satisfied myself that the island was cleared, I reformed the troops, and about five o'clock in the evening proceeded back, and the soldiers returned to their quarters at Amherstburg that night.

In all, the soldiers had been gone about thirty hours. Not one of them had slept during that time.

Upon reaching the Ohio shore, the remaining rebels were intercepted by American authorities, ordered to turn over their weapons, and held briefly before being allowed to return to their homes. For the greater Patriot movement, the defeat at Pelee Island would prove devastating. There would be no further incursions on the Lake Erie front; instead, the rebels decided to concentrate what remained of their resources along the St. Lawrence River. In the fall of 1838, they met government forces for one final, all-out assault near Prescott, Ontario, in what would become known as the "Battle of the Windmill." Once again, the battle was decided in the government's favour, effectively ending the Patriot threat to Canada.

The McCormicks would not return to Pelee Island for more than a year after the invasion. They resettled there permanently in the summer of 1839, but faced a daunting task in rebuilding. The farms and homesteads were heavily damaged and the settlers' possessions and provisions looted, while the island's lighthouse, built shortly before the rebellion, had been severely damaged by the Patriots, who took many of its fixtures with them back to Ohio. McCormick, whose home suffered miserably while it served as the invaders' headquarters for nearly a week, claimed £592 ($1,190) in damages to his own property from the colonial government, while seven other island farmers claimed a total of £472 ($950) — significant sums for such a small community.

The depressing work took an immediate toll on William. His health declined rapidly, and he died on Pelee on February 18, 1840, at the age of fifty-six. His elderly mother, Elizabeth Turner, had died barely a year before him at the family home in Colchester.

Colonel John Maitland, too, would not live long past the Battle of Pelee Island. He had suffered severe exposure to the bitter cold during the action, and finally died of its effects, nearly a year later, at Fort Malden on January 18, 1839. The announcement of his death, in the January 24

The *gravesite of William McCormick, the first non-Native owner of Pelee Island, at the Pelee Island Cemetery.*

edition of the *British Colonist*, reflected the sorrow many felt at his loss: "The great assistance which has been rendered by this highly valuable and much lamented officer in … various ways assisting and promoting the welfare of the community through a most eventful period has been most highly appreciated, not only by the Government but by the inhabitants at large, whose esteem and respect he had entirely gained."

As for the rebel prisoners, they would languish in a Toronto jail while the case became bogged down in legal difficulties, mainly relating to a dearth of defence witnesses and the American citizenship of the accused. They were eventually all returned to the United States.

Very little physical evidence of the Battle of Pelee Island remains today, and islanders mention it only in passing, if at all, and most often as a peculiar aside to Pelee's long history. But it should be remembered that the battle itself, and the greater rebellion, claimed many lives, caused considerable damage, and struck fear into the hearts of Upper Canadian colonists for

The monument to the five soldiers who fell at Pelee Island now stands in the front yard of an Amherstburg home.

many years. On a more positive note, the rebellion hastened the end of the hated Family Compact and contributed to the birth of the representative system of government that Canada enjoys today.

The only real commemoration of the Battle of Pelee Island on the island itself is a plaque erected by the provincial government at the north end. As for more lasting memorials, the only tribute to the brave men who died on the frozen ice of Lake Erie on that frigid March day is a stone monument erected in Amherstburg shortly after the battle. Now positioned awkwardly on the front yard of a house, in a subdivision not far from the centre of town, the weathered inscription reads simply: "This monument is erected by the inhabitants of Amherstburg in memory of Thomas McCartan, Samuel Holmes, Edwin Miller, and Thomas Symonds, of H.M. 32nd Reg. of Foot, and of Thomas Parish of the St. Thomas Volunteer Cavalry, who gloriously fell in repelling a band of brigands from Pelee Island on the Third of March, 1838."

Chapter 4

Raid on Johnson's Island

The evening of September 19, 1864, found western Lake Erie calm, the skies clear. Off the coast of Kelleys Island, Ohio, the sidewheel passenger steamer *Philo Parsons* followed its normal route, plodding its way toward its final destination for the day, the coastal town of Sandusky. To the naked eye, all appeared normal; the *Parsons* regularly ferried passengers from Detroit to Sandusky, often calling at Sandwich, Ontario (present-day Windsor), and Amherstburg, also on the Canadian side, and at many of the U.S. Lake Erie islands along the way.

But "normal" was probably the last word to describe what had happened on this day. One clear sign of trouble was that the *Parsons*, captained by Sylvester F. Atwood, a skipper known for his studiousness, and co-owned by the boat's clerk, Walter Ashley of Michigan, was running hours behind schedule. But this was not the only thing amiss; more unusual was the fact that neither man was even aboard.

After a routine trip to nearby Middle Bass Island, Atwood had returned to his home there, leaving Ashley in charge for the final push to Sandusky. But Ashley and the *Parsons*'s crew ended up getting more than they bargained for in the wake of this seemingly simple handover of command. For in the course of this last leg, Ashley would find himself staring down the barrel of a passenger's loaded pistol before being forced off the boat entirely. The end result was that the *Parsons* was now steaming for Sandusky under the command of hijackers who were part of a Confederate spy ring based in Canada.

The American Civil War, which had been raging for more than three years, had finally arrived on Lake Erie.

The *Parsons* was now in the hands of a band of twenty "Lake Erie Pirates" (as the Toronto *Globe* would later dub them), who were setting in motion the early stages of a secret plan first conceived several months before. On Johnson's Island, a tiny speck of rock in Sandusky Bay, stood a Union prison holding 2,500 Confederate officers. With John Yates Beall, a former privateer and a devoted partisan of the Confederate cause leading them, the hijackers were steaming to the rescue of this unfortunate lot. But this would be no easy prison break; first they had to overcome the formidable might of the fourteen-gun USS *Michigan*, the Union warship that guarded the island prison.

Confederate conspirator John Yates Beall.

With darkness setting in, Beall leaned over the *Parsons's* deck railing, straining his eyes into the darkness, keeping watch for the *Michigan*, which routinely rode at anchor at the mouth of the bay. Daniel Bedinger Lucas, a lawyer, poet, and close friend, provides a vivid description of Beall in his biography, *A Memoir of John Yates Beall*, published shortly after the war ended in 1865:

> ... he was stoutly built, with broad shoulders, flat chest, and measuring about five feet seven inches in height ... His hair was brown, and half covered the ear; the forehead high, the nose straight and regular, the complexion pale ... He wore a slight moustache, and whiskers coming to a point under the chin.

Suddenly, the *Michigan's* lanterns emerged out of the blackness. The Union gunboat was right where Beall expected it to be, settled in on the smooth water at the entrance to the bay. Beall ordered the *Parsons's* engines cut, and the steamer glided silently through the water, closing in on its quarry. As the minutes passed, an uneasy calm descended over the men aboard the *Parsons* as it drifted now so close to the *Michigan* that the warship's guns could be clearly seen against the blackness, its crew's voices heard lilting through the still evening air. Captain George Orr of the *Island Queen* (another passenger vessel serving the Lake Erie islands) who, through a set of equally incredible circumstances, found himself aboard the *Parsons* that night, described the scene to South Bass Island resident and historian Lydia Ryall, who published his account of that evening in her 1913 book, *Sketches and Stories of the Lake Erie Islands*: "It was about 10 p.m. The U.S. gunboat *Michigan* lay off Johnson's Island, her hull glooming through the night. The plotters were awaiting signals evidently which failed to appear. Three or four of the leaders went aside and held a consultation and I overheard Lieut. Beale *[sic]* say to the men: 'I have a notion to make the attempt, anyhow.'"

Orr was right. Beall had been waiting for a signal, possibly a rocket flare, which was supposed to be given by Captain Charles Cole, a Confederate spy who had spent the past two months befriending the *Michigan's* captain and crew. According to the plan, when the signal was given, Beall would pull the *Parsons* alongside and take his raiding party aboard.

But no matter how closely the raiders watched, nothing discernible changed about the *Michigan*. A dark feeling overcame Beall, and his men

Photo from *Lore of the Lakes*

The gunboat Michigan. *Confederate spies planned to take the ship and free the prisoners held on Johnson's Island.*

began to grow fearful, to the point of whispering openly about mutiny. If the *Michigan*'s crew had somehow been tipped off, the *Philo Parsons* would be no match for the powerful gunboat. The grand plan would quickly become a suicide mission. Confusion reigned aboard the *Parsons*. What had gone wrong? Why had the signal not been given?

A Fanatical Loyalty

John Yates Beall was born in Jefferson County, Virginia, on January 1, 1835. A quiet, withdrawn youth, Beall spent much of his time working on his grandfather's farm before heading to the University of Virginia in 1852 to study law and political economy. By all accounts he was a successful, though not particularly ambitious, student during his three-year academic career, leading Bedinger Lucas to note: "The modesty and reserve of his character combined to render the circle of his acquaintances very limited. With professors he had no recourse outside the lecture room …"

Beall's entire life could have been as listless as his academic career, had the Civil War not intervened. Fiercely loyal to his native Virginia, the twenty-six-year-old Beall was one of the first to enlist when hostilities erupted between the Union and the seceded states at Fort Sumter, South Carolina, on April 12, 1861.

Beall began his military career in the 1st Brigade of the Army of Northern Virginia, under the command of General Thomas Jonathan "Stonewall" Jackson. The General would go on to become a storied figure in American history, routing Union troops during a daring campaign in Virginia's Shenandoah Valley that ebbed and flowed through 1861 and 1862 before the general was fatally wounded by his own troops in what today would be termed a "friendly fire" incident. Struck by three .57-calibre bullets, Jackson struggled to recover for eight days before finally succumbing, uttering as he did so his now-famous last words: "Let us cross over the river and rest under the shade of the trees."

Beall would miss much of the action in the Shenandoah. He was on leave during the first major land battle between Union and Confederate troops, the First Battle of Manassas in his home state of Virginia (or the First Battle of Bull Run as it was known in the North), in July 1861. But like Jackson, Beall too would have his infantry career cut short on the battlefield. In October 1861, Beall was at Harper's Ferry, Virginia, the very place where another fanatic, antislavery campaigner, John Brown, had led an unsuccessful raid on the federal arsenal. Captured and hanged, Brown became a martyr to the cause and the subject of the famous song, "John Brown's Body," chanted by Union soldiers on the march.

Beall's trial by fire came on October 16, 1861; during a raid on a group of Union soldiers who had taken shelter behind a deserted brick house, he was cut down by musket shot. As Bedinger Lucas describes: "Beall emptied his musket twice, and had it raised to his shoulder in the act of aiming to fire again when a shot from the retreating party passed under his gun and, striking him obliquely in the right breast, broke three ribs and passed around his body. He discharged his own gun and fell."

To Beall's horror when he awoke moments later, the militiamen who accompanied him had fled. But fortunately, so had the enemy. Miraculously, he managed to hobble back to the Confederate line, and from there was taken to his mother's home in Jefferson County. Unlike Jackson, however, Beall would go on to almost fully recover from his wounds, no mean feat given the risk of infection and the limits of nineteenth-century medicine.

After a long convalescence, Beall was again well enough to travel, and he ventured deep into the South, stopping in Richmond, Tallahassee, and Virginia before riding west to Iowa, a Union state, and settling in the village of Cascade during the summer of 1862. But when suspicions of Beall's true political allegiance were spread by what Bedinger Lucas calls "the imprudence of his friends," Beall knew he could remain no longer. Late on the evening of September 2, 1862, he fled on horseback, crossing the border into Canada and taking refuge in the town of Dundas, near Hamilton. Here, he rested and followed news reports of Jackson's exploits in the Shenandoah before returning to the South in early 1863.

Though his first stay in Canada was uneventful, his experience travelling in the country, and the Lake Erie region in particular, would later prove valuable. But, in the short term, Beall was returning to the South a man with an injury that made it impossible to resume his career as a soldier.

He would have to serve the Confederacy in some other, more clandestine, way.

The Island Prison

The bloody defeat of Union forces at Bull Run was a grim wake-up call for the North, erasing all doubt about the Confederacy's determination to win the Civil War. It would not be the short military adventure that everyone had hoped for after Fort Sumter, but a long, bloody war of attrition that neither side could afford to lose.

As this realization began to set in on the fledgling Lincoln administration, it became clear that the Union would need more capacity to house prisoners of war. Northern Ohio, far from the frontlines, was seen as an ideal location, and in October 1861, Lieutenant-Colonel William Hoffman, the Union's commissary-general for prisoners, was ordered to build a new prison among the Lake Erie islands, off the state's northern coast — and to complete the project as quickly as possible.

Hoffman was a veteran regular army soldier who had served in the Mexican War before being deployed to Texas during the secession crisis that led to the outbreak of the Civil War. It was here that, in a quirk of history, Hoffman was made a prisoner of war before the conflict even officially began. With the Texas Secession Bill before the state legislature, his commander, Brigadier General David E. Twiggs, an elderly Georgian and Southern sympathizer, surrendered all Union forces in the state to the Confederacy in January 1861.

Twiggs's treachery had the unfortunate consequence of taking away any chance that Hoffman had to fight for the Union on a Civil War battlefield. The Confederates quickly paroled him, but the terms of his release stipulated that he could not take up arms against the South for the war's duration. So instead, Hoffman took the post of commissary-general for prisoners.

Hoffman hit the ground running when he arrived in Sandusky in mid-October 1861. It was late in the season, and if construction of the prison could not be started before the lake froze it would have to wait until the following spring, a serious delay in the face of a war that was continuing to escalate. Hoffman sailed the island chain in George Orr's *Island Queen* (a vessel that would play a recurring role in the Johnson's Island story) looking for an appropriate site, spending one night at the village of Put-in-Bay on South Bass Island and one night on Kelleys Island.

Finding a suitable location for such a massive facility on one of these small islands (at its peak, the prison would house 2,633 prisoners) presented more than a few challenges. Some of them, namely North Bass Island and Middle Bass Island, were too close to Canadian territory, making escape to the neutral British colony a constant temptation for prisoners, especially when the lake froze over in the winter. Another issue was security; the distance of these islands from Sandusky made them difficult to resupply, and left them almost entirely out of range after freeze-up. Other islands, like South Bass Island and Kelleys Island, were home to the region's emerging winemaking industry, which made it prohibitively expensive to acquire the necessary land. Hoffman also knew from his experience as a regular soldier that trusting the garrison to maintain its discipline in such close proximity to alcohol was a recipe for disaster.

With Kelleys Island and the Bass Islands effectively ruled out, Hoffman turned his attention closer to the Ohio shoreline, and it was here that he came upon the ideal spot. Nestled within the protective confines of Sandusky Bay, between the town of Sandusky and the Marblehead Peninsula, the 200-hectare Johnson's Island could easily be defended and resupplied, even in harsh weather. And, having no commercial value save for its timber, the government could lease half of the island (though it would have effective control over all of it) at a relatively cheap $500 a year. Johnson's Island was the obvious winner; Washington quickly approved Hoffman's choice and, wasting no time, Hoffman granted the construction contract to Sandusky builders W.T. West and Philander Gregg on November 15, 1862.

Recognizing the lateness of the season, West and Gregg got started right away. And as it turned out, good fortune would favour them; the winter of 1862 was unusually mild, allowing them to work without pause until colder weather finally arrived in early January. Another advantage was the natural supply of timber available for cutting on the island, which reduced the need to haul more across Sandusky Bay.

In the end, West and Gregg brought the project in on time and under budget. Johnson's Island prison was ready to house its first occupants by February 1862. At this early point in its life, the prison was intended to hold captives of all ranks, but a few months later it was designated for officers only.

While a cut above most prison camps in terms of amenities (there was a library, a laundry, and even two tailors, though most of these services were prisoner-run), the prison's thin-walled barracks robbed the inmates of any privacy whatsoever, and the conditions inside were downright life-threatening in winter. Johnson's Island inmate Henry Kyd Douglas describes the prison in his memoir, *I Rode with Stonewall*:

> The prison was an oblong, bare piece of ground enclosed by a high fence, and perched up on this fence, or barricade, at intervals, in sentry boxes, were armed sentinels. The barracks or prison houses were long buildings, hastily erected of wood and weatherboard, called wards. The weatherboarding was a single layer nailed to upright beams, and there was no plastering of any kind. The weatherboarding would sometimes warp, and in all the rooms there were many knotholes, through which one laying in bed could look out upon the moon or water; but when the weather got below zero, the scenery was scarcely compensation for the suffering. Bunks were

ranged along the walls — if they can be called walls — in three tiers.

With West and Gregg moving steadily forward on the construction front, Hoffman turned his attention to staffing the new facility. With the help of Ohio governor William Dennison, Hoffman put his administrative skills to work yet again, managing to pull off yet another minor miracle. Over the winter he raised a military staff of over one hundred local men, mainly by letting it be known that those who enlisted for duty on Johnson's Island would receive the same pay as soldiers in the field, with the advantage of being able to work near home — and not amongst the horror and death of the front lines.

Dennison, for his part, recommended that the new guard corps be named the Hoffman Battalion, in the commissary-general's honour; a suggestion that was readily adopted. In turn, Hoffman's recruiters ran the following ad in the January 1, 1862 edition of the *Sandusky Register*: "Hoffman Battalion! $100 Reward! Men enlisted to garrison Government section on Johnson's Island, receive above bounty in addition to good pay, excellent quarters and abundant rations. Men must be of good height, and between the ages of twenty and forty."

Photo courtesy of Sandusky Library Archives Research Center

Soldiers' barracks at the Johnson's Island prison. The Hoffman Battalion, which guarded the prisoners, is formed up in front.

With the final puzzle piece in place, and after a few delays caused by bad weather, the prison "welcomed" its first occupants on April 11, 1862. The Confederates, or "secesh" as the *Sandusky Register* derisively referred to them, arrived at Sandusky by train from Camp Chase in Columbus. Curious townspeople, eager to see the captives up close, gathered to watch as the prisoners were marched from the train to the *Island Queen* for the short trip across the bay and into captivity.

When the prisoners finally arrived on Johnson's Island, they found a place of both strict order and nearly endless boredom. Breakfast, served at six o'clock, consisted of coffee, bread, and beef, then the iceman and milkman came at seven-thirty. At eight o'clock the prison sutler, a private businessman who ran the general store, arrived to sell fruit and vegetables to prisoners who could afford to buy them.

The class system remained firmly in place among the prison population, and though Confederate ranks were not recognized, the ability to buy fruit and vegetables was far from the only way that well-to-do prisoners prospered behind the walls. They could also buy heavy coats and winter clothing from the sutler, though these could also be provided to poorer prisoners — with the recommendation of the medical officer. In an ironic twist, at least one slave-owning prisoner is thought to have brought his servant with him into captivity.

By far the most eagerly anticipated moment of the prisoner's day was mail call, with its packages and letters from loved ones. The sutler also returned at this time with the day's papers (available only to those who could afford them, of course). These consisted mainly of New York papers, plus the *Cincinnati Enquirer* and the *Sandusky Register*. All would be a day old save for the *Register*, the local daily, which was not popular among the prisoners because of its pro-Union stance. Likewise, the authorities would later ban the prisoners' favourite paper, the *Cincinnati Enquirer*, because of its pro-secessionist bias.

After lunch, the prisoners were free to spend the afternoon as they saw fit until dinner was served at sundown. Afterward, the men ambled back to their bunks, many engrossed in conversation about the progress of the war, others silently thinking of friends and family back home. Prisoner Edmund DeWitt Patterson, who was captured during the Battle of Gettysburg in July 1863, gives an apt description of the monotony of prison life in his diary:

> We ramble about through the pen, which comprises sixteen
> acres, during the day and at night retire to our quarters,
> some to read, some to write, and others to play chess, whist,

Old sledge, Euchre, Cribbage, and a dozen other games unnecessary to mention. We spend our time at this manner until half past nine o'clock, when at the tap of the drum, all of the lights must go out. And we retire to our "bunks," some to sleep — "aye, perchance to dream," and others to study of home and loved ones there.

The monotony aside, life at Johnson's Island was more bearable than at many other Civil War prison camps. Still, the Confederates endured periods of considerable privation. On a number of occasions, the sutler's services were suspended in retaliation for atrocities, real or imagined, suffered by Union prisoners in Confederate camps. There arose from this many stories of men eating rats in order to subsist, but these all seem to stem more from a sense of boredom and culinary sport among the Southerners rather than any real need.

So while there seems to have been enough food for the men at Johnson's Island, its nutritional value was certainly lacking. (According to Charles E. Fishman's authoritative book, *Rebels on Lake Erie*, fifty-six prisoners came down with scurvy, caused by a lack of vitamin C, between November 1, 1863 and March 20, 1865, even though the disease had been largely eradicated sixty years earlier.) In the face of protests from local townsfolk that the prisoners were treated too well — better than Union soldiers in the field, they argued — the health of the men at Johnson's Island remained generally stable, with roughly 200 prisoners being laid to rest in the prison cemetery during the prison's three-year career. By contrast, 13,000 of the 45,000 Union prisoners held at the notorious Confederate prison at Andersonville (or Camp Sumter as it was officially known) died from malnutrition, disease, overcrowding, and exposure in just fourteen months.

By far the greatest physical danger the Southerners faced was the brutal Lake Erie winter. As the mercury dropped through November and December, the men were left with nothing to do but hunker down as best they could, gathering around the pot-bellied stoves that heated the barracks and occupying themselves with chopping wood, which was delivered to the prison in one-metre lengths. To Henry Kyd Douglas, Johnson's Island "was just the place to convert visitors to the theological belief of the Norwegian that Hell has torments of cold instead of heat." Douglas also noted the lengths to which prisoners went to stay warm when, one night in January 1864, "two men would squeeze into one bunk so as to double blankets, would wrap themselves up head and feet, and in the morning break through crackling ice, formed by the congealing of the breath that escaped, as one has seen on the blankets of horses at sleighing time."

These dangers and discomforts notwithstanding, prison life was overwhelmingly monotonous for the Southern soldiers at Johnson's Island. Yet it was punctuated with more than a few moments of intrigue — and genuine terror. Escape attempts were not uncommon, and a few prisoners even managed to succeed against the keen eyes of the guards, the expanse of Sandusky Bay that separated them from the mainland, and Lake Erie's often treacherous weather. One such success story occurred on the brutally cold night of January 1, 1864, when five prisoners used a ladder to climb over the fence in a brazen attempt to catch the guards napping during record-setting cold temperatures. A heavy blizzard and violent gales had roared through the area the night before, nearly killing the lightkeeper and his family on nearby Green Island (see Chapter 6). Of the five who went over the fence that frigid night, one, who lacked proper clothing, chose to stay behind. The rest made their way across the frozen bay and eventually to Detroit. From there, another death-defying scramble across the partially frozen Detroit River brought them to Canada and safety. Lieutenant William E. Killen, another Johnson's Island prisoner, made note of the escape and the brutal weather conditions in his diary: "Jan. 2, 1864: Saturday. Still very cold. The thermometer must be from 12 to 15 degrees [Fahrenheit] below zero several prisoners made their escape. One was caught and brought back ..."

This, however, was one of the more audacious escapes from Johnson's Island. The handful of other prisoners who managed to get out did so in more mundane ways, by passing themselves off as parolees to the South or by hiding in the bottoms of the supply wagons that passed through the prison gates.

Executions also occurred at Johnson's Island, although these appear to have been relatively infrequent, and almost never involved prisoners of war but rather deserters from the Union army, suspected spies, and other criminals; these various types of lawbreakers were often held at prisoner-of-war camps. Perhaps the most intriguing case was that of Reuben Stout, who was put to death for desertion and murder on October 23, 1863. Stout had not returned to his post after his entire regiment had been captured by Confederate troops and subsequently paroled back to the Union. He later claimed his absence had been caused by illness, but in any case, he fell in with a secret society known as the "Knights of the Golden Circle," who were associated with the antiwar Copperhead movement in the North ("Copperheads," so known for the copper pins they wore to distinguish themselves, sympathized with the South, were largely proslavery and consisted mainly of Democrats opposed to the Republican Lincoln administration).

In the meantime, the army dispatched Solomon Huffman, a bounty hunter, to track Stout down. Four months later, Huffman found Stout hiding at his brother's home in Delphi, Indiana. A fight ensued, which ended with Stout shooting and killing Huffman with a pistol. Stout was subsequently sentenced to be "shot to death with musketry" on Johnson's Island.

The Johnson's Island cemetery gates stand as a haunting reminder of the Confederate prisoners once held here.

And so it came that on the morning of October 23, 1863, Stout found himself sitting on the end of his own wooden coffin on the south shore of Johnson's Island. The Hoffman Battalion formed up in front and the chaplain read portions of Stout's final statement (part of which appeared in the October 29, 1863 *New York Times*), in which he renounced both the Knights and the Copperheads, stating, "I was led by evil counsels, and my connection with a secret traitorous organization, to stay away from my post of duty in the army. I am truly sorry that I acted thus, or that I for a moment listened to these evil counsels …"

But there was to be no atonement in this life for Reuben Stout. When the chaplain finished, Stout was blindfolded and the firing squad given the fateful command. The musket claps echoed through the trees, and Stout's lifeless body slumped back over his coffin.

Beall's Privateers

It was just this kind of fate John Yates Beall was hoping to avoid when he set out for Toronto in August 1863. Unbeknownst to the Confederate government of President Jefferson Davis, Beall was on his way to meet Jacob Thompson, a former secretary of the interior under President James Buchanan, who was officially operating as a Confederate commissioner in Canada. Unofficially, however, Thompson's mission was more than mere diplomacy: armed with over a million dollars from his government, he was tasked with causing as much trouble for the Union on its northern flank as possible. This included everything from assisting the antiwar Copperheads to outright confrontation with the Union army.

There was, however, one major wrinkle: Thompson was under strict orders to respect Canadian, and by extension British, neutrality. To violate it risked bringing Britain into the war on the Union side; a chilling prospect for a Confederate army already stretched dangerously thin.

As for Beall, he had undergone a remarkable transformation over the eighteen months since he had returned to the South from Canada. Spoiling to get back into the fight, he had approached Confederate Secretary of the Navy Stephen R. Mallory and asked him for permission to launch a privateering mission on the Potomac River and Chesapeake Bay, where Beall could wreak havoc on the Union's waterborne supply line. Mallory accepted this proposal, and granted Beall a navy commission that made him an acting master in the Confederate States Navy.

It was a straightforward deal for Beall and his small crew (which never numbered more than twenty): the Confederate navy would give them arms and supplies, but nothing more. As with most privateering permits of the period, Beall's men received no direct pay from the government, but were entitled to keep all they could capture. On June 15, 1863, Beall departed Richmond with cutlasses and supplies, and set off for what he thought would be a rousing — and profitable — adventure.

But the expedition would get off to a disappointingly slow start, as Bedinger Lucas writes: "In the first month, nothing more was done than to surprise a camp of 'Contrabands,' killing one, capturing one, and putting to flight the remainder." The upshot was that over these opening weeks, the men captured just enough supplies to turn themselves into a reasonably effective raiding force. Operating from shore using two yawls (essentially small, two-masted sailboats), the privateers took five Union cargo vessels and fourteen prisoners between September 17 and September 20. One of the ships, the schooner *Alliance*, was carrying $200,000 worth of goods, a veritable fortune at the time.

Arguably the most brazen mission the crew undertook during the excursion was a raid on the Cape Charles lighthouse on Smith Island, in Chesapeake Bay, in early August 1863, just prior to the September raids on the five Union cargo vessels. As soon as the men landed, they quickly disembarked and scrambled for cover while Beall strode toward the lighthouse. "My friend," he called to the unsuspecting lightkeeper, "I am highly pleased with the lighthouse and your management of it, and I have a party of friends belonging to the Confederate States Navy who, I think, would like to look at it!"

With that, Beall gave a whistle, and his privateers sprang forward, storming through the door. Once inside, they set upon anything of value they could find, destroying or setting off with most of the lamps, machinery, and fixtures. They even managed to take three hundred gallons of oil off the island with them, which was of great value to the Confederacy, choked as it was by an ever-tightening Union naval blockade that had been in place since shortly after the war began. The raiders never laid a hand on the keeper, though it must have been a thoroughly terrifying experience for the man, who Bedinger Lucas describes derisively as "an illiterate and rough specimen."

As far as the Lake Erie raid was concerned, perhaps Beall's biggest acquisition in his Chesapeake Bay operations was the acquaintance of the man who would later become his chief lieutenant during the hijacking of the *Philo Parsons*. Born in Scotland, Bennet G. Burley had been drawn to the Confederacy by the lucrative but dangerous trade of blockade running. The privately owned vessels engaged in this activity brought everything from medical supplies to munitions and food to the Confederacy, and paid sailors handsomely. But after a short stint, Burley, too, decided to take a commission in the Confederate navy and join Beall for the privateering expedition, no doubt sensing that it had the potential to be even more lucrative.

Naturally, raids such as these soon began to attract the attention of the Union military. So much so, in fact, that it seems the generals overestimated Beall's strength when they dispatched a massive force, including a regiment of black infantry, two regiments of cavalry, and one artillery regiment to deal with the privateers. The Union force finally caught up with Beall at Tangier Inlet in early November 1862. Using no less than seven ships to seal off all available escape routes, the Union troops commenced a systematic search of the area. Characteristically undaunted, Beall ordered his two yawls into the inlet anyway, and quickly took a small schooner. Almost immediately afterward, he dispatched most of his men to shore in one of the yawls, while he kept a skeleton crew aboard the schooner, the idea being that fewer privateers on the captured ship would attract less attention.

But this time it was Beall who incorrectly estimated the size of the force opposing him. The men sent ashore were immediately captured and one of them, terrified, started talking, soon giving up the whole operation. Beall and his entire force were subsequently rounded up and transferred to the prison camp at Fort McHenry, near Drummondtown, Maryland. Astonishingly, even though Secretary of War Edwin Stanton ordered that the men be held "not as prisoners of war but as pirates or marauding robbers," they were exchanged back to the Confederacy in May 1864.

Spies and Saboteurs

Upon his return to Richmond, Beall took a much-needed break, again travelling and visiting old friends. His spirits rose with the extra rest, and in his journal he called this short period "the happiest two weeks of my life." He briefly considered a government offer to become a Confederate spy, but Beall, the consummate freelancer, was not yet ready to subject himself to superiors with whom he was almost certain to disagree. After taking up his musket to help with the defence of Richmond, around which the war was now tightening, Beall vanished from sight, finally reappearing in Toronto, where Jacob Thompson was headquartered.

Beall, in his journal, succinctly describes his first meeting with Thompson: "Immediately on my arrival in Canada I went to Col. Thompson at Toronto, and made application to start a privateer on Lake Huron. He informed me of a plan to take the *Michigan* (14 guns), and release the Confederate officers confined on Johnson's Island. I immediately volunteered …"

The Lake Erie raid would be a two-pronged strategy: Beall was to be responsible for organizing a raiding party at Sandwich that would procure a vessel to carry them to Sandusky Bay to attack the *Michigan*. The second part of the plan was already underway in Sandusky, right under the noses of the crew of the *Michigan*, and Beall immediately set off to judge things there for himself.

Upon arriving in Sandusky, Beall immediately sought out his contact, the spy Charles Cole, who was staying at the West House, a five-storey hotel near the waterfront, with his "wife," a woman variously known as Annie Davis or Emma Bison. Cole was posing as a wealthy oil baron, using generous amounts of Thompson's money to ingratiate himself to the crew of the *Michigan*, especially the captain, J.C. Carter. He ultimately planned to arrange a party for the crew aboard the ship, as part of the "oil man's" gratitude for the men's service to the Union. The champagne, however, was to be drugged, and when the crew fell unconscious, so the plan went, Cole would send a signal to Beall, who would be waiting nearby with a raiding party in his hijacked vessel.

During the summer of 1864, there were signs that Cole was having success. He wrote to Thompson in a letter that historian Charles E. Frohman later published in his 1965 book, *Rebels on Lake Erie*, that: "I have formed the acquaintance of Captain Carter, commanding United States steamer *Michigan*. He is an unpolished man, whose pride seems to be touched for the reason that, having been an old United States naval officer, he is not allowed now a more extensive field of operation."

With all seemingly going well on the Ohio side of the lake, Beall headed for Sandwich, where another surprise awaited him. His friend Bennet G. Burley, whom Beall had last seen during the privateering expedition on the Chesapeake, had managed to break out of captivity at Fort Delaware through a sewer that emptied into the Delaware River. Having thus gained his freedom, Burley showed even more bravado by choosing to join the Canadian operation, and when Beall arrived in Sandwich he found Burley there waiting for him. Beall must have been thrilled to have the experienced

Burley at his side for what would surely be the pair's toughest test yet. Naturally, Beall made Burley his second-in-command.

The Taking of the *Parsons*

Walter Ashley described the beginnings of the plot to take the *Philo Parsons* at Beall's military trial, held in New York in January 1865 (the proceedings of which Bedinger Lucas included in his *Memoir of John Yates Beall*):

> On Sunday, the 18th of September, about six o'clock in the evening, I was onboard the steamboat *Philo Parsons*, in the cabin alone, at the boat's dock in Detroit; she being a boat sailing from Detroit to the city of Sandusky, touching regularly at the Canadian port of Amherstburgh, and occasionally at Sandwich ... Mr. Bennet G. Burley came aboard the boat, and inquired for Ashley. I told him my name was Ashley. He then said he intended to go down as a passenger, in the morning, to Sandusky; that three friends were going with him; and he requested that the boat stopped at Sandwich, a small town on the Canada side of the river below Detroit, and take on those three friends as passengers. I remarked that it was not customary for the boat to stop at Sandwich. He then asked it as a personal favour that the boat would stop and take on his friends. I then agreed, provided that he, Burley, would take the boat himself at Detroit, and let me know for sure that his friends would be ready to come on board at Sandwich ... The next morning, being the 19th of September, the boat left Detroit at eight o'clock in the morning, with freight and passengers. As the boat was swinging away from the dock, Burley came to me and reminded me of my promise to stop the boat at Sandwich. At the time the boat left Detroit, Capt. S.F. Atwood was in command of her, but he stepped off at Middle Bass Island, where he resides. I told Capt. Atwood that the boat would have to stop at Sandwich, and he stopped and took these three friends of Burley at Sandwich.

The three men picked up at Sandwich, whom Ashley described as "gentlemanly in their appearance," paid their fare, stating they were "taking a little pleasure trip," with no particular destination. Still, this was a relatively normal morning aboard the *Parsons*, save for the unusual stop at Sandwich. When describing the stop at Amherstburg, a short way downriver, however, Ashley's testimony takes a slightly more suspicious tone:

> ... twenty-five men got onboard there at Malden [Amherstburg], and they paid their fare also ... all the baggage brought on board by the party was a very old trunk with cord, a rope, tied around it. It was taken in at the after gangway by two of the roughest looking subjects of the party; most of the party were roughly dressed in citizens' dress.

At this point Ashley thought he had taken on a group of "skedaddlers," or men who had crossed into Canada in order to evade the draft and were now heading home. Such men were not uncommon passengers on the *Philo Parsons*'s cross-border route.

From Amherstburg, the *Parsons* left the Detroit River and crossed the open lake to the small settlement at North Bass Island, then onward to Put-in-Bay, at South Bass Island, before proceeding to Middle Bass Island, and finally on to Kelleys Island, closer to the Ohio shore. It was while the boat was at Middle Bass that Captain Atwood disembarked to spend the evening with his family at his home on the island, leaving De Witt Clinton Nicols, the *Parsons*'s mate and Atwood's son-in-law, to sail the rest of the way to Sandusky and back the next morning, when Atwood planned to rejoin the *Parsons* on its return trip to Detroit. Ashley remained on board to look after what he called "the affairs of the boat."

It was as the *Parsons* was leaving Kelleys Island, at approximately four o'clock, that the hijacking got underway. Ashley was standing at the door to the ladies' cabin when he was approached by three of the men who had boarded at Amherstburg, each armed with pistols. Burley, who had been at the stern, rushed to join the attackers. Ashley recalled Burley's simple words to him while testifying at Beall's military trial: "Get into that cabin, or you're a dead man."

Beall then started counting, and by the time he had gotten to three, Ashley was well inside the cabin. Burley and his men then locked the door and posted guards outside. Ashley's testimony at Burley's Canadian extradition trial in December 1864 (which was closely followed in the Toronto *Globe*) illustrates the rampage the clerk then witnessed through the ladies' cabin window:

> From the cabin I observed the whole party gather round the old trunk; the cords were cut, the lid taken off and the whole party armed themselves with revolvers from the trunk; most of them had two revolvers each, and a belt around their waist with a revolver in it; some of them carried a hatchet … the prisoner [Burley] then with an axe smashed the luggage room door open; I do not know for what purpose … he then went forward and smashed the saloon door in the same manner … he had charge of the main deck, and for about an hour took charge of the vessel … he took charge of everything, and ordered the freight to be thrown overboard; the freight consisted of thirty tons of pig iron; I saw them commence to throw the iron overboard …

Meanwhile, a similar scene was unfolding in the *Parsons* wheelhouse, where De Witt Clinton Nicols was at the controls. His testimony at Burley's Canadian extradition trial neatly tells the story: "… I was in the pilot house when a man came up and said, 'I am a Confederate officer; I seize this boat and take you prisoner; submit to what I demand, or if not there (showing a revolver) are tools to make you.' I submitted and did as I was told." That man, whom Nicols mistakenly thought had gotten on at Amherstburg, was none other than John Yates Beall.

Once they had control of the boat, the Confederates shuffled the *Parsons*'s passengers, including Nicols, into the hold, where they could be easily monitored. Within thirty minutes, Beall's men were in complete control of the *Parsons* and were sailing directly for Sandusky Bay and the *Michigan*.

But just as the men began to celebrate their early success, another problem presented itself; there was not enough wood aboard the *Parsons* to power the boat's boilers for the seven to eight hours Beall estimated he would need. They would have to return to Middle Bass to take on more. With his quarry, the *Michigan*, nearly in sight, Beall angrily ordered the *Parsons* turned around.

The *Parsons* had been at the dock at Middle Bass taking wood, her "crew"

Photo courtesy of Lore of the Lakes

The Island Queen, *which was taken by Confederate operatives and partially sunk on Chickenolee Reef.*

doing their best not to arouse suspicion, for about fifteen minutes when their problems were compounded even further: George Orr's *Island Queen*, which was on its way to Toledo with a stop at South Bass Island, pulled in alongside to take on wood as well. With the increased activity on the dock that the *Queen*'s arrival attracted, it was getting more difficult for Beall's men to hold their cover. Even worse, the *Island Queen* was carrying between forty and fifty Union soldiers who were returning to Toledo, plus several Middle Bass Islanders, for a total of one hundred passengers in all. There was no choice — Beall would have to seize the *Island Queen* or risk being overrun by the soldiers aboard her. George Orr describes what happened next:

> Here the *Queen* was taken possession by the armed conspirators, who leaped aboard from the *Parsons'* upper decks. The men comprising the crew and passengers of the *Island Queen* were compelled to go into the *Parsons'* hold, while the ladies and children were all ordered into her upper cabins.

Unfortunately, the taking of the *Island Queen* was not done without some bloodshed. According to Orr, "Engineer Henry Haines was ordered out of the engine room, and told that if he did not come they would shoot him. He refused and they shot him in the face, causing a flesh wound and filling his face with powder." In order to disperse the crowd gathering on the dock, the Confederates fired indiscriminately into it, seriously wounding Lorenz Miller, a resident of Put-in-Bay.

Beall was out of time. He had to get the *Parsons* away from the dock — immediately. He quickly ordered the passengers of both boats, save for Orr, the wounded engineer, and the *Island Queen*'s clerk, put ashore, under the condition that they not inform anyone of what had happened for twenty-four hours. (The passengers quickly violated this quaint convention of nineteenth-century warfare and set off by rowboat to tell the residents of nearby Put-in-Bay about the Confederate raiders. But by the time they got there, the danger had long passed.)

Beall ordered the *Island Queen* taken in tow, and the two vessels lumbered away from Middle Bass, heading for Chickenolee Reef, just south of Pelee Island, in Canadian waters. There, a small group of raiders boarded the *Island Queen*, cut the steamer's water feed pipe, and cast it adrift. It eventually came to rest on the reef, partially submerged in just under three metres of water.

With the *Queen* conveniently disposed of, and Beall back in firm control of the situation, there were no more obstacles to be overcome. Beall ordered the *Parsons* to Sandusky Bay. With the time now around 10 p.m., the *Parsons* cut her engines three kilometres outside of the channel buoy, with the *Michigan* in uncomfortably close range. Beall had done all he could. All that remained now was the signal from Cole.

It would not come. What Beall could not know was that an informant had somehow managed to get word through to Captain Carter about the plot to take his ship and, specifically, Cole's role in it. There are numerous stories as to exactly how Cole was apprehended, but what is clear is that he and his "wife" had packed their bags, no doubt ready to make an escape to Canada, when Cole was captured and taken to the *Michigan*. Ironically, as Beall and his men were nose to nose with the Union gunboat in Sandusky Bay, Cole was likely aboard the *Michigan* — in the brig.

A full thirty minutes had passed since the *Parsons* had arrived at Sandusky Bay and still the *Michigan* rode silently ahead at anchor. When word got out that Beall was considering making the attempt anyway, tensions reached a breaking point. Seventeen of the raiders were now convinced that such an action would be folly, and it was time to head back to Canada. When they expressed this opinion, Beall flew into a furious rage. But the men would not be moved. Finally, even the fanatical Beall realized he had no option. He would order the *Parsons* back to Canada, but not before each of the hijackers signed a sworn statement of what Beall described as their insubordination, which they proceeded to do on the back of a bill of lading.

With this, the *Philo Parsons* sped back toward the Detroit River, her boiler being kept in a "tremendous heat," according to George Orr, because the Confederates were burning old coal oil barrels that had been left aboard. During the return journey, Beall ordered the Confederate flag hoisted up the *Parsons's* mast.

It would be the only time the "Southern Cross" would fly above a vessel on the Great Lakes during the Civil War.

When they reached Amherstburg at around eight o'clock in the morning, two of the raiders fled ashore in a small boat that had been taken from the *Island Queen* before she was scuttled. The next stop was Fighting Island, a small, uninhabited isle further up the Detroit River. There, Orr, the engineer, and the clerk were put ashore. Then, as Orr says, "they continued up the river to Sandwich, where, after removing the piano and other valuables, the *Parsons* was set adrift, but afterward picked up by a tug. The raiders then scattered into Canada as fast as possible."

Endgame

With that, the Lake Erie raid came to its ignominious end. Cole, ironically, would be sent to Johnson's Island for the duration of the war, and would be one of the last remaining prisoners at the facility before it was finally closed on September 5, 1865. He was sent to Fort Lafayette, in New York Harbor, where he was finally discharged five months later, on February 10, 1866.

The presence of the Confederate agents on Canadian soil proved to be a major headache for the Canadian government in the months following the Lake Erie raid. Relations between Canada and the Union had been frosty for much of the Civil War, mainly because Northerners tended to view Canadians as Southern sympathizers, and the Lake Erie raid only further spread the Union belief that the colonies were a haven for Confederate spies and saboteurs. The September 22, 1864, *Detroit Free Press* captures this sentiment concisely:

> We trust, for the credit and reputation of our friends across the river, that this action of ferreting out and insuring punishment to the scoundrels will be vigorous and prompt. They do not and cannot be allowed to stand before the world as harborers of thieves and pirates.

The Canadian authorities launched an extensive manhunt in the days following the raid, catching up with Burley in Guelph, Canada West (now Ontario), days after the events on Lake Erie, though they at first thought he was John Yates Beall. To the Crown's further embarrassment, an illegal warrant was used in Burley's arrest, forcing his release, after which he was quickly rearrested, specifically for being a member of the party that had attacked the *Philo Parsons*, and for stealing articles belonging to the crew. His case was front-page news in the Toronto *Globe*. The judge's ultimate decision — to allow Burley's extradition to the United States — was greeted with scorn by many Canadians, who saw the decision as caving in to pressure from the Union. Ironically, the entire legal ordeal would make absolutely no difference to Burley's long-term fate. After being extradited from Canada, Burley was waiting for yet another trial at a jail in Port Clinton, Ohio, when he managed yet again to elude his captors. It happened on the afternoon of September 17, 1865, just days before the one-year anniversary of the Lake Erie raid. The sheriff took his family on a visit to the countryside, locking only the outside door of the jail as he left, leaving Burley, the only occupant at the time, with the run of the place. When the sheriff sent a man to give Burley his supper, he found the building empty, the sheriff's keys missing, and the outside door unlocked. The only evidence Burley left behind was a note that read: "Sunday — I have gone out for a walk — Perhaps (?) I will return shortly."

Burley crossed back into Canada before returning to his native Scotland a short time later. There, he would change the spelling of his name to "Burleigh" and go on to write several books — though he never did write a single word about his adventure on Lake Erie — and become a distinguished war correspondent for the *London Daily Telegraph*, covering, among other conflicts, the South African War (1899–1902) and the Russo-Japanese War (1904–1905). He died in London on June 17, 1914.

For John Yates Beall, on the other hand, old habits proved difficult to break. He was finally arrested on December 16, 1864, at Dunkirk, New York, on the American side of Lake Erie, while trying to sabotage the railroad tracks used by freight trains travelling to Buffalo. His criminal trial took place in New York in January 1865; the outcome was never in doubt. He was found guilty of treason and sentenced to death by hanging at Fort Columbus, on Governor's Island, between twelve and two o'clock on the afternoon of February 24, 1865. His remaining friends, including Bedinger Lucas, did their best to win a reprieve from President Lincoln, but it would not come. There has been conjecture in the years since that

Lincoln's refusal to grant Beall a reprieve was one reason why John Wilkes Booth assassinated Lincoln, but this is based on a wide variety of speculative claims (including the spurious notion that Beall and Booth were cousins) for which there is no evidence.

Beall spent the morning of his execution enjoying a last meal and dressing himself with "his usual care and neatness," according to Bedinger Lucas, before being led to the scaffold at one o'clock, escorted by a cortege of regulars, with whom Beall, perhaps recalling his days as a soldier, kept step.

After a short delay, Beall mounted the platform and took his seat below the rope, his coffin, a rough pine box, waiting for him at the foot of the gallows. After the adjutant had finished reading the charges against him, Beall quietly rose and announced his readiness before turning to dutifully face his beloved South. His last words before the hangman did his work were simple: "I protest against the execution of this sentence. It is a murder! I die in the service and defence of my country! I have nothing more to say."

—⚬—

The end finally came for Johnson's Island on September 5, 1865, five months after the end of the war, when the last of its prisoners were transferred to other facilities. By November 5, prison fixtures were being auctioned off and the walls were torn down.

The island returned largely to its natural state, with little activity other than farming occurring there until 1894, when a small resort, was constructed, only to fail three short years later. Another attempt was made in 1904, but it, too, quickly succumbed, this time to Cedar Point, just across Sandusky Bay. Cedar Point's owners bought Johnson's Island and relocated the buildings to their resort. Cedar Point is now one of the premier amusement parks in the United States.

Today, little remains of the Johnson's Island prison, and the island itself is mainly home to a few small, private cottages and, of course, the graves of those who died there. The quiet cemetery's crude wooden headstones were long neglected after the dismantling of the prison, but in 1890 a group of Sandusky citizens replaced them with marble markers displaying each prisoner's name, rank, regiment, and company (where known). According to a plaque at the site, there are 206 individual markers, though 267 sets of human remains have been located using ground-penetrating radar. All of the men interred here, both the known and unknown, are watched over by "The Lookout," a bronze statue of a

Confederate soldier created by Confederate veteran Sir Moses Ezekiel and dedicated in 1910.

Though the Johnson's Island prisoners have been finally, and properly, given an official memorial, it is the hundreds of unofficial remembrances, perhaps, that best mark the grim and fading memories of a place like the Johnson's Island prison. The following poem, likely written by a young,

Photo by author

A Confederate grave at the Johnson's Island cemetery. The original wooden markers were replaced with marble ones in 1890.

war-weary captive yearning for home, was found etched on one of the prison walls after the prisoners had been shipped back to their homes in the South. Lydia Ryall made sure it wasn't lost to history by recording it in *Sketches and Stories of the Lake Erie Islands*:

> Farewell to Johnson's Island
> Hoarse-sounding billows of the white-capped lake
> That 'gainst the barriers of our hated prison break,
> Farewell! Farewell; thou giant inland sea;
> Thou too, subservest the modest of tyranny —
> Girding this isle, washing its lonely shore.
> With moaning echoes of thy melancholy roar.
> Farewell, thou lake! Farewell, thou inhospitable land!
> All, save the spot, the holy sacred bed,
> Where rest in peace our Southern warriors dead.

Chapter 5

Captives of Time:
Lake Erie Shipwrecks

Harlan Hatcher, in his seminal 1945 book on Lake Erie, titled simply *Lake Erie*, had this to say about the men who crewed the lake freighters of the time:

> There is a quality of loyalty and devotion about them which borders on the sentimental. They live in a tight little world of their own into which outsiders gain only an occasional glimpse. It is practically self-contained. As soon as the shipping season starts in April the men go aboard the ships to which they have been assigned, and they seldom leave them again, except for an hour or two in port or for a few minutes while they take on bunker coal or lock through the Sault, until the ice closes over and they tie up for the winter in late November or early December.

This could easily describe Great Lakes crews a hundred years before Hatcher wrote his book, and much of it is just as applicable to those who staff today's advanced vessels. For even though modern conveniences have made lake freighters far more comfortable than they have ever been, life aboard ship remains inherently lonely. And although a spirit of closeness and brotherhood often pervades freighter crews, these men and women never stop thinking of friends, family, and the comforts of home. It is a sentiment that is often most visible in times of great danger. Stories of ships fighting storms or fires at sea are often riddled with crewmen worried, in their most desperate moments, about how their loved ones will get by without them, or others who simply drop to their knees and pray that they will get the chance to see those loved ones again.

And there is never a shortage of such dangers on Lake Erie. The shallowest of the Great Lakes, it has long been known as a graveyard for ships, with a reputation for weather so fearsome that it has proven itself capable of grabbing one of the giant vessels that roam across it and driving it to the bottom without a trace, sometimes keeping the gloomy secret of its victim's fate for a century or more.

The four stories that follow exemplify the heroism and camaraderie that is often revealed when people decide to take on the challenge that is Lake Erie. At Long Point, Ontario, Abigail Becker, a young mother, risked everything to save the crew of the grounded schooner *Conductor*, while the men aboard the cargo steamer *Clarion* found themselves pushed to the limit while battling both a roaring fire and treacherous shoals off Point Pelee. The crew of the whaleback *James B. Colgate* put their uniquely designed vessel up against the worst storm in Lake Erie's modern history, the so-called "Black Friday" maelstrom of 1916, and, on a foggy night in 1852, Amund Eidsmoe, a Norwegian immigrant hoping to give his family a better life in the American Midwest, got far more than he bargained for aboard the passenger steamer *Atlantic*.

While these stories only scratch the surface of the human drama that has played itself out time and again as crews have fought against Erie's rage, they do show how the human spirit can persevere against even these long odds. And the countless wrecks that remain pay silent tribute to those who never returned to the families they left behind.

A Bump in the Night: The Loss of the *Atlantic*

Amund Eidsmoe gazed out over Lake Erie and saw a road to a better life. The Norwegian immigrant and his small family had arrived in Buffalo in late August 1852, after a four-month odyssey that had taken them across the Atlantic Ocean and then by rail from Montreal.

Eidsmoe was born in 1814 among the rolling hills and valleys of the Valdres region of Norway. His upbringing had been a humble one: with his parents struggling to raise six children, there was little time for the young boy to engage in the usual childhood pursuits — he had to go to work as soon as he was able. But he was more than up to the challenge, quickly mastering the lathe and, with the help of his brothers, turning out a wide range of trinkets, from pepper grinders to spinning wheels. It wasn't much, but every little bit helped the Eidsmoes make ends meet.

At the age of sixteen, Eidsmoe's father sent him to a seminary to study. Two years later, he graduated with the recommendation: "very quick in learning: a teacher and choir leader position." Upon his return home, Eidsmoe took the hint and became a teacher at a small school in his neighbourhood. But even though he enjoyed the work, he took the job mainly because his church had financed his studies and expected a return on its investment. Eidsmoe's new job was a seven-year commitment and offered very meagre pay.

On top of that, his domestic life was changing, as he describes in his own unpublished account, which he penned in 1901, very late in his long life:

> When I had served the seven years I was compelled to, I received an increase in salary and taught in all 16 years. In that time I had married and two children were born of this union, one boy and one girl. My wife died after four and a half years of married life and our little girl died at the age of two and a half years. I married again in 1849. Then I became aware of the fact that the school salary was going to be too small and decided to wander out to America.

What had been drawing Eidsmoe and his Norwegian countrymen, along with most other immigrants, to the New World over the previous two hundred years was straightforward: cheap land. As the United States expanded westward, there was an abundance of opportunity for hardworking men like Eidsmoe. He planned to be among the first of what would become a large number of Norwegians to settle in the American Upper Midwest.

But the trip to Buffalo had already been plagued by obstacles; after Eidsmoe and his family, which now included the boy from his previous marriage and a little girl, had said goodbye to their relatives for what they all must have known would be the last time, they arrived at the port city of Drammen only to learn that the ship on which they had booked passage had already departed. This unexpected hardship forced the Eidsmoes to find temporary accommodation in Drammen and the surrounding area for a total of nine weeks until another vessel could be fitted out for the journey.

To their great relief, the day of departure finally arrived. The Eidsmoes brought aboard their own food supply, which was already stretched by the unexpected layover, and all of their possessions in a few small trunks. Eidsmoe provides his perspective of the voyage: "On the ship we were always in danger of falling from the heaving and plunging of the waves and in our rooms we were thrown from one wall to the other, now up and now down. It continued in this manner for eight weeks and four days until we arrived at Quebec."

The steamer took them down the St. Lawrence River as far as Montreal, where the Eidsmoes and their fellow Norwegians were unloaded and moved onto a train bound for Buffalo. But their misfortune was far from over: while the baggage was being offloaded from the ship, one of the Norwegians slipped off the pier and fell into the harbour. Passersby scrambled to try and reach the panicked man, but he was hopelessly trapped between the ship and the dock. Finally, he disappeared beneath the surface and did not reappear. On the train, Eidsmoe and his family found themselves sharing a seat with the man's newly widowed wife and child. "She was overcome with grief," wrote a still-saddened Eidsmoe almost fifty years later. "It was a pitiful sight to see and think about."

But as they started their rail journey, things started to look up. The immigrants were, after all, now into the last leg of their ordeal. Eidsmoe, able to see Niagara Falls out the window as the train sped by, wrote: "From our car we could see in the distance the Niagara Falls, where grandeur is beyond my power of description."

From Buffalo, Lake Erie beckoned. When Eidsmoe and his family laid eyes on the vessel that would carry them into the U.S interior, the practically brand-new paddlewheel steamer *Atlantic*, their hearts must have soared.

—ɷ—

The *Atlantic* was barely three years old when she sailed from Buffalo on the evening of August 19, 1852. She was a big ship, clocking in at eighty-one metres in length. And elegant: she was endowed with eighty-five staterooms and could carry over three hundred passengers. The *Atlantic* was also no

Illustration from the collection of Walter Lewis

LAKE ERIE STEAMBOAT ATLANTIC, 1848.

The Atlantic, *one of Lake Erie's most luxurious steamers, was only three years old when it was lost in 1852.*

slouch in the speed department, and made her owner, E.B. Ward of Detroit, proud by setting a Lake Erie speed record up to that time, cruising clear across the lake, from Buffalo to Detroit, in 16.5 hours.

The Eidsmoes and the more than one hundred other Norwegians aboard would know little of the luxuries the *Atlantic* had to offer. Many scattered across the deck, searching for any corner in which they could spread out and get a decent night's sleep. But none felt terribly put out. After all, they would be safely in Detroit by the next afternoon.

Later that evening, the *Atlantic* steamed into Erie, Pennsylvania, to take on even more passengers, again mostly new immigrants. The sidewheeler was now so overloaded that seventy had to be left behind on the dock. As it turned out, these would be the luckiest people involved with the *Atlantic* saga, though they certainly didn't feel so at the time.

The *Atlantic*'s clerk later estimated that there were between 500 and 600 people aboard when they left Erie, or about 300 more than there should have been. One hundred fifty squeezed into the cabins and 350–450 more scattered about the deck. By this period, Great Lakes skippers knew well not to tempt Lake Erie's unpredictable weather. The *Atlantic*'s captain, J. Byron Petty, showed a serious lack of judgment by letting so many passengers onto his boat. It would be the first of many decisions taken that night that would have horrific consequences.

It was about eleven o'clock by the time Petty ordered the wheelsman to ease the *Atlantic* out toward the open lake. While the crew settled in for what looked like another routine crossing, things were far from comfortable down on deck, as Eidsmoe notes:

> There were many people and all wanted to find a place to sleep. As many as found room went down into the cabins, but many had to prepare their beds upon the deck. I and my family were among the latter. The deck was crowded with every conceivable thing: baggage, new wagons, and much other stuff. So we lay down to rest but sleep was not of long duration.

The lake was calm, and various sources are unclear on the level of visibility, recording conditions as different as a light mist and a heavy fog. What is clear is that as the *Atlantic* steamed toward Long Point, a sandspit protruding some forty kilometres out from the Ontario shoreline, it would have been difficult to see much.

At about two o'clock, the *Atlantic* passed the Long Point lighthouse. In the wheelhouse, the second mate, James Carny, and the wheelsman, Morris Barry, strained their eyes into a mist Carny later described as "smoky." Barry, quoted in the August 23, 1852, Buffalo *Daily Republic* tells what happened next:

> We passed Long Point light at two o'clock on our usual course … Should think in twenty minutes after, the 2nd Mate, who was on watch, called my attention to a light on our larboard bow … It was two small lights, very dim, couldn't tell what it was, but I saw no signal lights supposing it to be a vessel. Had no idea on what course she was sailing.

The light was from the freighter *Ogdensburg*, headed in the opposite direction, toward the Welland Canal, having departed Cleveland around noon with a load of grain. She was a propeller-driven vessel about the same size as the *Atlantic*, and in her wheelhouse a similar scene was playing out as her crew tried in vain to see what might be looming ahead. De Grass McNeil, the *Ogdensburg*'s first mate, was on duty that night. At a coroner's inquest on August 21, McNeil gave his version of events, which were published in the Buffalo *Daily Republic* of the same date:

About half past one saw the steamer. She had a light aloft and two white lights at the center and another signal light in front of the wheelhouse. When I first saw her she was probably three miles distant … I judge from her course that we should pass a half mile south of her, upon nearing her, she appeared to have changed her course and to be making across our bows. I now ordered our engines stopped. It was about ten minutes before the collision seeing that we were likely to strike together. I ordered the engine to back, and the wheel to be put hard a-starboard. I shouted as hard as I could.

The *Ogdensburg* caught the *Atlantic* on her port side, about ten metres forward of the paddlewheel, her bow slicing the steamer open down to the waterline. As the *Atlantic* shuddered with the impact, the passengers on deck were rudely awakened to see the *Ogdensburg's* prow suddenly towering over them. Instantly, pandemonium broke out as they scrambled out of the way of falling masts, toppling trunks and cracking timbers. Below, cabin passengers were already beginning to flee rooms that were starting to flood.

But, amazingly, the atmosphere in the vessels' wheelhouses was a stark contrast. Obviously unaware of the severity of the damage to the *Atlantic*, Carny decided to keep the paddlewheels turning at full speed, but ordered the steamer's course changed toward the Canadian shore.

Meanwhile aboard the *Ogdensburg*, McNeil ordered a full reverse, and just as quickly as she had come, the *Ogdensburg's* bow eased out of the gash she had carved into the side of the passenger steamer and disappeared into the fog. Then, probably noting that the *Atlantic* was continuing on under full steam, McNeil ordered the *Ogdensburg* put back on its regular course. Two kilometres on, he decided to order the boat stopped so the crew could check her over for damage. It was then, just as the hum of the engines was dying off, that the *Ogdensburg's* crew picked up the first signs of trouble; though they didn't want to believe their ears at first, there was no denying it. The sounds they heard wafting through the calm, damp air could only be human screams.

—∿—

Aboard the *Atlantic*, things quickly went from bad to worse. With the engines still under full steam, large amounts of water rushed in through the gash in her side and flooded the lower decks, soon extinguishing the boilers. Now beginning to panic themselves, the crew quickly lost control of the situation, starting with Captain Petty, who emerged from his cabin to help launch one of the first lifeboats. But just as the craft was being lowered, he slipped and fell headfirst into it. Probably concussed, Petty was made a bystander to the terrible events that were only beginning to engulf his ship. Eidsmoe tells what he saw:

> It seemed as if even the wrath of the Almighty had a hand in the destruction. The sailors became absolutely raving and tried to get as many killed as possible. When they saw that people crowded up [trying to come up from the lower decks] they struck them on the heads and shoulders to drive them down again. When this did not help, they took and raised the stairway up on end so the people fell down backwards again. Then they jerked the ladder up on the deck. All hopes were gone for those that were underneath. Water filled the rooms and life was no more.

By this time, passengers had begun throwing whatever they could find that might float — trunks, deck chairs, even bedding — over the side before leaping themselves. The Norwegians, many of whom could not even understand English, were among the first to do this, thinking, perhaps, that it would be the best way to escape the chaos that was now at full rage aboard the passenger steamer. But, as the ship continued to sink, and more and more passengers jumped in after them, many of these unfortunate souls were pulled beneath the surface as the mass of humanity now writhing in Lake Erie's waters desperately grabbed for anything that would float. Of all the immigrants who were aboard the *Atlantic* that night, it is estimated that more than half never lived to see the end of the long journey they had started so many months before.

As it turned out, the safest place to be was aboard the ship itself. When the bow slipped beneath the surface, an air bubble buoyed up the stern, giving those who remained there enough time to wait for the return of the *Ogdensburg*, whose lights many had noticed were growing larger as she raced back toward the scene. When the freighter arrived, these fortunate survivors simply stepped across to her deck.

The Eidsmoes had a more difficult time of things. When the bow went under, the water washed over and swept them into the lake. Miraculously, they were able to stay together and, with his wife and two small children clinging to his back, Eidsmoe treaded water for several minutes until crewmen from the *Ogdensburg* spotted them and pulled them to safety. Of his unexpected salvation he wrote: "When I discovered that all of my family were alive, I was full of joy, as if I had become the richest man in the world, despite the fact that we had lost all of our goods."

The *Ogdensburg* circled the debris field three times, until well after dawn, her crew pulling survivors from the water as they came across them. But eventually an eerie silence fell over the wreck site, and there were simply no more lives left to be saved. At seven o'clock in the morning, about an hour after the *Ogdensburg* had sailed away, the air bubble that had been supporting the *Atlantic*'s stern finally seeped away, and it, too, slipped beneath the surface.

The scene aboard the *Ogdensburg* as it steamed back toward Erie with its wretched human cargo must have been heartbreaking, as frightened and exhausted mothers searched for lost children, and wives scoured the deck looking for their missing husbands. Because of the haphazard manner in which the *Atlantic* had been loaded, there is no way to know exactly how many went to the bottom of Lake Erie with her on that dark night, but the estimate is somewhere between 200 and 300, making the *Atlantic* tragedy the fifth-worst in the history of the Great Lakes.

For many years, it looked as though the *Atlantic* story might end here. Aside from a series of dives immediately after the wreck to retrieve the purser's safe, which contained US$36,000, divers appear to have paid little attention to the *Atlantic*. As time passed, her location was eventually forgotten.

But all that ended with a bang in 1991, when Mar Dive Limited, a salvage company based in Los Angeles, announced that it had rediscovered the wreck in the summer of 1989. Mar Dive's president, Steve Morgan, quoted in the June 26, 1991, Kitchener–Waterloo *Record*, said: "We knew we found it when we saw it. We could tell just by the size of her wheels." At the time it was rumoured that the *Atlantic* contained up to $60 million in gold coins.

There were a couple of obstacles facing this claim: one was an objection by Mike Fletcher, a professional diver from Port Dover who quickly refuted the company's assertion that it had discovered the *Atlantic*. "I've had almost 100 dives on the wreck," he said in the June 28, 1991, Kitchener–Waterloo *Record*.

And then, of course, there was the tricky matter of sovereignty. The *Atlantic*, though an American vessel, rests well inside Canadian waters. Responding to the increasing tension over ownership of the *Atlantic*, the Ontario government ordered the Ontario Provincial Police to patrol the site and arrest anyone trespassing on it. This they did, both by boat and, according to the August 19, 1992, *Toronto Star*, through a sophisticated electronic monitoring system placed in the Long Point lighthouse. If a vessel remained too long over the *Atlantic*, the device would send a signal to the OPP office, which would then dispatch patrol boats. This was to be the state of things until the courts decided who spoke on behalf of the *Atlantic*.

In Toronto on December 20, 1996, Mr. Justice Douglas Lissaman handed down a 117-page ruling handing the right to the *Atlantic* over to the Province of Ontario. "This is good for the ship, and for shipwrecks in general," said Fletcher, quoted in the December 21, 1996, *Toronto Star*, but he admitted he was concerned that all the publicity would attract more attention to the beleaguered wreck.

So, has the end of the *Atlantic* story finally been written?

As with all matters involving our heritage shipwrecks, only time will tell.

—m—

Amund Eidsmoe and his family made it to Wisconsin, but not without the help of Milwaukee's German community, which raised US$450 in cash and forwarded $350 worth of clothes for the *Atlantic* survivors. Of their generosity, Eidsmoe wrote:

> ... the Germans were very kind to us and had taken up contributions so we were all supplied with money and clothes. A merchant, named Carlsen, was very kind to us and gave me a suit of clothes and $30.00 in cash. There were probably those who received more, but I was glad that they had helped us this much.

From Milwaukee, it was out to the Wisconsin countryside, where the Eidsmoes finally got down to the business of farming. But it was not quite over for them; two years later, a rival claim on their property forced them to abandon everything once more and move to Green County, where

Eidsmoe's brothers were settled. While still a humble farmer, Eidsmoe couldn't resist his original calling and became the first teacher in the newly formed English school division there.

And he never lost his optimism, even during the hard times. In his twilight years, he wrote:

> On the first of January, 1900, our children had a postponed Golden Wedding for us (November Thanksgiving, 1899). Two weeks later my wife died quietly and peacefully, after an illness of but three days with lung fever. I thank God earnestly for his care over me so far. If he has laid a burden on me he has also, fatherly, helped me to carry it. If I could prepare myself for a blessed departure from this world and my passing away be as my dear wife's, my wish would be fulfilled. God help me ... Amen.

Unlike many of his fellow passengers on the doomed *Atlantic*, Eidsmoe lived a long, full life. On November 11, 1903, scarcely two years after writing his account, he passed away. He was eighty-nine years old.

Abigail Becker: Long Point's Lifesaver

Abigail Becker had put in a long night.

It was the morning of November 24, 1854, and the young mother hadn't slept a wink. Instead, she spent hour after hour staring up at the ceiling of her small, drafty cabin among the sand dunes on the south shore of Long Point, Canada West (present-day Ontario). Outside, the wind was howling at gale force, whistling through the cracks in the small cabin's walls and whipping Lake Erie into a frenzy. To make things worse, the temperature had dropped below freezing early in the evening, lowering the temperature inside the cabin with it, and bringing a blizzard that left the sparsely populated peninsula thinly blanketed with snow.

The Becker home was located not far from what was referred to as the "Old Cut," a natural canal created by another violent storm that had hit Long Point over twenty years earlier, in November 1833. The Cut bisected Long Point near its base, not far from the current gates of Long Point Provincial Park. It offered a shortcut for mariners, who used it as a way to avoid having to navigate all the way around the end of the forty-kilometre sandspit, with its hundreds of treacherous and ever-shifting sandbars, and to wait out nasty weather on the other side, in the shelter of Long Point Bay.

To accommodate this new and unexpected shipping route, the colonial government sent a lightship to mark the bayside entrance to the Cut in 1840. It remained there until, in 1879, the Old Cut lighthouse was built on the lake side, which was the more important position in terms of safety. The Old Cut lighthouse, now privately owned, remains in good condition, though it looks wildly out of place today, for the Cut itself disappeared just as it had been born — it was filled in by a violent storm in 1906. The storm ended Long Point's brief history as an island and turned it back into a peninsula — and left the Old Cut lighthouse high and dry.

But, in 1854, shipping through the Old Cut was in its heyday, and on that cold November morning, Abigail's mind was almost entirely on her husband, Jeremiah. The previous day, he had set off in the family's rowboat for the nearby settlement of Port Rowan with a load of furs to trade for supplies. Just before he left, perhaps sensing his wife's unease about the wind, which was already beginning to gather, Jeremiah promised he would stay close to shore the entire way. Still, Abigail worried. She prayed he was safe and warm in Port Rowan, carrying on his business or waiting out the storm.

So Abigail rose earlier than usual the next morning and, before her children began stirring, groggily made her way down to the beach to fetch some water. But just before she dipped her bucket into Lake Erie's still churning waters, something bobbed into her line of sight, less than a kilometre in the distance, near the shore. Straining her eyes, she began to make out a white, rectangular form, and as she did, a sense of dread filled her. She hoped in vain that it was an illusion, but it was not to be. The floating form could only be one thing — an overturned rowboat.

Abigail trembled with fear as the realization set in: sailors had been out in last night's storm. What's more, if they were lucky enough to still be alive, they were no doubt shipwrecked nearby. Not missing a beat, Abigail dropped her bucket and sprinted down the beach toward the small craft.

Little did she know that her fears were about to be compounded. For when Abigail reached the rowboat, her eyes fell on an even more terrible sight: in the near distance, the tattered rigging of a ship protruded from the surface of the water. She was sure she could see human forms clinging to it.

—⚒—

Abigail Jackson was the first-born in a family of Dutch Loyalists from Pennsylvania, who eventually settled in Norfolk County. At age seventeen, she married Jeremiah Becker, a local trapper and fisherman of humble means. Jeremiah was a widower who was significantly older than Abigail and already had five children of his own. That number would later swell to thirteen, as Abigail would bear eight more — three girls and five boys.

While the Beckers had few of the comforts of life, their home was largely a happy one, as her stepdaughter Margaret Wheeler (a product of Jeremiah's first marriage) told Reverend R. Calvert many years later. Calvert would transcribe and publish Wheeler's retelling of Abigail's life in 1899 as *The Story of Abigail Becker: The Heroine of Long Point*:

> When my father met Abigail Jackson, she was a slender young girl. She worked hard and devotedly to make us comfortable, and has often since expressed her pleasure in us. We are, you may be sure, proud of her. She really raised three families, seventeen children in all. It is her boast that she raised her eight boys and not one of them uses tobacco or liquor.

Shortly after their marriage, Jeremiah built the small cabin on Long Point, mainly out of logs and driftwood.

By all accounts, Abigail enjoyed life on Long Point, despite the loneliness and isolation she endured when Jeremiah was away. And she seemed to have had a knack for being in the right place when help was needed, as Margaret Wheeler notes, "… she [Abigail] saved a child from drowning in a well, and a man from a similar fate at Nanticoke by throwing him a plank and holding him up till assistance came."

Then came the first Long Point shipwreck that Abigail was caught up in. Again, Wheeler provides a detailed description:

> There was an iron-laden vessel wrecked on Long Point Island, near the lower lighthouse [the Old Cut light], the crew of six escaping to land. On reaching the lighthouse they found the keeper had gone for the winter … Only four of the six succeeded in walking to our place; the other two gave out about a mile and a half away. Mother sent the boys with food and raiment for them. A little later they were able to get to the house.

Illustration courtesy of the collection of the Norfolk Heritage Centre.

Abigail Becker displaying the medal she was awarded for saving the crew of the
Conductor.

One can only imagine Jeremiah's surprise the following day when he returned to find six exhausted and frostbitten sailors sprawled out across the cabin. Over the next several weeks, the generous Abigail nursed all of them back to health.

It was a harbinger of events to come.

—ww—

Little did Abigail know that just as she was seeing Jeremiah off to Port Rowan on the chilly morning of November 23, a far more fateful voyage was beginning far to the west. At Amherstburg, on the Canadian side of the Detroit River, the two-masted schooner *Conductor*, under Captain Henry Hackett, an Amherstburg native, was easing its way out of its berth and edging south toward Lake Erie, its hold stuffed with 8,000 bushels, or over US$10,000, worth of corn. Hackett planned to sail east through the Pelee Passage, around Long Point, and into the Welland Canal, which would deliver the *Conductor* onto Lake Ontario and the short trip to Toronto, where it would deliver its cargo.

But as the ship made her way east and night fell, the weather began to take a turn. The ship's barometer fell, the wind came up and, just as she approached Long Point, the *Conductor* was beset by blinding snow squalls.

Like many lake captains before him, Hackett made the decision to change course and head for the safety of the Old Cut.

But the storm made finding the mouth of the Cut something of a needle-in-a-haystack proposition. Hackett circled several times in vain, but, unable to spot the channel, he could wait no more; he gave orders to make a run for the tip in hopes of rounding into the Point's lee side. With that, the *Conductor* slowly came around. In such conditions, the ship was barely manageable, but just as the *Conductor* began to respond, the unimaginable happened: the schooner gave a hard lurch and came to a dead stop. Even though the crew could see very little because of the blizzard, they were hung up on a sandbar, less than 200 metres from shore. Shortly, the waves began to curl up over the side, and were soon washing over the deck of the swaying and creaking schooner. As a final indignity, the lake swept away the ship's only lifeboat. The heavily laden *Conductor* was both sinking and being torn apart.

The crew was out of options; they knew their chances of surviving in the freezing water, in the dead of night, were next to none. So, with the captain leading the way, they climbed the rigging. Once there, they lashed themselves down and, with the screaming wind and blinding snow whipping their exposed bodies, proceeded to put in what was undoubtedly the longest night of their lives.

—⚉—

By the time Abigail got back to her cabin, she was completely out of breath. "Children," she called, "there is a vessel ashore about a mile up the beach.

Edward, you go and see if we can help them." The boy went, and shortly returned with a blunt assessment: "If they cannot get to shore," he said, "they will all perish."

Abigail needed time to formulate a plan. She left the cabin and climbed up on one of the nearby sand dunes to see for herself what kind of shape the men were in. There were eight of them clinging to the rigging, and to Abigail it didn't appear that they had much strength left in them. Time was not on her side. Nor was the lake, whose roiling, freezing waters made any attempt at rescue by boat or raft impossible. There was really only one chance: get to the beach opposite the wreck and try to encourage the men to swim for it.

When she returned to the cabin, Abigail gathered her oldest children and headed for the beach opposite the helpless *Conductor*. When the men in the rigging saw her coming, they let out a cheer. Soon, Abigail had a roaring fire going on the beach, on which she put a kettle of water for making tea. She then waved to the half-frozen men to let them know that if they would swim for it, she would help them. Margaret Wheeler remembers the results:

> He [Captain Hackett] pulled off his coat and shoes and plunged into the water. The waves carried him down the beach a great distance. He was becoming exhausted and Mother, who was tall, waded in and caught him by the hand. She dragged him to the fire and gave him some hot tea, and then beckoned for the rest to come.

And they did, again according to Wheeler:

> The mate was the second to make the attempt. Edward, my brother, who was lame and walking with crutches, wanted to help, and he tried to go in to his mother's assistance, but the sea was so heavy he could not stand, and she had to get them both out of the water.

Over and over, Abigail continued this routine, sometimes wading into the frigid water all the way up to her neck to drag the men ashore. Some, particularly toward the end, lost consciousness and Abigail had to drag them all the way up to the warmth of the fire by herself. There was only one problem: The cook could not swim a stroke, and with the lake still running high, he had no choice. The poor fellow would have to face another night in the *Conductor*'s rigging — but this time all by himself.

By nightfall, Abigail had returned to the cabin, bringing the men along with her. The other children had already started a fire, around which the haggard crew of the *Conductor* gathered and dried out their tattered clothes.

For Abigail it would be another sleepless night, this time spent worrying about the *Conductor*'s stranded cook. By morning, the lake had calmed and she called the men together to make another attempt. When they got to the beach, they could see the cook still holding fast to the rigging. Moving quickly, they built a raft out of wood that had washed ashore from the ship and set out for the wreck. The cook was unconscious, but alive, and had lashed himself tightly to the rigging to keep from being swept away. They brought him back to the cabin, where Abigail placed his frozen feet in a bucket to draw out the frostbite. According to Wheeler: "The men were very grateful for what had been done for them. The captain remarked to Mother that it was a good work she had done that day, for not one of them was prepared to die."

For Abigail, the adulation quickly poured in. The March 7, 1855, edition of the Toronto *Globe* raved: "Such noble conduct deserves more than a passing notice. She is a woman of the most humble position in life, but showed herself, on this occasion, a true heroine, and possessed of the noblest qualities of heart and soul."

When it was learned that two of the *Conductor*'s crew had been Americans, the Lifesaving Benevolent Association of New York, an organization dedicated to helping shipwreck victims and their families, sent Abigail a gold medal. The May 26, 1857, Buffalo *Daily Courier* describes it:

> The medal, which we have had an opportunity of examining, is a very fine one; on one side is an inscription stating the object for which the medal was given, and on the reverse is the device of the association — a ship in a gale driving on a lee shore, on which is seen a small building in which the life-saving apparatus is kept; and close to it a mortar ready for use, a shot from which carries a line to the vessel, followed by a hawser, upon which the life car is slung.

A letter from Queen Victoria soon followed and, in 1860, Abigail was thrilled to get a visit from the Prince of Wales while he was hunting at Long Point.

But by far the most valuable gift was a sum of money donated by Buffalo's merchant and sailor communities. Totalling $550, an impressive sum for the time, the money was placed in the care of the customs officer at Port Rowan. With this, Abigail bought a fifty-acre farm north of town (though the customs officer, when she came to get the money, would only release $535).

The farm was not a great success in the early going. Two cows soon died (one when a tree fell on it), and Jeremiah quickly lost interest in the operation and returned to Long Point to hunt and trap. Then came the most debilitating blow. Wheeler recalls:

> He [Jeremiah] went over there [to Long Point] and was only there a few days when a heavy storm came up. He was obliged to leave his shanty. He seems to have hoisted his trunk upon the roof, where it was found, and part of his clothing frozen to it, as if he had been sitting upon it. Afterwards he had apparently tried to make his way to another shanty some three miles distant. He had gone about two miles when he seems to have sat down on a log and frozen to death. His body was not found for nearly three months.

In the wake of such a loss, and considering the few opportunities available to single women on the frontiers of nineteenth-century Canada, one could be forgiven for thinking that this would certainly mean a sad end to Abigail's story. But as she had shown many times before, Abigail Becker was at her best when times were hard. She also had a number of young, strong sons among her brood of thirteen to draw upon. By pulling together, the family managed to make the farm modestly profitable, though it was far from easy, particularly for Abigail, who sustained a number of injuries during her farming career, including four broken arms and a number of broken toes that she suffered when her horses bolted as she was unloading hay.

By the time she married again, a few years after Jeremiah's death — to Henry Rohrer, who brought with him even more children — Abigail was a seasoned survivor. She lived out the rest of her days quietly and with little notoriety on her small farm, passing away there in 1905 at the age of seventy-four.

Today, there are few permanent memorials to Abigail Becker in the Long Point area, save for a plaque erected by the Ontario government in a park in Port Rowan. But Abigail's is a story that almost transcends monuments or plaques. Simply mention her name to anyone who has spent any time in the area, particularly anyone connected with the marine community, and the recognition is instant. Long Point, it seems, needs no reminder of the heroic deeds of its favourite daughter.

"A Seething Furnace": The sinking of the *Clarion*

"Fire!" cried one of the crewmen as the freighter *Clarion* fought her way through Lake Erie's treacherous Pelee Passage.

Up on the bridge, Captain Thomas Bell felt an immediate sense of dread. Fire aboard a lake freighter is one of the most terrifying situations any sailor can encounter. And it couldn't have come at a worse time, for Bell and his crew were already dealing with one of the most vicious Great Lakes storms in recent memory.

His many years of experience told Bell, a veteran Great Lakes skipper from Ogdensburg, New York, that he had a desperate situation on his hands. As he slowly turned toward the ship's stern, he caught sight of what was causing the commotion: a red glow flickering out of one of the hatches just before the aft deckhouse. Just as he was beginning to take this in, a crewman barged onto the bridge behind him and announced that the *Clarion*'s hold had become "a seething furnace."

It was the evening of December 8, 1909. And the *Clarion* was about to sail into Lake Erie folklore.

—⚓—

The iron-hulled propeller steamer *Clarion* had begun life some twenty-eight years earlier, sliding into the Detroit River from her dry dock at Wyandotte, Michigan, at three o'clock on the afternoon of July 27, 1881. The July 28 Cleveland *Herald* reported the event matter-of-factly:

> The propeller *Clarion* was built at the Detroit Dry Dock
> Company's iron shipbuilding yard at Wyandotte, under
> the supervision of F. Albert Kirby, the drawings, etc.,
> being furnished by Frank E. Kirby, of the Dry Dock
> company. She is, in appearance, the exact sister to the
> propeller *Lehigh*, launched at the same yard last fall, the

only difference between the ships being in the boiler and the machinery.

Iron-hulled vessels were still a relatively new innovation on the Great Lakes at this point, and the *Clarion* was impressive ship, though not overly large. Operated by the Anchor Line of Buffalo (the lake division of the Erie and Western Transportation Company), the *Clarion* was 78 metres long and 11 at the beam. She had only a single deck covering her hold, and often carried a crew of twenty-one. Because she operated in conjunction with the railway system, the *Clarion* also carried the odd passenger, especially in her early days.

But the *Clarion*'s career on the Great Lakes did not get off to the most promising start. While her home port was listed as Erie, Pennsylvania, she ranged far and wide, calling at big-city and small-town ports alike and hauling essentially anything that could be carried in a railroad boxcar. During one of these runs, while passing through the St. Clair River, the *Clarion* was involved in a collision with the wooden schooner *Hercules*. The *Clarion*'s iron hull made short work of the old sailing vessel, as the June 16, 1883 *Marine Record*, quoting the *Detroit Free Press*, notes:

> At about six o'clock on Wednesday evening the propeller *Clarion*, bound up, collided with the schooner *Hercules*, which was sailing up, and damaged her to such an extent that she filled and went to the bottom at once, giving the crew barely time to save themselves. It was broad daylight at the time, and great indignation is manifested by those who saw the accident against the officer in charge of the propeller … The *Hercules* lies on her starboard side a short distance above the Club House, on the Canada side of the St. Clair River. The hull is completely under water, and the topmasts broken. Her sails are set.

But despite this regrettable incident, the *Clarion*'s long years of service on the Great Lakes were largely uneventful. She was a sturdy ship, and even though newer, faster, and larger vessels were constantly coming on stream, she remained in steady service without any further reported problems. Until the night of December 8, 1909, that is.

—∿—

The men who toiled aboard the Great Lakes freighter fleet in the early twentieth century always dreaded the "last trip down." December is usually when the weather is at its nastiest. On top of that, there was always a frantic race for cargo as captains crammed their ships into port in an attempt to get loaded, on their way, unloaded, and into winter lay-up before their insurance ran out for the season.

The *Clarion*'s chief engineer, A.E. Welch, was no different. Welch had split his time between the *Clarion* and another Anchor Line boat, the *Conestoga*, for more than twelve years. His career had kept him away from home for many long weeks at a time, and no doubt Welch was looking forward to putting the *Clarion* to bed at Erie just as soon as she was finished unloading her cargo at Buffalo.

The *Clarion* had left Chicago early on the morning of December 7, loaded mainly with flour and corn feed. The trip had gone well; she steamed southbound on the Detroit River the following afternoon alongside the freighter *Denmark*, past Detroit and Windsor, Ontario, headed for the open waters of Lake Erie. But here things took on an ominous feel: the skies had started to darken and the wind had picked up from the west-southwest. And the forecast offered no good news for the men on Lake Erie that night — nothing less than fierce winter gales and towering waves awaited them. As the *Clarion* emerged onto the lake and Captain Bell swung his vessel around to the east for the entrance to the Pelee Passage, he knew his crew was in for a long night.

Out on deck, the temperature had dropped to a bone-chilling -12˚C degrees Celsius, and Lake Erie, true to form, was throwing a late-season tantrum. Thomas J. Thomas provides a dramatic description in an article he wrote about that fateful night in the April 1911 *Wide World Magazine*:

> The waves were running mountain high, lashed by the cold December wind. To make matters worse, a heavy vapor, rising from the foaming water, was instantly converted into a dense fog, which, being quickly frozen was driven with stinging force against the faces of the men on the bridge.

The Pelee Passage was and still is one of the most dangerous places on the Great Lakes. It covers the stretch of water between Pelee Island to the north and the tip of Point Pelee, on the Canadian mainland, to the south. The water is about twelve metres deep in the Passage itself, but there are three major shoals here: the Middle Ground Shoal, which extends northeast from Pelee Island, the Southeast Shoal, extending out from the Point, and Grubb Reef, near the entrance to the Passage. The shallow water and unpredictable conditions here have made many a captain anxious. And this is just one of many such places on the lakes, and just one kind of condition, that sets the captains of the big lakers apart from their ocean counterparts, as the January 10, 1910, *Marine Review* bluntly points out:

> It is no disparagement to say that even the most skillful average coast master would absolutely refuse to undertake some of the things which are matters of every day to the lake skipper. It is merely to say that he has not grown up amidst the conditions peculiar to the lakes where maneuvering big ships in narrow channels and crowded harbors loaded and light, with many times but a few inches of water between him and a big job for the dry dock or the wreckers, is an every day occurrence, and has resulted in a skill which is unequalled in the world.

Today, the Southeast Shoal, at the eastern entrance to the Pelee Passage, is marked by an unmanned light station, but in 1909 only the tiny lightship *Kewaunee* marked the spot where vessels cleared the Passage and headed out into the open lake. And it was here, just as the *Clarion*'s exhausted men were searching through the dense fog and blinding snow for the comforting glow of the *Kewaunee*'s light, that one of them noticed the fire bursting through the cargo hatch in front of the boat's aft deckhouse.

Immediately, the chain of command began to break down as the men struggled with the *Clarion*'s steam-powered fire extinguisher. Very early on, the fire disabled the boat's steering, leaving the freighter at the mercy of the lake and drifting beam-on to the raging water. More frighteningly, she was now headed in the general direction of the *Kewaunee* — and the shallow waters of the Southeast Shoal.

In the midst of the bedlam, James Thompson, the boat's mate, performed the first of a long list of valiant acts that night, grabbing a hand-held fire extinguisher and dashing down into the hold to search for the fire's origin. His crewmates never saw him again. Welch had a theory about what happened to his unfortunate crewmate: "He must have been overcome by the smoke, which soon began to roll out of the hatchways in dense volumes," he later told a reporter. Nearly a century after the event, author James Donahue made sure the engineer's perspective wasn't lost by including Welch's retelling in his book, *Terrifying Steamboat Stories.*

Meanwhile up on deck, the fire quickly spread, fanned by the whistling gale. By the time the men actually got the boat's fire extinguisher working and water began to spit from the end of the hose, it was far too little, too late. The fire was totally out of control. The *Clarion* was entering the final hours of her life.

As the men did their best to prolong the inevitable, a haunting wail, which Thomas J. Thomas fancifully describes in *Wide World Magazine* as "like the shriek of an animal in agony or terror," bellowed out from the stricken ship. It was the *Clarion*'s whistle at full cry — Captain Bell had returned to the bridge and was pulling the *Clarion*'s whistle rope desperately, hoping against hope that another vessel might respond.

Miraculously, far off in the distance, one did.

Faintly, a steamer whistle could be heard wafting through the din of the roaring fire and crashing waves. Bell yanked the rope again, and again came the response. Louder and louder the other boat's whistle grew, until finally the men could see her lights emerging out of the darkness, and then her hull, which passed so close astern they could actually see the faces of the men on the other steamer by the light of the flames. But then, to their horror, just as quickly as she had appeared, the mystery ship was gone, her hull and then, finally, her running lights winking out in the fog and the mist.

The steamer was the freighter *E.C. Pope*, under the command of Captain Balfour. Probably afraid of grounding his own ship on the treacherous shoals, Balfour proceeded on without attempting a rescue. But he did send out the first wireless message indicating that the *Clarion* was in trouble. The *Pope* was one of at least three ships who passed by that night, saw the stricken *Clarion*, and carried on.

Aboard the lightship *Kewaunee*, which was now barely three kilometres away, the three-man crew could also see the *Clarion* drifting by, and the smoke and fire billowing from her deck. But there was nothing they could do, either: they had their hands full managing the tiny lightship, which was encrusted with ice and, anchored to the bottom, was being whipped by the fierce gale. Even if they were to attempt a rescue, launching their small yawl in such seas would have been suicide. Instead, they repeatedly blared the boat's horn and rang her bell, so that if the men of the *Clarion* did decide to take to the lifeboats, they would at least know where to steer.

Aboard the burning freighter, this is exactly what was being contemplated. Their abandonment by the *Pope* made it clear to the crew that rescue was simply not in the cards. Worse, the fire had divided the men into two groups, with twelve at the bow with Captain Bell and seven at the stern with Welch, who recounts what happened next:

> We saw Captain Bell and the forward crew launching the big metallic lifeboat and we turned to the light wooden boat on the davit's aft. Her lines were covered with ice, and long before we got them clear, Captain Bell and the other members of the crew succeeded in getting away.

To all appearances, Captain Bell and his companions had managed a narrow escape, while the half-dozen men left aboard were condemned to a bitter fate. But events were to take a strange turn that night.

While one lifeboat pulled away, circumstances were pointing to a grim conclusion at the stern of the *Clarion*. The last lifeboat, an old wooden craft, was the only hope for those remaining aboard. But even this was quickly dashed — as the men were lowering it, a large wave suddenly grabbed the tiny launch and smacked it high against the *Clarion's* hull, tearing it from its ropes and capsizing it.

Just as the group was absorbing this shocking development from the deck, one of their number, an oiler named Joseph McCauley, made a snap decision. Grasping the deck railing, McCauley vaulted over the side and into the freezing water. With his stunned mates looking on, McCauley struggled toward the overturned lifeboat in a vain attempt to bring it under control. But just as the plucky oiler reached out his hand, another wave suddenly swept him up and carried him away into the darkness. Helpless, he likely took a few futile strokes toward the distant lightship before going down for good.

This grisly scene utterly destroyed the morale of the remaining six men, who could now feel the heat of the fire bearing down on them as they huddled at the stern.

Their choice was becoming clearer and clearer: they could either burn to death on the *Clarion* or follow McCauley into Erie's dark waters.

—⚏—

Little did they know that help was indeed on the way. Two other freighters, the *L.C. Hanna* and the *Josiah G. Munro*, under the command of Captain Matthew B. Anderson and Captain C.B. Sayre, respectively, had heard the

Pope's wireless message. Both were steaming toward the *Clarion*'s position. The *Munro* was the first to get there, but because of her size (at 162 metres, she was more than double the length of the *Clarion*), she ran hard aground on the Southeast Shoal before she could get close enough. Stranded but otherwise safe, Sayre was forced to leave the job, and the lives of the six men on the *Clarion*, in the hands of Captain Anderson.

Born in Norway in 1864, Matthew Anderson had been through too many things in his seagoing career to give up on the rescue effort easily. He had been sailing from the time he was a boy, and had served on ocean freighters before coming to the Great Lakes. Those who served under him recall a man with a great sense of humour and a deep compassion for his crew. On this dark night on Lake Erie, he was steaming for Cleveland with a load of iron ore. But fate had more immediate plans for Anderson and his men.

As he closed on the *Clarion*'s position, a lone light on the stricken freighter's stern caught Anderson's eye (this turned out to be an oil lantern that Welch was holding in his hand). He brought the *Hanna* around in a wide circle so as to be able to bring his boat's side up against the *Clarion*'s stern, essentially forming the two vessels into a "T" shape. This type of maneuver, with the wind and waves pushing the two ships in all directions above the dangerous shoal, would push the *Hanna* to her limit. Even so, slowly but steadily, Anderson managed to ease the ice-covered *Hanna* up against the *Clarion*'s burning stern, just — but only just — brushing up against it as he did so.

The men aboard the *Clarion* simply could not believe their eyes. But as the *Hanna*'s lights grew brighter and brighter, they came to realize that her captain meant business. As she glided past, they steeled themselves. Then, one by one, they leapt. But not all of them, as the *Marine Review* describes: "The sixth man, benumbed with cold and advanced in years, was unable to make the leap in the precarious footing on an ice-covered ship, rolling deep, broadside to a raging sea, and as the *Hanna* passed on, threw up his hands in despair."

That sixth man was none other than Welch. As the *Hanna* passed on into the darkness, it appeared to him that all hope was exhausted. The fire was now so close that it was only a matter of time before he would have to make the same horrible choice that all of the remaining men were contemplating only minutes before. He held onto the deckrail and prepared himself for the end.

Welch had no way of knowing that Anderson had no intention of leaving him to die. He had seen Welch throw his hands up into the air from up on the *Hanna's* bridge, the lantern clasped in one of them. Anderson resolved to try again.

Skillfully guiding the *Hanna* abeam of the wind to the south, away from the shoal, Anderson looped around in a wide arc, making his way around again to brush the burning stern of the *Clarion*. This time, his crew was ready: as the ships touched, they reached out to Welch. Staring straight ahead, the engineer threw his lantern into the lake and leapt. As he did, the *Hanna's* men latched onto his arms and, at the last second, snatched him from Erie's grasp.

With every one of the *Clarion's* remaining men now safely aboard, Anderson proceeded on his way, bringing to an end one of the most incredible rescues in Great Lakes history, and leaving the tough little *Clarion* to founder, alone, off the Southeast Shoal.

But it was oh, so close. As Welch said humbly in the days afterward: "The intense heat had driven us to about the limit of endurance when we were rescued."

They had been fighting the fire and the storm for over four hours.

—⋙—

The days following the horrible storm of December 8, 1909, were marked by confusion and sorrow. As news reports trickled out, it became clear that the *Clarion* was not the only ship to go to her grave that night. The massive railcar ferry *Marquette & Bessemer No. 2* had left Conneaut, Ohio, at about the same time as the men of the *Clarion* were fighting the blaze on their ship and had disappeared, taking her thirty-two-man crew with her. And off Buffalo Harbor, the steamer *W.C. Richardson* had run aground and sank, killing five before the rest of her crew could be taken off by another vessel.

The men of the *Clarion* eventually made their way to the Anchor Line offices in Buffalo before being reunited with their anxious families. A search was immediately launched for Captain Bell and the men in the lifeboat, but there was little to be hoped for, as the December 10, 1909, Toronto *Globe* glumly reported:

> Somewhere on Lake Erie a steel lifeboat containing, it is believed, the bodies of the ill-fated thirteen sailors from the steamer *Clarion*, is aimlessly drifting with wind and current. Corpses, rigid in death, are encased in caskets of ice formed by the flying spray. The boat itself can now

be little more than a big cake of floating ice, and this fact will probably delay its finding. Although all hope has been abandoned for the thirteen missing men, the big steel tug *Alva* is sweeping the lake in the hope of finding the lifeboat.

But neither the boat nor any of the "encased" corpses would ever turn up. Most likely, it overturned in the high seas shortly after launch, dumping the thirteen unfortunate souls into the frigid waters where, like the young oiler Joseph McCauley, they never stood a chance.

Remarkably, A.E. Welch chose to continue serving on Anchor Line boats, and returned the very next season to the *Clarion*'s identical sister, the *Lehigh*.

Captain Matthew Anderson was lauded as a hero for his incredible tenacity in the face of such long odds. His remarkable seamanship that terrible night was on a level that has not been seen, before or since, anywhere on the Great Lakes. In the days following the disaster, the *Clarion*'s owners presented the flattered captain with a ship's bell clock honouring his bravery, to which he reportedly gave pride of place on his mantle until his death in February 1952. The inscription read simply: "Presented by The Erie and Western Transportation Company to Captain M. Anderson of the steamer *L.C. Hanna* in grateful recognition of his bravery in rescuing six of the crew from the steamer *Clarion* while burning on Lake Erie December 8, 1909."

The *James B. Colgate* vs. Black Friday

When the ferry's whistle first shook Captain Walter Grashaw from his fitful sleep, he must have thought it had all been a terrible dream.

The newly minted captain was stretched out on a tiny wooden life raft, bobbing along on a calm Lake Erie morning off Rondeau Park, Ontario. He was freezing cold, his shredded clothes were soaked completely through, and he was well into the state of delirium that often precedes death at sea. Yet ironically, Grashaw was surrounded by tranquility: the gentle motion of the waves as they sloshed against the side of the raft, the fresh autumn breeze and, overhead, just a hint of sunlight piercing the slate-grey sky.

To the casual observer, it would have been hard to believe that just two days earlier, in the early morning hours of Friday, October 20, 1916,

Grashaw had steamed out of Buffalo full of confidence in his boat, the freighter *James B. Colgate*. It was a vessel he knew well, having served aboard as mate for over ten years before being given command a mere two weeks earlier. Loaded with coal, the *Colgate*'s destination had been Fort William, Ontario (present-day Thunder Bay). Grashaw commanded a crew of twenty-one men who, like most freighter crews of the day, were young; twenty of them, in fact, were less than thirty-two years of age.

But now there seemed little evidence that any of them, or the *James B. Colgate* itself, had ever existed. There was only Walter Grashaw, alone, bobbing along on his little raft.

With his last ounce of strength, he lifted his head to see where the whistle had come from. The appearance of the railcar ferry steaming toward him, her crew waving from the deck, must have seemed equally unreal.

The *James B. Colgate* glided into the still waters of Lake Superior at Superior, Wisconsin, over twenty-four years earlier, on September 21, 1892. Ninety-four metres long and 11.5 metres wide, the *Colgate* was not a particularly large boat for her day. But her hull design definitely made her unique. The *Colgate* was what was referred to as a "whaleback" freighter. Derisively named "pigboats" by the men of the Great Lakes shipping trade, the whalebacks were a revolutionary take on the cargo steamers of the time.

The design, which consisted of a single wheelhouse astern perched atop a nearly cylindrical, flat-bottomed hull, was the brainchild of Captain Alexander McDougall, a man who, as evidenced by the peculiar appearance of the whaleback itself, was hardly averse to taking a few risks. And he had quite literally done it all: a renowned seaman, inventor, real-estate developer and entrepreneur, McDougall had scratched his way up from the very bottom to become one of the giants of the Great Lakes shipping business.

He was born in 1845 on the Island of Islay, off the west coast of Scotland. McDougall's family had left their ancestral homeland behind for the wilds of North America while he was still a young boy. Like many Scots before them, they came to Canada and made their way to the rapidly industrializing Great Lakes region. But although the McDougalls were no longer the tenants of autocratic landowners, as they had been in Scotland, life in the Ontario countryside (the McDougalls had settled in the mainly Scottish village of Nottawa, near Collingwood) had not been easy, either, as

Whaleback freighters passing through the locks at Sault Ste Marie, Michigan. The James B. Colgate *is at the top left.*

McDougall points out in his autobiography, titled simply *The Autobiography of Captain Alexander McDougall*: "When eleven and twelve years old I was able to cut our wood and occasionally spend a few days at the log schoolhouse nearby. At night in the village I used to cut wood for others, to earn money with which to buy my school books."

In July 1861, at the age of sixteen, young McDougall took a job as a deckhand on the passenger and cargo steamer *Edith*, mainly because, in his words, "I was to receive $12.00 a month, the first real sum of money that had ever come into my hands."

Although he couldn't have known it at the time, this hesitant first step would prove to be the launching pad for his wildly successful shipping career. And his timing couldn't have been better, for the American Civil

War was by then driving demand for raw materials through the roof — and fuelling the need for men to handle the ships that moved them.

Over the next two decades, McDougall worked his way steadily upward, spending many long weeks at a time away from home, until he finally got his own command. From 1871 to 1873, he carried passengers and freight from Chicago to various Lake Superior ports as captain of the *Japan*, a new iron-hulled boat that McDougall had helped build for Buffalo's Anchor Line. The experience of building the *Japan*, along with its identical sister ships, the *China* and the *India*, introduced McDougall to the art of shipbuilding and, combined with his sailing experience, planted the seed of the whaleback idea in his mind. McDougall himself explains his conception of the whaleback in his autobiography:

> While captain of the *Hiawatha*, towing the *Minnehaha* and *Goshawk* through the difficult and dangerous channels of our rivers, I thought of a plan to build an iron boat cheaper than wooden vessels. I first made plans and models for a boat with a flat bottom designed to carry the greatest cargo on the least water, with rounded top so that water could not stay on board; with a spoon-shaped bow to best follow the line of strain with the least use of the rudder and with turrets on deck for passage into the interior of the hull.

McDougall was late in his storied career when he got around to designing the whalebacks. And though he had earned the respect of his peers in the shipping business, the response to his design, particularly from other lake captains, was scathing. According to McDougall, the comments ranged from the ignorant ("She will roll over, having no masts to hold her up") to the insulting ("You call that damn thing a boat — why it looks more like a pig"). None of this deterred McDougall. When he financed and built the first whaleback barge, *No. 101*, on his own property in Duluth, and brought it to Two Harbors, Minnesota, to have it loaded with coal bound for Cleveland, he found his business office there "full of lake captains, all making fun of my boat, and I joined in good-naturedly with them." Even his wife wasn't so sure. As *No. 101* slid down the skids at Duluth in 1888, she reportedly turned to her sister-in-law and uttered, "There goes our last dollar."

Luckily, success came quickly for the whalebacks. And no doubt the captains weren't laughing so hard when they heard that McDougall's odd little barge had caught the eye of Colgate Hoyt, a colleague of legendary American industrialist John D. Rockefeller. McDougall showed Hoyt the model for his next barge, *No. 102*, which was planned to be almost twice the size of *No. 101*, and Hoyt, a methodical, no-nonsense businessman with a large amount of iron ore to ship, was immediately impressed. He knew a good idea when he saw one, and moved quickly, proposing that he and McDougall join forces in an attempt to change the way shipping was done on the Great Lakes. The pair registered a new venture, called the American Steel Barge Company, to which McDougall sold all of his patents and plans for the whaleback for US$25,000 in stock, with 20 percent of the remaining shares being held by the company for McDougall until he could pay for them.

Now flush with cash, McDougall got right to work on building his first whaleback freighter. Soon, the *Colgate Hoyt*, named for McDougall's new business partner, slid into Lake Superior at Duluth. She came in on time and under budget and, according to McDougall, achieved "such good results in operation that the lake fraternity feared competition more than ever."

In December 1889, McDougall moved his operations to a lot in Superior, where, by June 1890, barely five months later, he had constructed a brand new, state-of-the-art shipyard. As usual, the frugal captain had done it all for less than US$90,000, a modest sum for such an ambitious project.

Between 1890 and 1897, the American Steel Barge Company turned out thirty-seven whalebacks, which works out to an impressive average of over five a year. Of those, twenty were barges, sixteen were freighters, carrying mostly iron ore and wheat (although two were rigged as oil tankers), and one, the *Christopher Columbus*, held the title of the world's only whaleback passenger steamer. Built almost entirely by hand for the Chicago World's Fair, the *Columbus*'s durable hull was tested to carry up to 8,000 passengers. McDougall himself drew up the plans, built the models, and tested them in a pond before closing the deal to build the boat on August 26, 1892. She was launched by December 3 and, on May 13, 1893, barely five months later, the *Columbus* departed Superior for Chicago, making the trip in thirty-three hours and reaching speeds as high as thirty-two kilometres per hour. During its first year of operation, shuttling revelers from downtown Chicago to the fair site, the *Columbus* carried two million people. After the fair ended, she went on to carry passengers between Chicago and Milwaukee before the Great Depression finally put an end to her career in 1931. McDougall had an almost fatherly pride in his only passenger liner, calling it "probably the most wonderful ship contracted for and constructed up to that time."

The *James B. Colgate*, the twenty-first whaleback hull to roll down the skids (and the fifteenth built at McDougall's Superior shipyard), was an exact replica of the *Colgate Hoyt* and the other whaleback freighters that had preceded her. They were utilitarian vessels that, in order to reduce construction costs, rarely deviated from McDougall's original design specifications. They were tough, practical ships that, unlike their immaculate cousin the *Christopher Columbus*, carried few creature comforts. What's more, when the freighters were loaded, the main deck, with little freeboard already, sank perilously close to the water, making working on it at sea a perilous proposition for the crew, something akin to working on the deck of a rolling submarine. The design also left the ships' hatch covers exposed to the ravages of the water, a danger the *Colgate*'s crew would become all too familiar with.

Even still, the whalebacks boasted an excellent safety record. But they were not immune to the human error and technological shortcomings that often plagued nineteenth-century shipping. The *Colgate* and ships of her generation were not even equipped with radios and this, combined with an ever-increasing number of vessels roaming the lakes, was a recipe for disaster. Collisions were common, and the *Colgate* was involved in four documented ones during her Great Lakes career, including a particularly severe impact with the wooden schooner *Duvall* on December 6, 1905, while the *Colgate* was steaming southbound on the St. Clair River. The Buffalo *Evening News* reports:

> The steamer *James B. Colgate* and the schooner *Duvall* collided off Tashmoo Park, St. Clair River, Tuesday night. The schooner drifted down and finally sank near Muir's Landing, the crew escaping in the lifeboat. The steamer was run ashore above Muir's Landing on the Canadian side to prevent her sinking in deep water.

Miraculously, workers managed to remove forty-five tonnes of ore from the *Colgate*'s forward section, raising the damaged part of her hull just above the water so that a temporary patch could be welded into place. With that, the *Colgate* pressed onward and successfully delivered her cargo.

With such a proven track record of dependability, which the whalebacks undoubtedly possessed, it's no wonder the *Colgate*'s new captain, Walter

Grashaw, had few worries about taking his ship out into the maelstrom that was beginning to gather over Lake Erie in the early morning hours of October 20, 1916.

—⁂—

The storm that hit on what came to be known as "Black Friday" was undoubtedly the most ferocious in the history of navigation on Lake Erie. When it unleashed its fury, it almost immediately drove all but the very largest freighters (and the bravest captains) into port, effectively shutting down shipping, as the October 21, 1916, Toronto *Globe* reports from Sarnia, Ontario, at the mouth of the St. Clair River:

> Storm signals are flying at this port, and a score of large freighters are lying at anchor or are tied up to the docks here or at Port Huron [Michigan]. The wind is in the southwest, and is blowing strong. Downbound vessels report heavy seas getting up on Lake Huron. Only the largest freighters are taking chances and proceeding.

On Lake Erie, all of the passenger steamers of the Detroit & Cleveland Navigation Company were moored solidly to their docks. This was because A.A. Shantz, the company's vice-president and general manager, had learned that a ninety-kilometre gale was by now raging over the lake. The savvy Mr. Shantz, the *Globe* reported, "decided to take no chances."

But at the eastern end of the lake, one vessel was doing just that. Just after midnight, the whaleback *James B. Colgate* had made its way out of Buffalo Harbor. Captain Grashaw set off bound for Detroit, the same port where Shantz's passenger steamers were wisely tied up, with a load of coal.

Walter Grashaw harboured none of Shantz's concerns. His long experience as mate of the *Colgate*, and a strong confidence in both his own abilities and those of his young crew inspired him; after all, he had seen his vessel, with its innovative whaleback design, stand up to a good number of blows, and it had successfully prevailed over every one of them.

It wasn't long before Grashaw's confidence was put to the test. About a third of the way to his destination, with the *Colgate* nearing Long Point, the wind picked up, pushing the waves into a steady chop, considerably slowing the freighter's progress. Still, Grashaw remained unperturbed. Unbelievably, only one day after he was rescued by the rail car ferry *Marquette & Bessemer*

No. 2 (which had been replaced by a nearly identical boat of the same name after the original was lost in the same 1909 storm that claimed the *Clarion*), the captain was able to pen his own account of Black Friday, which was published in the October 23, 1916, edition of *The Cleveland Leader*. In it, he justifies his decision to press on:

> The steamer ran into rough weather last Friday afternoon. We couldn't make much headway in the face of the storm and about 6 o'clock it became apparent that we were in for a severe fight with the weather. Blackness set in and the wind blew a seventy-five-mile [121-kilometre] gale. We tossed about like a cork. The crew gathered aft, every one confident we would weather the storm.

By eight o'clock, the unrelenting winds were still lashing the *Colgate* and the waves towered over ten metres high. Ceaselessly, they rolled over the whaleback's low deck, which, with the boat fully loaded, swayed perilously close to water level. Over the next several hours, Lake Erie tested the *Colgate*'s hatches, sloshing tonnes of water over them and washing away anything that wasn't tied down. The crew, knowing full well that any attempt to work on the viciously swaying deck would be suicide, could only stand by helplessly and watch. Grashaw paints the grim picture:

> We headed her into the sea, but it soon became apparent that it was only a question of a few hours before she went under. Then some of the men dropped on their knees and prayed. Others talked of the folks at home. They all held together to the last. There was no panic.

But Alexander McDougall's whaleback design didn't go down without a fight, holding up to Black Friday's vicious onslaught for nearly eleven exhausting hours in total. But by late evening the water had fully penetrated the deck hatches, first in dribbles, then in torrents. Finally, many of the hatches simply crumpled and gave way.

Grashaw was up in the wheelhouse, flashing the *Colgate*'s powerful spotlight over the lake in a desperate bid for help when he began to feel the boat settle deeper into the water. He provides a vivid written account of the *Colgate*'s last moments in the *Leader*:

> ... I turned the light on the steamer itself. My fears were
> confirmed. The boat was awash nearly to her hatches. Then
> I knew everything was gone. I made ready for the jump
> and as she seemed about to plunge beneath the waves, I
> dived from the bridge far out into the sea.

Here, fate intervened; when Grashaw poked his head above the surface of the roaring, frothing water, he immediately bumped into the side of one of the *Colgate*'s small life rafts, something that is nothing short of miraculous considering that the *Colgate*, after taking such a long beating from the storm, had left no significant wreckage behind for the men in the water to cling to. Hurriedly, Grashaw clambered aboard, along with two other crewmen. In his own words: "It was every man for himself. I climbed aboard the raft but it went over. When it finally righted and I pulled myself aboard again, I found that there were two others on with me, a coal passer whose name I do not know, and Harvey Ossman [the *Colgate*'s second engineer]."

Throughout the terrible night, the frozen, terrified men clung helplessly to the tiny raft, doing their best to stay on top of it and out of the freezing water, capsizing many times in the effort. During one of these terrifying incidents, three hours after the sinking, the coal passer, exhausted, slipped from Grashaw's grasp and was never seen again. The next morning the lake claimed Ossman, leaving only Grashaw, alone, exposed, and at the full mercy of the elements. But even though the storm had largely blown itself out by this point, his ordeal was far from over; he would remain adrift for another twenty-four hours, and be passed by at least one steamer that failed to see him, before the sweet sound of his ultimate salvation — the whistle of the car ferry *Marquette & Bessemer No. 2* — finally rang in his ears.

Grashaw was in no position to witness the ultimate demise of the rest of his crew, which, for him, was perhaps the only fortunate thing about that terrible night on Lake Erie. The October 23, 1916, *Cleveland Leader* speculates that, "Nineteen of them were sucked down to death the instant the big steel boat foundered in the storm." While we will never know for sure, it would have been a horrifying scene; those poor souls who didn't drown in the immediate aftermath of the sinking would not have lasted long in the freezing, towering waves.

Sadly, the lost crew of the *James B. Colgate* would make up less than half of the death toll from a storm that claimed a total of four vessels on Lake Erie that night — and cut short the lives of fifty young sailors.

Some of McDougall's whaleback fleet would remain in service for another forty years after the loss of the *James B. Colgate*, but they were already beginning to fade into the annals of history by the time Black Friday howled over Lake Erie. As industrialization quickened in the run-up to the First World War, newer, larger bulk carriers were built to carry ever-increasing cargo volumes, and the whalebacks simply weren't big enough. Apart from this, their cylindrical hulls made them difficult to load, meaning that any spillage from their hatches inevitably went over the side and into the lake. Still, the old boats hung on for a time, with some being converted into oil tankers and one, the *City of Everett*, even seeing ocean service, but by the 1920s the writing was clearly on the wall for the pigboats. And just as his ships were beginning to disappear, the father of the whaleback himself, Alexander McDougall, died in 1923.

Today only one whaleback, the S.S. *Meteor*, survives. After serving as an oil tanker, it was converted into a permanent museum dedicated entirely to these unique and intriguing Great Lakes workhorses. Even though the old freighter is no longer in top shape, it remains at Superior (though no longer in the water), and is open to the public during the summer months. The longevity of the *Meteor*, truly the last of her kind, is a testament to the skill and determination of its inventor, and to the many hardworking young men who served on these unique vessels.

Chapter 6

Shelters from the Storm:
Lake Erie Lighthouses

The lightkeeper's job bears two unique but opposite distinctions: it is both the most tedious job on the Great Lakes and the most terrifying. Lake Erie, with its treacherous mix of shallow water and ferocious storms, poses risks even for today's technologically advanced vessels. But during the Age of Sail, many sailors who plied these waters in their wooden ships never returned home.

Expected to keep the lights burning and to save crews' lives when their vessels were in peril, lightkeepers on both the Canadian and American sides faced huge obstacles. In both countries, lighthouse services were drastically underfunded, leaving keepers ill-equipped and often lacking basic shelter near their places of work. At Pelee Island, Ontario, for example, keepers often had to hike several kilometres from their homes — or sleep on the beach. But by far the most difficult aspect of the job was the nearly endless boredom. Keepers worked late at night, often alone. While these long hours were occasionally punctuated by the excitement of setting forth to rescue sailors or by the sheer terror of witnessing horrific disasters, the vast majority of their time was spent doing tedious maintenance work.

Although there are dozens of lighthouses on Lake Erie, all with intriguing personalities and stories of their own, the four covered in the following pages are typical of the types of challenges Lake Erie lightkeepers faced. At the Pelee Island lighthouse, privation was the major problem, with keepers often running out of oil during the navigation season while, at the same time, they tried to build homes and farms on the untamed, isolated island. On nearby Green Island, in American waters, a terrible midwinter fire nearly cost keeper Charles F. Drake and his family their lives. At the Marblehead lighthouse, Benajah Wolcott, the first keeper and one of the area's earliest settlers, survived one war, and was displaced by another. His successors would see even more armed conflict in the area. And at Point Abino, Ontario, the crew of Lightship *No. 82* went head-to-head with the Great Storm of November 1913 — the worst ever to hit the Great Lakes — and lost.

With over 200 years of history on the Great Lakes, lighthouses are among the last remaining monuments to a time long past — when lake vessels formed the backbone of the economies of two nations, bringing raw materials to settlers who would go on to build the lakeside towns and cities that many of us call home. The continued presence of historic lighthouses on Lake Erie is the result of the hard work and resourcefulness of scores of dedicated volunteers. Behind nearly all of the lighthouses studied for this book, there was a group of citizens striving to keep their community's lighthouse preserved for future generations. The work of these groups is vital to maintaining the nautical heritage of both Canada and the United States, and their efforts should be given our greatest support.

Pelee Island Lighthouse: The Limestone Fortress

Of all the lightkeepers on Lake Erie, those who kept their vigil on the lake's remote islands faced perhaps the toughest challenge. Today, the islands are mostly well-developed vacation spots, but this is a fairly recent development. Not so long ago, they were untracked forest. Separated from the mainland by the lake's often-dangerous waters, these stalwart keepers regularly endured long, lonely stretches of time totally cut off from the outside world and, when disasters or critical shortages struck, they were often left to face the peril on their own. This was the case for the men who tended the lighthouse built at the northeast corner of Pelee Island in 1832.

In 1819, Canadian explorer and cartographer David Thompson passed through the area while on a border survey as part of the Treaty of Ghent, which formally ended the War of 1812. The venerable Thompson was winding down his illustrious career by this point, but in the course of the previous thirty-five years he had managed to explore and map much of western Canada. During his survey, he crossed the volatile Pelee Passage, the stretch of open water between Pelee Island and the Ontario mainland, in an open boat. He wrote of the hostile environment he found on the island in his journal entry of August 31:

> ... the country is nothing but a pestilential marsh on the level of the lake surrounded by a ridge of sand made burning hot by the sun and the marsh full of rattle and black snakes, the latter very large and bold. We have twice seen them coming some distance from out in the lake with fish 6 in. long in their mouths. The rattle snakes are also large and fat.

As the crew of the *Clarion* would learn the hard way nearly a century later (see Chapter 5), the Pelee Passage is, quite simply, a graveyard for ships. In 1821, a trip through the Passage during a fierce storm nearly cost American surveyor Joseph Delafield his chartered schooner, the *Sylph*, and the lives of her entire crew. He describes the event in harrowing detail in his official record of his journeys, entitled *The Unfortified Boundary*:

> During the night they [the *Sylph*'s crew] had been endeavouring to beat off the coast and attempted to weather Point aux Playes [Pelee Island] on one tack, or Stockwell's Point [the Ontario mainland] on the other; that they soon carried away so much of their rigging as to be without the use of the main sail and, finding that they were losing ground, the Capt. had resolved to beach his boat, but the gleam of day inspired them with hope; they kept under way until, finding all exertions vain, they tried to hold by their anchor, and fortunately rode out the gale.

Ironically, the *Sylph* would be wrecked among the Lake Erie islands only a few years later, one of the many vessels that met their end on the archipelago's constantly shifting shoals, which consist mainly of sandbars formed by storms and currents.

At the same time, the lands surrounding the western basin of Lake Erie were booming. In the peace following the War of 1812, settlers began moving in, building small farms and homesteads and, in turn, boosting passenger and freight traffic on the lake. In 1818, Lake Erie saw its first steamship, the *Walk-in-the-Water*, which, while crude compared to the regal steamers that would follow, did a brisk business ferrying both cargo and passengers. But, like the *Sylph*, the *Walk-in-the-Water* would soon be lost on Lake Erie, running aground near Buffalo in 1821.

The influx of settlers also meant an increase in demand for wood and stone for construction. Pelee Island and the neighbouring Lake Erie islands had both in spades — sturdy limestone that formed the bedrock of the islands and abundant forests. An ever-growing number of ships were now routinely calling among the islands.

All of this activity made the task of alerting captains to the dangerous, shifting shoal at the southern extreme of the Pelee Passage all the more critical. As the number of lost vessels mounted, the Upper Canadian administration finally responded. On February 13, 1833, it passed legislation ordering the construction of a lighthouse on Pelee Island. Eight months later, the lighthouse was finished.

The lighthouse, described in the late 1800s by journalist and historian Lydia Ryall, who lived on nearby South Bass Island, as "a stately structure, romantic as to environment," was built from limestone supplied by Pelee Island's first non-Native owner, William McCormick. Its fixed white light was nearly fourteen metres above the water, and was visible fifteen kilometres offshore, covering almost all of the Pelee Passage. McCormick would prosper from the lighthouse's presence on his island — not only did the lighthouse help speed Pelee's development, but he was also hired as the first keeper. The post almost naturally fell to him because, beyond his own family, there were few other settlers on the largely marsh-covered island.

From the beginning, difficulties plagued the new lighthouse and its keeper. The government did not supply McCormick with enough oil, forcing him to leave the light dark for many nights during its first season. Interestingly, one of the only mentions of the lighthouse in McCormick's private papers is a September 1834 protest to William Hands, an official in Sandwich (present-day Windsor), about this very problem:

> The lighthouse has been out of oil for several weeks past.
> I think you had better authorize me to buy oil from
> Buffalo, where I think it might be got of better quality

than has been furnished. I have ascertained that it was not of that quality used in lighthouses and will never make a good light.

Compounding the oil supply problem was the fact McCormick was at the time mainly concerned with relocating his large family from the Canadian mainland to the new settlement they were constructing on the island. The move, and the backbreaking work of building his home, often kept McCormick away from his lightkeeping duties. This was no small problem, and did nothing to improve the safety of shipping in the Passage.

The lighthouse also fell victim to a number of acts of vandalism in its early years. In 1835, it was paid a visit by a young Robert E. Lee, later the most storied of Confederate commanders in the Civil War, then surveying the Ohio-Michigan boundary as an officer of the Army Corps of Engineers. While there, Lee found the lighthouse in a state of "considerable disrepair" and, after killing a snake that was laying at the door, forced his way inside, climbed to the top of the tower, and proceeded to use it to take a position reading. On the way out, for good measure, he stole some lampshades. His later report on the raid to his superiors was the source of confusion for years afterward. Portraying the snake he had killed as the "lightkeeper," Lee wrote that the keeper was "irascible and full of venom" at the presence of the Americans, and "an altercation ensued which resulted in his death." He later refers to the keeper as a "Canadian Snake." Had Lee really killed the keeper? As McCormick lived another five years and the murder of a lightkeeper on Canadian soil by an American surveying crew would most certainly have sparked an international incident, it appears that Lee, perhaps bored by his surveying duties, was having a little fun with his superiors.

Only three years later, the Upper Canadian Rebellion of 1837 (see Chapter 3) wreaked yet more havoc on the lighthouse. It was looted again, this time by members of a 450-strong raiding party that seized Pelee Island in late February 1838. These self-styled "Patriots" meant to use the island as a springboard to invade Upper Canada, overthrow its government, and turn the colony into an American-style republic. They stole furniture and fixtures from the lighthouse before being driven back to American territory by a force of British regulars and Canadian militiamen dispatched from Fort Malden, in nearby Amherstburg, Ontario.

Little changed for the lighthouse after William McCormick's death in 1840. His son Alexander took over, but the supply problems continued. It would appear that Alexander, like his father, was too busy with his duties as the island's landlord, and the light often went unlit, prompting more than a few complaints from passing mariners.

Finally, in 1850, James Cummins took over the tending of the lighthouse, and maintained the position, with the exception of four years, until 1889. The diligent Cummins introduced a more professional approach to lightkeeping on Pelee Island. When he complained that the lack of a keeper's house often forced him to sleep on the lighthouse steps, the government ordered a small dwelling built next to the light.

The lightkeeper was also expected to act as a rescuer for sailors in distress, and even though he was provided with little equipment for this, Cummins saw a number of vessels get chewed up on the shoal, and even managed to save some lives. On July 3, 1869, the robust Irishman pulled Andrew Poustie, the master of the schooner *George Warren*, from the raging surf after the ship had capsized in a fierce storm. A little more than a year later, on December 5, 1870, Cummins was credited with saving the captain and crew of the schooner *Tartar*, which was smashed to pieces on the shoals of the Pelee Passage. For his bravery, Cummins was awarded a gold watch by the Canadian government.

But by this time the lighthouse's heyday was slowly drawing to a close. As shipping traffic through the passage continued to increase, the Canadian government responded by placing lightships and stationary markers in the Pelee Passage itself, which eliminated the need for the Pelee Island lighthouse. The order to suspend operations came down on April 15, 1909 and was signed by Prime Minister Sir Wilfrid Laurier himself (from Ronald Tiessen's *Brief History of the Pelee Island Lighthouse*):

> ... the Lighthouse Board, Department of Marine and Fisheries, are of the opinion that the light hitherto in operation on Pelee Island, Ontario, is no longer required, as it is not now used for vessels, and recommending that after the 30th June, 1909, the above mentioned light be discontinued and the services of Mr. J.R. Lidwell as keeper dispensed with ...
> Wilfrid Laurier [signed]

With this, the last keeper, J.R. Lidwell, put the lantern out for the last time, descended the spiral staircase, and locked the door behind him.

For many years, this looked like the end of the Pelee Island lighthouse's story. By the late 1990s, all that remained was the hollowed-out limestone tower, its powerful lantern long since removed. The tight spiral staircase, which had carried successive lightkeepers up to their perch for the night, was almost completely rotted away. And erosion of the beach below was threatening the lighthouse's very existence. As for the keeper's dwelling, it did not survive much past the the lighthouse's closure in 1909. There is no evidence of it at the site today.

But, behind the scenes, a plan was quietly unfolding to bring the old lighthouse back to life. In January 2000, helped by funding from Human Resources Development Canada, the Pelee Island Heritage Centre, Ontario Parks, and the donations of many individuals, a team of architects, carpenters, and even a blacksmith began drawing up plans for its reconstruction. By May, they were hard at work on the site, and on August 19 the completed lighthouse was unveiled to the public, fully restored to its former beauty. The *Windsor Star* covered the ceremonial luncheon to mark the opening of the restored lighthouse, and reported the event in its August 21, 2000, edition. There, Pelee Island Heritage Centre curator Ronald Tiessen, who was one

Photo by author

The interior of the Pelee Island lighthouse prior to its restoration. The spiral staircase was nearly rotted away.

Photo by author

The Pelee Island lighthouse was threatened by decay and shoreline erosion before it was restored in 2000.

of the principals in the restoration project, neatly captured the reason why so much effort went into the restoration of the lighthouse: "Because it's a beautiful structure."

Green Island Lighthouse: Trial by Fire

In the lonely lighthouse on Green Island, just twenty kilometres southwest of Pelee Island in American waters, Colonel Charles F. Drake faced a situation more isolated and dangerous than perhaps any other lightkeeper on Lake Erie.

Tiny Green Island, barely eight hectares in size, is not a place you'll find on many tourist maps. Even many sailors have spent their entire lives on the lake know little of it. At first glance it would appear that the island, barely three kilometres west of South Bass Island and its small settlement at Put-in-Bay, would be a relatively safe place to build a lighthouse. When Lake Erie's fury erupts, however, there is precious little shelter to be found on the island's rocky shores, and the scramble for the safety of South Bass can quickly become a long and difficult ordeal. Drake and his small family would learn this lesson the hard way on the evening of December 31, 1863.

Photo by author

The Pelee Island lighthouse, restored to its original beauty.

Green Island's story actually begins in October 1820, when surveyor Joseph Delafield, conducting the same border survey that would bring him to Pelee Island the following summer, landed at Green Island with his small party and, much to his surprise, uncovered a rich deposit of strontium among the rocks on the island's eastern shore. In the nineteenth century, strontium was prized for two of its rather unusual abilities; it produces a red tint when used in fireworks and flares, and it was (and remains) useful to farmers for extracting sugar from sugar beet molasses. Delafield excitedly recounted his find in *The Unfortified Boundary*:

> They [the strontium crystals] were of no uniform shape or size. The crystals would weigh from half a pound to four pounds, and we found broken pieces of crystals that must have weighed entirely much more ... Some are in tables and some in prisms ... [the strontium] is white, blue and now and then tinged with green, and sometimes a little yellow appears on the white that is transparent.

This small island would go on to become a significant source of strontium. But by the turn of the twentieth century, the deposits had been completely exhausted by industry and collectors from across the globe who had come to see the rare mineral for themselves.

The Green Island lighthouse was built to help guide ships through the treacherous southern passage stretching between the U.S. Lake Erie islands and the Ohio mainland. The American government bought Green Island from Judge Alfred Edwards, owner of a number of islands in the archipelago, in 1851. By 1855, the new lighthouse was finished and fully operational.

Unlike most other lighthouses on Lake Erie, the lightkeeper's house at Green Island was connected directly to the light tower and, although the tower appears to have been built mainly of locally quarried limestone, the attached quarters were made of wood. The fifty-four-year-old Drake was named the first keeper, and he and his small family — his wife Mary, daughter Sarah, and son Pitt — quickly took up residence there.

The Drakes enjoyed a relatively peaceful eight-year term on Green Island, where Charles, suffering from asthma, likely enjoyed the warm, clear summers of what at the time was still mainly unsettled frontier country. Supplies were brought in by rowboat, and the Drake children often took day trips over to Put-in-Bay, which by this time had started on its way to becoming the lively resort town that it is today.

December 31, 1863, dawned clear and sunny. The weather was unseasonably warm, with the mercury topping out at 15 °C by midday. The citizens of Put-in-Bay were thrilled at this unexpected respite from the bitter winter, and took to the streets, busily socializing and running errands in preparation for that night's New Year's celebrations. On Green Island, the Drake family, too, was preparing a holiday feast, while Pitt Drake planned to spend his New Year's at Doller's Hall at Put-in-Bay, where the youth of the Bass Islands were planning their own New Year's party. Early in the afternoon, he set off in the family's rowboat.

Then this day of strangely warm weather took an even more unexpected, and dangerous, turn. Late in the afternoon, the wind quietly swung around to the northwest and began to pick up, steadily pushing the temperature down as it gained strength. By evening, it had escalated to a gale, and a dusting of snow began to descend on the Lake Erie island chain. As day turned to night, the thermometer dropped an incredible 47 °C, from 15 °C to -32 °C, breaking a low-temperature record in the process.

To the excited partygoers at Doller's Hall, the first sign of trouble was a sudden chill in the building's temperature, which quickly drove them from the dance floor to the warmth of a nearby pot-bellied stove. All around them, the building groaned under the force of the intensifying gale.

Suddenly the crowd, gazing out through the window as they tried to keep warm, became transfixed by what appeared to be bright flames shooting up from behind the treetops. A stunned moment passed, then someone burst into the hall and shouted: "Green Island lighthouse is on fire! Green Island lighthouse is on fire!" Local historian Lydia Ryall describes what happened next in her 1913 book, *Sketches and Stories of the Lake Erie Islands*:

> A thrill of horror swept over the group, as swiftly upon each dawned the significance of such a disaster to the light keeper, Colonel Drake and his family alone on the little isle, the wild storm, the darkness, and the tremendous sea cutting them off from all human aid. The keeper's son, Pitt Drake, who was present in the hall, became frenzied with forebodings concerning their safety, and only with the greatest difficulty could the young man be restrained from launching forth in a small boat, which would have meant to him certain death.

Any bid to rescue the Drakes was quickly ruled out. The raging lake, whipped into a frenzy by the high winds, was covered in slush and far too dangerous to cross. The waves now reached over nine metres, and literally froze as they crashed onto the shore. Despite Pitt Drake's anguish at his helplessness, his family was on its own.

On Green Island, the Drakes — Charles, his wife, his son-in-law, and two daughters — had just sat down to dinner when Charles heard a crackling sound. Stepping outside to investigate, he was no doubt astonished to find the whole upper portion of the tower engulfed in flames, fanned by the gale-force winds. He rushed the rest of the family out of the house; they gathered what few possessions they could before fleeing into the raging blizzard.

The Drakes made every effort to fight the blaze, with Charles's son-in-law climbing a ladder and using damp clothes and pails of water that Drake's wife and daughters rushed up from the lake, but it was pointless. After emptying nearly thirty bucketfuls, it became obvious that the fire was simply too powerful, and that without the shelter of the keeper's house, which was attached to the burning tower, the family was at the mercy of the storm.

Charles made one last dash into the house in a bid to find blankets, clothing, or whatever could provide warmth. Finding only an old mattress and a couple of mattress covers, he emerged from the smoke-filled house and led his weary brood to the island's sole remaining structure — the outhouse. There, squeezed together in the dank and frigid little building, they covered themselves as best they could and proceeded to put in a truly dreadful night.

Back on South Bass, Pitt Drake waited, hoping his family could somehow survive the maelstrom. By dawn, the storm had abated, and the lake now stood silent, its surface frozen over, though precariously so. Pitt quickly roused a small rescue party and, ever so slowly, they made the crossing on wooden planks, placing them end over end, one after the other, until they finally landed at Green Island late in the morning. Full of trepidation, the rescuers fanned out over the island, and were overcome with relief when the found the entire Drake family, partially frozen, but very much alive in the outhouse. Drake's daughter Sarah was the most affected by the ordeal, with both of her arms frostbitten. Fortunately, however, they were rescued in the nick of time and she made a full recovery. The *Sandusky Register* picked up the story the following week:

> It [the fire] caught from a stovepipe in the upper part of the building and had made such progress, and the wind blowing a gale, that very little was saved. As this was the only house on the Island, and the night so rough that they could not get off, both residents and guests were obliged to shelter themselves in a small outbuilding for the bleak night ... The light was kept by Col. Charles F. Drake, formerly of this city, who ... managed to save only two

beds, a marine clock and some small articles. The loss to the government will be from $6,000 to $8,000.

In the aftermath of the disaster, the Drakes were given temporary housing at Put-in-Bay, and the government, evidently learning its lesson, quickly replaced the lighthouse with a new structure made completely out of limestone. The new light was in operation by the middle of the summer of 1864. This station would go on to a much longer and far less harrowing career than its predecessor, being tended by many keepers, some of whom kept chickens, cows, and other livestock, which had the run of the island. The light was finally decommissioned in 1939 when, as in many other places on the Great Lakes, lightkeeping on Green Island became an automated affair. It sat vacant while its job was taken over by a light mounted on a metal tower.

Events on Green Island came full circle in April 1974, when the venerable old lighthouse, long deserted, ironically met the same fate as Green Island's first lighthouse. Two passing fishermen landed on the island and set a small fire, only to lose control of it. The ensuing inferno raged for an entire day. In an eerie parallel to that fateful night in 1863, the flames were visible from the surrounding islands, and subduing the fire was not easy, as northeast Ohio's *News Herald* reported in its April 15, 1974, edition:

> One 40-foot utility boat was dispatched from the Marblehead station but, because of the wind-whipped lake and lack of docking facilities on the long-abandoned island, had difficulty landing men on the island.

Today, Green Island sees few visitors. Its valuable strontium now long gone, this lonely little island is now home to a wide variety of bird species and the ghosts of not one, but two Lake Erie lighthouses.

Marblehead Lighthouse: A Lake Erie Pioneer

In a picturesque park at the tip of the Marblehead Peninsula, near Sandusky, Ohio, stands the Marblehead lighthouse. White, red, and subtly bell-shaped, the old lighthouse, along with its keeper's dwelling, is in a perfect state of preservation. An ideal place for a picnic, the Marblehead lighthouse has

Photo by author

The Marblehead lighthouse, the oldest continuously operating lighthouse on the Great Lakes, had two female keepers.

appeared in countless postcards, photographs, and paintings, and was even commemorated with a postage stamp in 1995 — one of only five American lighthouses to be honoured in this way.

But this old sentinel is more than just a pretty picture. First lit in 1822, the twenty-metre limestone tower, now equipped with an electric light, still guides vessels through Lake Erie's difficult South Passage, making it the oldest continuously operating lighthouse on the Great Lakes.

And its services are still very much in need: the South Passage, which covers the distance between the U.S. Lake Erie islands and the Marblehead Peninsula, is one of the most dangerous places on all of the Great Lakes. With no headlands from the Lake Erie islands all the way to Buffalo at the eastern end of the lake, the winds there can be violent, indeed. As residents of the U.S. Lake Erie islands will tell you: "islanders respect a northeaster," and when one blows up, it can howl for days at a time, making the Passage a dangerous place for ships, even today.

The Marblehead lighthouse also marks the mouth of Sandusky Bay. Here, there are areas of incredibly shallow water, some less than two metres, creating a nightmare for sailors and increasing the size and strength of the waves during a strong wind. As Harry H. Ross noted in his 1949 book, *Enchanting Isles of Lake Erie*:

> Sandusky Bay is so shallow in places in midsummer that when the water is exceptionally low and calm, one can walk on a sandbar from the Marblehead shoreline almost to the Cedar Point channel [to the east], skirting the west shore of Cedar Point, in water a few inches deep.

The Marblehead lighthouse finds its roots in the very earliest days of settlement on Ohio's northern coast. Following Oliver Hazard Perry's victory over the British in the Battle of Lake Erie during the War of 1812 (see Chapter 2), the area saw an influx of settlers. At the same time, the opening of the Erie Canal in 1825 and, four years later, the Welland Canal, began to push the Great Lakes from five isolated bodies of water toward the integrated shipping network they are today. More and more ships appeared on Lake Erie and, as in the Pelee Passage to the north, shipwrecks became all too common in the South Passage, often with great loss of life.

By 1819, the need for a lighthouse in the area had become painfully clear. That year, Congress allocated $5,000 for its construction, which was totally insufficient to even start the job, causing it to be delayed until the following year, when, under increased pressure to get the project under way, the federal government doubled the amount to $10,000. Stephen Woolverton, one of the Sandusky area's earliest residents, was contracted to do the job and he, in turn, subcontracted it to William Kelly, who had built some of the young community's first stone houses. The hardworking

Kelly, whose crew included his thirteen-year-old son, managed to make up for much lost time, and by June 1822 the Marblehead lighthouse was up and running. Built of local limestone, it featured thirteen whale oil-powered lamps. Thomas Foster, an official from Erie, Pennsylvania, visited the site that June and came away impressed, crowing in a letter to Stephen Pleasonton, the government's general superintendent of lights, that the lighthouse and its buildings were "completed in a masterly workmanlike manner."

Benajah Wolcott, a veteran of the revolutionary war and one of the two earliest settlers on the Marblehead Peninsula, was named the first keeper on June 17, 1822. The pioneering Wolcott is an intriguing figure in Ohio's history. One of the first two settlers on the Peninsula, Wolcott cleared a small parcel of land and built a small log cabin there for his family during the spring and summer of 1809. The Wolcotts had made the long journey from the eastern seaboard to Marblehead, both on foot and by sleigh, over the previous winter. And there was certainly no civilization waiting for them at Marblehead. All that greeted them when they arrived was a dense, untamed wilderness that was sparsely inhabited by Natives of the Ottawa and Wyandot nations, along with a few French traders. To make matters worse, the area's residents were sharply divided amongst themselves; in the tense environment leading up to the War of 1812, many Ohio Natives were sympathetic to the British, mostly because of what they had deemed to be incursions by American settlers onto their tribal lands. In this environment of fear and terror, it is not difficult to imagine the fear Wolcott must have felt for his young family. He kept his musket close at hand, and vigilantly watched over the surrounding woods for bands of marauding Native warriors.

Fortunately, Wolcott found himself a most unlikely ally. Nearby, on the present site of the city of Sandusky, lived Chief Ogontz of the Ottawa Nation. Perhaps because he sensed how vulnerable his situation was, Wolcott went out of his way to befriend this chief and, in the process, made a valuable contribution to Ohio history by recording the chief's story and later retelling it to Joseph M. Root, another settler, who in turn passed it on to *Fire Lands Pioneer* magazine in 1863. Handing the story down still, generations later, was Ohio historian Charles E. Frohman, who recorded it in his 1969 book, *Sandusky's Yesterdays*.

Ogontz had come to Ohio with two tribes of Ottawa from Canada in the years following the American revolutionary war. Taken to Quebec by French Roman Catholic missionaries as a young boy, Ogontz had been given a Catholic education. The priests, no doubt recognizing his value in converting other Natives to Christianity, then sent him across the colony, including a sojourn to nearby Detroit, to preach to local tribes and teach them French. It was during this time that Ogontz came to develop a fierce dislike for the British-controlled government that ruled the colony, and decided that he would no longer subject himself to its rule. So, interestingly, Ogontz accompanied the two tribes to Sandusky, acting as their priest and spiritual mentor. Some French traders, who in Ogontz's words "liked the British no more than I did" came along as well, and this uniquely intermingled band formed some of the very earliest settled communities in the area. Ogontz also had a grim prediction for Wolcott:

> A war between your people and the British is close at hand, and when that comes we must fly from here — all of us. Indians are great fools for taking part in the wars of white people, but they will do so. Ottawas will join the British and Wyandots will join your people. I will not fight in such a war. I wish your side success; but I must go with my people. Still, whilst we are neighbours let us all be friends.

The chief's words turned out to be prophetic: a short time later, the War of 1812 stormed ashore in Ohio in the form of a party of Ottawa Natives, who, in keeping with the Ogontz's predictions, had allied themselves with the British. Landing only steps from Wolcott's cabin, they were met with stiff resistance from local Natives and American settlers. According to an Ohio historical plaque that marks the site, forty Native warriors were killed in the ensuing fight, along with eight Americans, but the raiding party soon retreated.

This and other incursions proved too much for many settlers in the area. Again following Ogontz's prediction, many fled. A number of families went only a short distance, to Sandusky, while the Wolcotts packed what belongings they could and journeyed to the Cleveland area to wait out the war. The following two years proved to be a time of great struggle for Wolcott: not only had he and his family lost nearly all of their material possessions, but his beloved wife Elizabeth contracted a fever during their exile and died, leaving him to care for their three children alone.

But Wolcott's luck would soon take a turn for the better. At war's end in 1814, the family limped back to Marblehead Peninsula and, in a sign of happier days ahead, found their cabin largely unscathed from the fighting and subsequent looting. Seven years later, on March 10, 1822, just before he signed on as keeper of the Marblehead lighthouse, Wolcott remarried, taking Rachel Miller, a young Sandusky schoolteacher, as his wife.

But, just like the Wolcotts' early days on the Peninsula, life at the Marblehead lighthouse would be anything but dull for Benajah and his successors, who, as we shall see, kept the job in the family for some time.

It was during this time that the "Patriots" were active on the northern Ohio coast (see Chapter 3). These rebels, consisting mainly of Americans who loosely allied themselves with Canadian rebel leader William Lyon Mackenzie, were working to raise volunteers in northern Ohio through late 1837 for a planned invasion of Upper Canada. On February 26, 1838, they ventured across the ice to Pelee Island, quickly driving off the inhabitants, taking others prisoner and, after a week of looting and pillaging, were finally driven off after a short, bloody exchange on the frozen lake by a contingent of British regulars and Canadian militia from Fort Malden.

After fleeing back across the ice, a number of the rebels ended up spending the night on the lighthouse grounds before being picked up by local authorities who, after seizing their weapons, dispatched most of them to their homes.

This would not be the last time the Marblehead lighthouse would see military action. In 1862, a prison camp for Confederate soldiers was set up on tiny Johnson's Island in Sandusky Bay (see Chapter 4). From behind the prison walls, the prisoners could plainly see the light beckoning from the lighthouse, a terrible reminder of the close proximity of the freedom they were being denied. Marblehead would also serve as the backdrop for the only Confederate "naval action" on the Great Lakes during the war, when a group of Confederate spies operating in Canada took command of the steamer *Philo Parsons* in a daring and brazen attempt to use the passenger liner to land a party on the Union gunboat *Michigan* and use it to free the men on Johnson's Island. The plot was foiled, however, when the men of the *Michigan* were informed of the plan. The raiders were driven back to the Detroit River, where they scuttled the *Parsons* and escaped.

When Benajah died in 1832, Rachel Wolcott dutifully took over the lightkeeping duties at Marblehead, making her the first woman to tend a lighthouse on the Great Lakes, though there was little notice of this fact taken at the time. It is difficult to imagine how Rachel, in a situation similar to the one fellow settler Abigail Becker would find herself in only a few years later on the Canadian side of the lake (see Chapter 5), managed. Now a single parent of three responsible for tending both a home and a farm (and a lighthouse), Rachel was living in what was then still largely unsettled frontier country. But manage she did — the light was thought to have been kept consistently lit during the shipping season, with its lanterns in very good repair. As keeper, Rachel was also responsible for keeping a log of all passing ships and, of course, helping to save lives when disaster struck. In a reflection of the times, when Rachel married Jeremiah Van Benschoten, a widower from the nearby village of Vermilion, in 1834, he was immediately appointed the new lightkeeper — no questions asked.

Prior to its automation, fifteen keepers had tended the Marblehead lighthouse. And Rachel Wolcott was not the only woman. Like Rachel, George McGee's wife, Johanna, took over the lightkeeping duties when her husband died in 1896. She served for seven years, until her retirement in 1903. If you include the time she helped her husband tend the light, Johanna devoted an astounding thirty-three years of her life to the Marblehead lighthouse — a feat virtually unheard of at the time, especially for a woman.

Another notable Marblehead keeper was Charles F. Drake, who was keeper for an eight-year term, beginning in 1843. In 1851, he went on to tend the Green Island lighthouse for another eight years until it burned to the ground in a fierce winter storm on December 31, 1863, forcing Drake and his family to seek refuge in an outhouse until their rescue the following day.

Though it appears much the same today as it did the day it opened, the Marblehead lighthouse has seen no shortage of technological innovations over its nearly 200 years. Then it burned mainly whale oil. But, as supplies became more and more scarce, thereby driving up the price, more efficient and cleaner burning kerosene was introduced. Shortly after the turn of the twentieth century, the lantern was upgraded with a new lens ordered from France, which was installed after first being displayed at the 1904 St. Louis World's Fair.

Unlike many other lighthouses in the area, however, automation came relatively late to Marblehead — not until 1946. Today, even though it is no longer permanently staffed, the old lighthouse still echoes a long-gone era. This timeless old beacon is showing no signs of slowing down in its old age.

Point Abino Lighthouse: The Great Storm of 1913

"Goodbye, Nellie. Ship is breaking up fast. Williams."

This haunting message, carved into a wooden ship's hatch cover, was found by a fisherman on the beach near Buffalo, two days after the largest storm ever to hit the Great Lakes swept through, leaving in its wake an unprecedented path of death and destruction. What mariners used to call the "Big Blow" is more commonly known to history as the Great Storm of 1913; the hatch cover had come from United States Government Lightship *No. 82*, which, a few days earlier, had been stationed just off Point Abino, Ontario, twenty-five kilometres outside of Buffalo Harbor.

Today, the ornately sculpted Point Abino lighthouse, first opened by the Canadian government in 1918, but unused since 1996, stands in memory of the lost crew of Lightship *No. 82*. The identity of the man who wrote the cryptic note on the hatch cover remains a tantalizing mystery, but a few things are known: the writer was almost certainly a member of the six-man crew of Lightship *No. 82*, and the note was written in the very last moments of his life, as the helpless vessel, anchored to the bottom and with nowhere to run, was being bashed to pieces by monstrous fifteen-metre waves.

Lightships have a long history on the Great Lakes. The vessels were heavily used by the United States Lighthouse Service at the turn of the twentieth century, and were permanently moored to the bottom in areas where hazards, such as shoals and rock shelves, threatened shipping. They first appeared in 1891, when the first three vessels, *Nos. 55, 56,* and *57* took up station in northern Lake Michigan. These wooden ships, each about thirty metres long, remained at their posts continuously from early April until the last of the big freighters crossed the lakes in early December. Because of these lengthy tours of duty, they were often outfitted with more creature comforts than most lake ships. Lightship *No. 82*, for example, featured upholstered chairs, French plate glass mirrors, and even a small library. Still, these luxuries were no substitute for the company of friends and family.

Though they were only intended as a stopgap until permanent lighthouses could be built, these early lightships were around for an unexpectedly long period, with the last one still in service, *No. 56*, finally retired in 1928. Their main drawback was expense: Point Abino's *No. 82* cost nearly

US$45,000 to outfit when she was launched in 1912, and US$8,000 was needed every year to properly maintain and staff each lightship. This was a massive drain on the already tight finances of the Lighthouse Service.

Another problem with lightships, which *No. 82* would go on to demonstrate, was safety — when a storm hit, it was very difficult to keep a vessel that was permanently moored to the bottom from being swamped by the high waves. What's more, there was often no safe port for the lightships, held fast by their mushroom-shaped anchors, to find refuge in. On the contrary, lightships were most necessary when the wind and waves were at their most threatening, and their crews were duty-bound to hold their stations for the sake of the lake freighters that depended on them to find their way. As Mary Williams, the wife of *No. 82*'s captain, said when asked if she thought her husband had tried to make a run for safe harbour during the Great Storm: "Certainly not. Captain Williams and his crew... would remain at their station until blown away or ordered to move."

Lightship *No. 82* was built in Muskegon, Michigan, and though it was somewhat smaller than many other lightships, measuring just under twenty-five metres in length, she was considered state of the art in terms of safety.

Photo courtesy of Lower Lakes Marine Historical Society

A rare photo of Lightship No. 82 *under way, taken shortly after she was launched in 1912.*

Unlike its wooden predecessors, *No. 82* was outfitted with a steel hull and a whaleback-shaped forecastle deck, both of which enabled it to more easily handle rough weather and high seas. Her crew, Captain Hugh H. Williams of Michigan, mate Andrew Lehy of Ohio and his brother Cornelius, the assistant engineer, Chief Engineer Charles Butler of Buffalo, Cook Peter Mackey of Buffalo, and Seaman William Jensen of Michigan, first took up station off Point Abino on August 12, 1912. It is not hard to imagine the confidence these young men must have had in their brand new steel-hulled ship as they settled into the ebb and flow of shipboard life. What they could never have imagined was the bizarre confluence of weather that would soon conspire to cut their careers, and their lives, frightfully short.

—⚓—

The violent storm that raged over the Great Lakes from November 7 to 10, 1913, was actually the result of two gigantic weather systems smashing into one another. As the November 10 edition of the Toronto *Globe* describes:

> The storm of which Toronto was the pivotal point at eight o'clock last night was the result of a fusion of two storms off the Atlantic coast off Maryland and the other from the Canadian northwest. At the meteorological office last night it was learned that this storm was directing its attention to Ontario and its environs. Storm signals were hoisted at all lake ports Saturday, and the weather man declared that the hurricane which vented its fury on Lakes Erie, Huron and Superior was the most pronounced on record.

Of all the lakes, Huron was the one that took the brunt of the storm, with 188 lives lost and 24 vessels sunk or damaged, many of them the pride of the Great Lakes shipping fleet. Because of this staggering loss of life, history tends to record the Great Storm primarily as a Lake Huron disaster, but what is not as well known is that Lake Erie ranked a not-so-distant second with seventeen vessels affected. The city of Cleveland took the hardest blow, suffering US$5 million in damage. As C.P. Staubach, who was on his way home to Detroit via Cleveland by train, recalled to Frank Barcus in his definitive 1960 book on the storm, *Freshwater Fury*:

... the railroad tracks were blocked by telegraph poles and wires; the wires were tangled around them in one unholy mess. It was the same damned mess around every signal tower and station. Gangs of men were out ahead of us all day, chopping away the poles and clearing the railroad track for us. It took twelve hours to work the train through the city of Cleveland itself, a run which normally takes twelve minutes.

As Barcus also notes, because of the downed telegraph lines, Cleveland was very slow to learn that it would actually bear a significant piece of the storm's human toll as well: twenty of the freighters out on the lakes during the maelstrom were Cleveland-based, and one hundred eighty-six Clevelanders lost their lives.

Still, on Lake Erie, there were only six men who failed to return home after those fateful November days — those aboard United States Government Lightship *No. 82*.

The first sign that there might be trouble off Point Abino came on the morning of Tuesday, November 11, when a buoy and some debris bearing the markings of *No. 82* were found at the beach near Buffalo Harbor. When this was reported to the area's lighthouse inspector, Roscoe House, he immediately dispatched the lightship tender *Crocus* to investigate. In turn, the assistant lighthouse inspector chartered the tug *Yale* as well, and the crew of the Buffalo lifesaving station, already exhausted after the storm's four-day pounding, took to the beaches to look for wreckage. All came back empty-handed.

The search resumed early the next day, November 12. By now, Mrs. Williams had arrived to personally assist in the search for her husband. By all accounts, Mrs. Williams was a skilled sailor in her own right and, like many sailors, was quite superstitious, especially when it came to matters of the sea. Believing that if she personally went out onto the lake, she might be able to find her lost husband, she insisted on being taken aboard the *Crocus*.

By coincidence, it was also on November 12 that a fisherman came across the hatch cover bearing the message, which was immediately assumed to be a final farewell from Captain Williams to his wife.

Not entirely, according to Mrs. Williams. While she believed the message was indeed from her husband, she was also convinced that it had been written for the captain by Seaman Jensen. Her husband, she insisted, had never called her Nellie. But Mrs. Williams's theory stood in stark contrast to statements made by the wife of Thomas Joseph, keeper of the lighthouse at nearby Horseshoe Reef. The Williams family had stayed with the Josephs throughout the summer of 1912, and Mrs. Joseph insisted that Captain Williams had indeed called his wife Nellie. A subsequent check of Williams's signature on an invoice seemed to indicate that the handwriting was his, but it was difficult to be certain, given the terrible conditions under which the message was written. There is also the possibility that the message itself was a fraud, carved into the hatch cover by someone in one of the surrounding communities. But as the cover was found so soon after the disaster itself, this seems unlikely.

So were these last thoughts really the captain's? Or were they those of another crewman? And who was Nellie, if not Mrs. Williams? We will probably never know.

With the lake threatening to ice over for the winter, little more could be done for the lost lightship. Roscoe House, faithful to the rules of the Lighthouse Service, recommended to the Secretary of Commerce in Washington that the positions of the crew of Lightship *No. 82* be discontinued as of November 10, 1913. The assiduous House even went so far as to publicize the salaries of the lost crewmen, which ranged from US$37 a month for Seamen Jensen to US$900 per year for Captain Williams — a pittance, even in 1913 money, in light of the endless tedium and very real dangers that these men faced.

With that, the matter was laid to rest until the following spring. Finally, on May 9, 1914, the search vessel *Surveyor* located the missing lightship lying a full three kilometres off her station in nineteen metres of water. Dave Beaudry, a diver who surveyed the wreck, reported that her steel hull was relatively intact, but that the interior and the ship's wooden superstructure were horribly damaged. He could find no bodies in this initial search, though *No. 82* was by this time largely filled with sand.

Her investigation complete, the *Surveyor* left a buoy behind to mark the location of the wreck, and the government set about the task of contracting the job of raising *No. 82*. After two attempts (the first failed due to the sand-filled wreck's astounding weight), Lightship *No. 82* was returned to the surface of Lake Erie on September 15, 1914, at a staggering cost of US$36,000 — nearly as much as a new vessel. When the steel hull rose out of the surf, there was hope that the ship would finally yield the bodies of her lost crew who, it was assumed, had made the vessel fast against the storm as best they could before sealing themselves below.

But these expectations were quickly dashed. A thorough search of the vessel revealed no trace of the crew, and of the six, only one was ever found; later that fall, the body of Chief Engineer Charles Butler was pulled from the Niagara River near Buffalo. His widow identified him by his coat, a gold cuff button, and a missing finger on one of his hands.

The wreck, however, revealed much about the ferocity of the "Big Blow." The vessel's steel hull and whaleback-shaped foredeck had indeed done their jobs, but the storm had created waves so high that they carried right over the hull and bashed into the vessel's aft wooden superstructure. Once they tore off the mast and lanterns, the waves crashed into the interior, filling the hull from the inside, violently swamping the ship — and likely killing her trapped crew instantly — before tearing her completely off her moorings and dragging her to her final resting place. It also appeared that Mary Williams had been right: Captain Williams had decided to stay on his station, but in such conditions there was nowhere for the tiny vessel to go, even if it had tried.

And perhaps, even more surprisingly, this was not the end of Lightship *No. 82*'s story. Once refloated at Buffalo, the ship was towed to Detroit, rebuilt, and used as a relief lightship. *No. 82* held stations on Lake Michigan and Lake Huron before being retired at the end of the 1935 navigation season. From there it went to Boston, where it was permanently docked and used as a summer retreat for retired Navy men. But ironically, Lightship *No. 82*'s ultimate demise would come not from a storm at sea, or even from old age: in 1945, vandals boarded her and sank her at her dock. By now, Lightship *No. 82* had run out of lives — after being refloated a second time, she was finally sent to the scrapyard.

Today, the lighthouse stands abandoned at the tip of Point Abino, roughly midway between the towns of Fort Erie and Port Colborne. After the loss of Lightship *No. 82*, two other lightships temporarily held the position before the Canadian government finally got around to building the ornate lighthouse, complete with an attached keeper's dwelling, in time for the 1918 navigation season. With this, and a lighted buoy marking the nearby shoal, lightships were no longer necessary.

With its twenty-eight-metre white concrete tower, the Point Abino lighthouse is a rarity among Lake Erie lighthouses. Constructed in Greek Revival style, it spurns the utilitarian look of most Great Lakes lights, instead

Photo by author

The Point Abino lighthouse, an architectural rarity on the Great Lakes, faces an uncertain future.

projecting an almost regal appearance that nearly masks its once-vital role of guiding vessels safely into Buffalo. It was manned for far longer than most other lights on the lakes, with the last keeper, Lewis Anderson, finally turning off the lantern in January 1989, when the lighthouse was fully automated. Quoted in a January 3, 1989, *Toronto Star* article, Anderson was blunt about his feelings: "Lighthouse keepers have been around since the time of the ancient Egyptians. Now we're going the way of the dodo bird."

But Anderson's thirty-year term can hardly be described as boring. In December 1985, the keeper found himself in the middle of yet another fierce Lake Erie gale, with waves blowing so high they completely entombed the lighthouse in ice, blowing out the windows and completely destroying Anderson's office at the base of the tower. When Anderson and his crew arrived the next morning, they had to use fire axes to get in. "There was five feet of ice," he said in the same *Toronto Star* article. "It took three months before it thawed, and we had to dry everything with industrial-sized heaters." On other occasions, Anderson was forced to ride out storms for days in the lighthouse.

After Anderson left, automation would only extend the old light's life for another seven years. With the advent of the Global Positioning System and other tools of modern navigation, the Point Abino lighthouse, like the lightships that had preceded it, was no longer needed. At the close of the 1996 navigation season, the Point Abino lighthouse fell dark — for good. But as with Lightship *No. 82*, this is a story with many endings.

Almost from the moment the Point Abino lighthouse was deactivated, local citizens began to put together a concerted effort to preserve it. The building was almost immediately designated a National Historic Site by the federal government in 1998, which was something of a pyrrhic victory, since no money was allocated for its maintenance. Further, the land behind the lighthouse, and the only access road leading to it, is owned by private interests.

But all was not lost. A group of nearby residents organized and began to press local politicians to act. In 2001, they did, and the town of Fort Erie bought the lighthouse from the federal government. Later, a deal was worked out with the landowners to allow limited public access. While far from a permanent solution, something of a reprieve has been granted. But much work remains to be done if the future of this unique Lake Erie landmark is to be secured.

Chapter 7

Bootleggers and Blind Pigs:
Rum-running on Lake Erie

"Prohibition Comes In Without Disturbance," announced the headline on the front page of the September 18, 1916, Toronto *Globe*.

And so it appeared, for a short time at least, that eliminating the heartbreak and destitution caused by what was then known as the "liquor traffic" was as simple as passing a law. As the *Globe* goes on to report:

> The bars that closed on Saturday as purveyors of intoxicating liquors open today as restaurants for temperance drinks. The shops stay closed. The passing of King Alcohol was tame and orderly in Toronto, save for a bit of isolated roystering. There was no celebrating, no "rough-housing." Hotelmen combined with officialdom to preserve order.

Along the shores of Lake Erie, the story was much the same. The Windsor *Evening Record* didn't even bother to run a story about the dawn of a "dry" Ontario, and instead devoted most of its front page to reports from the world war that was raging an ocean away on the bloody battlefields of France.

But the cracks in the Ontario Temperance Act, or OTA, the law behind Prohibition, soon began to show. The law marked the end, or so it was thought, of the free sale of liquor in Ontario, wiping out just about any place a cocktail could be enjoyed in the company of friends. The only exception was private homes, and even then, in the words of the OTA itself, the stuff couldn't be "purchased and received from any person in Ontario." In other words, it could still be imported, and it was, in record amounts, mostly from neighbouring Quebec.

And this was far from the only way to get around the OTA; there were countless other loopholes. For one, doctors could still prescribe liquor to patients in need, and this privilege was widely abused. The problem was most obvious during the Christmas season, when "illness" ran rampant across the province, causing long lines of "patients" to snake their way out the doors of their local pharmacies.

Clearly taken aback, the province tightened restrictions on doctors and druggists, but as with many of Prohibition's more stringent rules, these merely had the opposite effect of encouraging drinkers to find other, more creative ways to wet their whistles. Locally produced wines were still being sold, and the pipeline from Quebec remained open, but for the more stout-hearted, there were less legal ways to get one's hands on alcohol.

In the United States, the advent of Prohibition followed a similar route, but the Eighteenth Amendment, which took effect on January 16, 1920, was much more strict than the OTA, doing away with "the manufacture, sale, or transportation of intoxicating liquors within, the importation thereof into, or the exportation thereof from the United States..." But unlike the OTA, which still allowed alcoholic beverages to be made and exported, the Eighteenth Amendment was firm: no alcohol was to be produced in America. Period. It was a crucial distinction. And it was what the whole lucrative enterprise of smuggling booze across Lake Erie and into the United States rested upon.

The Prohibitionists

"Mr. Dobson, I told you last spring ... to close this place and you didn't do it. Now I have come with another remonstrance. Get out of the way ..."

With that, Carry Nation, a six-foot-tall temperance crusader from Kansas, went on a rampage, hurling bricks and bottles in all directions, smashing the mirrors and liquor bottles that the bar's owner, the aforementioned Mr. Dobson, kept neatly stacked behind the bar. Terrified, Dobson and another man standing beside him hit the deck.

It was June 7, 1900, in Kiowa, Kansas, and the legend of Carry Nation had been born.

Through the rest of that day, she smashed two more bars, and was heard calling to one young bartender: "Young man, come from behind that bar. Your mother did not raise you for such a place." She then threw a brick at the mirror, and though it didn't break, "the brick fell and broke everything in its way."

Nation was a fervent Methodist whose first husband, a doctor, had paid for his alcoholism with his life. Until she died eleven years later, Nation firmly believed that God had charged her to go to Kiowa that day to demolish the bars and gin joints that she believed were spreading the disease of alcoholism among the men of the community. According to Nation's memoirs, which she penned in 1905 under the title *The Use and the Need of the Life of Carry A. Nation*, she had prayed before going to bed the previous evening for "the Lord to use me in any way to suppress the dreadful curse of the liquor." Her prayers were quickly answered, as she describes:

> The next morning before I awoke, I heard these words very distinctly: "Go to Kiowa and" (as in a vision here my hands were lifted and cast down suddenly) "I'll stand by you." I did not hear these words as other words; there was no voice, but they seemed to be spoken in my heart. I sprang from my bed as if electrified, and knew this was directions given me, for I understood that it was God's will for me to go to Kiowa to break, or smash, the saloons.

Over the years, the eccentric Nation would become arguably America's best-known "dry" advocate, and over time her methods would change. Switching from hurling pieces of brick to wielding a hatchet in order to cause as much damage as possible, Carry would come to call her visits to the pubs "hatchetations," and proclaim that she was saving their clientele from "a drunkard's hell." The police did what they could to control Carry, but she had many deep-pocketed supporters who were willing to help her pay the many fines she ran up. As for the barmen of Kansas, many lived in constant fear of Nation's wrath, and some closed up shop entirely.

Southern Ontario's answer to Carry Nation was the Reverend J.O.L. Spracklin, also a Methodist and another rabid prohibitionist. Spracklin was the pastor of the Sandwich Methodist Church in Sandwich, which was then a town of its own (it would later be amalgamated with Windsor). Through 1919 and early 1920, he had been publicly pressuring the police to do something about what he considered lax enforcement of the OTA in the southwest. His argument centred on the huge amount of liquor that was being smuggled across the Detroit River, something that was getting more and more out of hand as Windsorites, from everyday citizens to professional rum-runners in expensive speedboats, came to realize the fast buck waiting to be made by "exporting" booze to their nearby American neighbours.

Almost immediately after Prohibition became law in the United States, the river came alive with bootleggers. Although it is impossible to know for sure, three-quarters of the alcohol that entered the U.S. from Canada during the dry years is said to have come this way, earning the river the nickname the "Windsor–Detroit Funnel." From Windsor, all the way down to Lake Erie, the river was lined with docks devoted exclusively to the "export trade," on which were built plain sheds where the booze could be housed until it was smuggled across. (The close proximity of the Hiram Walker Distillery, located on the Detroit River shoreline in nearby Walkerville, didn't hurt, either.) Day and night, rowboats, speedboats, and even steamers loaded with liquor crowded the river. Not even the bitter winter could stop the parade; rum-runners simply built sleighs or put chains on the tires of their cars and drove them across, often bringing planks of wood along in case they had to drive over cracks in the ice. There were even rumours of underwater cables and pipes running to the Detroit side, and a host of other bizarre contraptions built with one goal in mind: to get as much booze as possible past the authorities and into American "speakeasies" and "blind pigs" — underground bars and clubs where booze was sold in outright defiance of the Eighteenth Amendment.

Spracklin was one of the leading voices against this kind of lawlessness, and the pastor knew how to use his talents as a speaker to maximum effect. He made headlines across the province by appearing at a Sandwich town hall meeting on July 19, 1920, and dramatically presenting a handwritten charge against Sandwich's police force for, according to a report in the next day's *Border Cities Star*, "... gross negligence and inefficiency in the discharge of their official duties, and further, that by such negligence and inefficiency on their part, drunkenness, disorderly conduct, the illicit traffic in strong drink, and indecency have for some time past flourished to an alarming degree in the town."

Not willing to stop there, Spracklin went after the chief of police himself, according to the July 20, 1920, *Toronto Globe*:

> Mr. Spracklin also charges open neglect on the Chief of Police, Alois Masters, citing in particular the night of June 20, 1920: "during which date between the hours of 9:20 p.m. and 11:45 p.m., when the chief remained in front of the Chappell House [a Sandwich hotel], except from 11:40 to 11:55 p.m., when he was inside the place, that men and women staggered from said place evidently under the influence of strong drink, and the Chief of Police during that time failed to enforce the law of the land."

The *Globe* called Spracklin's colourful oration at the town hall meeting, given with a number of Sandwich's prominent citizens standing behind him, nothing less than "the biggest sensation ever in town." A spectator captured the mood best when he told a reporter from *The Border Cities Star*: "This man Spracklin has, tonight, lighted a torch which shall not die out until the whole province of Ontario is awakened to the conditions existing along the Essex border."

And Sandwich's police were not the only ones feeling the heat; the fiery preacher's outspokenness was also proving to be an embarrassment for the provincial government, which at this point was desperate to find a solution to the ever-worsening situation in the "wild west." But the province's new attorney general, William E. Raney, had a plan. Instead of trying to silence Spracklin, as American authorities had tried to do with Carry Nation years earlier, Raney decided to harness the pastor's boundless energy — and use it to bolster the OTA along the border. To the shock of many, less than ten days after Spracklin's outburst at the Sandwich town hall meeting, Raney gave the pastor a temporary appointment as a provincial liquor license inspector, armed him, and allowed him to hire as many men as he needed to bring the bootleggers to heel.

Not surprisingly, Spracklin wasted no time putting his newfound powers to use, hiring a squad of fellow license inspectors to help him, including William H. Hallam and S.M. Hallam, two Windsor brothers who were known around town for being little more than petty thugs. Still, if Spracklin was going to operate in the dark and seedy world of the bootleggers, he figured he would need some added muscle.

But it wasn't only gangsters and small-time smugglers who had to worry about a visit from the "fighting parson" and his anti-liquor squad. The high and mighty were not safe, either. Little more than two weeks into Spracklin's appointment, he and S.M. Hallam took down the mayor of nearby Amherstburg, Doctor W. Fred Park, and Sam Renaud, one of the town's constables. The pair, according to the license inspectors, had received 230 cases of whiskey, which they had stashed in Park's barn after loading some of the hooch into a small boat. Park explained that he didn't own any of the liquor, but was simply storing it, in the words of the August 27, 1920, *Border Cities Star*, "in the public interest, so that it might not be stolen."

None of this washed in the eyes of Magistrate Alfred Miers, who promptly slapped Park with a $1,000 fine for possessing liquor in a place other than a private dwelling.

For a churchman, Spracklin was also remarkably cavalier about using his gun — something that would later come back to haunt him. Early on the morning of August 26, 1920, Spracklin and S.M. Hallam stopped four boats on the Detroit River and arrested nine men, all Americans, on grounds that they were smuggling whiskey into the United States. Three of the boats came quietly, but one, a large cruiser called the *Eugenia*, needed a little coaxing before yielding to Spracklin and his men, who stalked the rum-runner in a government-supplied speedboat appropriately named the *Panther II*. The agents fired on the slower-moving boat, no doubt scaring the life out of the rum-runners aboard. In a sense, Spracklin and his agents were lucky that night; although the *Eugenia* had reportedly been equipped with a rifle, there were no guns aboard when it was loaded with whiskey at a nearby Windsor hotel and sent on its way. All nine bootleggers were charged with violating the OTA, and the license inspectors asserted that, according to the August 20, 1920, *Border Cities Star*, they were using the tiny fleet for "transporting liquor from the border to Toledo or some other downriver point."

Although it appeared on the surface that Spracklin was having some success in controlling the carnival atmosphere that hung over the border, any gains he made were obscured by the conflicts that arose shortly after the Sandwich pastor became an overnight lawman. Complaints about his methods quickly sprang up, including a charge by a Windsor lawyer that Spracklin's men were carrying pads of blank search warrants and simply filling in the names as they went along. Throughout the region, people's cars were being searched at random — even while they attended Sandwich Methodist on Sunday mornings. Worse, the bootleggers responded to Spracklin's raids in the only way they knew how: with violence. Death threats were phoned and mailed in to Spracklin's home, and on Halloween night in 1920, the house was sprayed with bullets, with one whistling past the pastor's wife before burying itself in a wall. In one particularly strange incident, bootleggers even tossed Spracklin into a canal near the town of La Salle. Far from getting better, the situation along the border seemed to be getting more brutal with each passing day.

The event that would put an end to Spracklin's short-lived reign of terror over the bootleggers and gin joints along the Detroit River came early on the morning of November 6, 1920. Predictably, Spracklin turned his attention back to the Chappell House, in his own backyard of Sandwich. The hotel was owned by a man called Beverly "Babe" Trumble, who, aside from being an old childhood rival of Spracklin's, was flouting the OTA by selling liquor on the premises — and doing very little to hide the fact. What caught Spracklin's eye that morning was the shadowy form of Ernie Deslippe, a Sandwich local, sitting on the sidewalk in front of the Chappell House with Trumble standing over him. As Spracklin and his squad got out of their cars and approached, according to Spracklin, Trumble muttered something about Deslippe being injured. And poor Deslippe was certainly in bad shape; aside from being drunk, his face was bloodied, suggesting that there had been a fight at the Chappell House that night. But before Spracklin could ask any more questions, Trumble disappeared into the hotel and locked the door behind him.

The pastor, seeing this as his chance to finally put an end to the illicit goings-on at the Chappell House, demanded that Trumble let him in. When Trumble failed to answer, Spracklin forced his way in through a ground-level window. It was then that things turned ugly. Once inside, Spracklin caught up with Trumble near the bar, where he allegedly pulled a gun on Spracklin and threatened him. According to Spracklin's testimony at an inquest into the events two days later: "'Babe' Trumble pressed his gun against the pit of my stomach. 'Damn you, Spracklin,' he said, 'I'm going to shoot you.' I knew then that it was his life or mine." Spracklin then pulled the trigger, striking Trumble in the abdomen. The innkeeper stumbled and fell. In the panic that followed, someone in the bar called a local doctor, who arrived moments later, but Trumble's wound, a severe internal hemorrhage, was simply too serious. Twenty-five minutes after being shot by Spracklin, Beverly Trumble succumbed to his injuries. A terrified Spracklin had fled the hotel immediately after the shooting and turned himself in to Windsor police. The minister was said to be severely shaken when he arrived at police headquarters, and he had no idea that by this time Trumble was lying dead on the floor of the Chappell House.

The courtroom was packed when Spracklin's trial opened over four months later, on February 21, 1921. The pastor and his lawyers seemed optimistic about the outcome, but they were far from cocky. Standing in their way was Trumble's tough-minded widow, Lulu. She had been with her husband when he was shot, and had been stubbornly contradicting the pastor's story from the beginning. Most troubling to the defence was that during her testimony she swore over and over that her husband had never even owned a revolver. Later in the trial, one of the witnesses even stated that he had seen Mrs. Trumble herself wielding a pistol at the time of the shooting. The February 23, 1921, *Border Cities Star* recorded the courtroom's response to this interesting bit of testimony:

> Spectators realized that a startling statement had been made and a number of persons applauded. Sir William Mulock [the judge] ordered Sheriff C.N. Anderson to have the persons responsible for the demonstration arrested and held in contempt of court. He expressed the opinion that if they were men they would stand up.

The Spracklin trial was rapidly becoming a circus. And Mrs. Trumble wasn't helping. When she was recalled to the stand to be questioned about whether or not she was armed, she deadpanned, "If I had had a gun, there would certainly have been another murder."

In the end, the jury was unable to bring itself to believe Lulu Trumble, and it took its members only fifty-nine minutes to unanimously acquit Spracklin on February 24, 1921: "I have made no plans for the future," Spracklin told the *Border Cities Star* five minutes after the verdict had been read, "I am not sure what I shall do, now that I am finally free from this charge."

One thing the "fighting parson" would never do again was prowl the Detroit River in search of rum-runners. His appointment as a provincial liquor license inspector had actually ended months earlier, in the days after the Chappell House shooting, when Attorney General Raney finally came to his senses and appointed a former police officer, W.J. Lannin of Stratford, to take over the fight against liquor trafficking on the border. The *Border Cities Star*, clearly lamenting the loss of Spracklin and his inspectors (and the wealth of stories they provided), glumly reported in its November 22, 1920 edition: "The border bids goodbye to the picturesque little band of freelancers who, under the leadership of Rev. J.O.L. Spracklin, waged such a spectacular warfare against the bootleggers and rum-runners who plied their trade across the Detroit River."

And the changeover came not a moment too soon: further doubts about Spracklin's competence seemed to surface almost daily through late 1920, and early 1921. The most glaring was a lawsuit levelled by Oscar E. Fleming of Windsor over a raid that Spracklin had carried out on Fleming's yacht, the *Kitty Wake*, while Fleming's son was hosting a party onboard. The *Kitty Wake* had just sailed from Windsor toward Lake St. Clair on the evening of September 17, 1920, when Spracklin and the Hallam brothers, cruising in the *Panther II*, spotted it and gave chase. According to Oscar Fleming Jr., his pursuer showed no running lights, even though it was dark, and followed at a distance. Finally, when the *Kitty Wake* dropped anchor between Belle Isle and Peche Island, the license inspectors drew alongside and clambered aboard. The younger Fleming tells what happened next in the testimony he gave during the suit, the opening of which was reported in the December 11, 1920, *Border Cities Star*: "Mr. Spracklin appeared in the cabin … with a flashlight in his left hand. His right hand was in his coat pocket. The pastor inquired who owned the pleasure boat and when informed it was the Fleming yacht, the minister, according to the witness, said that he would not have boarded had he known this."

Still, the Fleming name didn't stop Spracklin from searching the yacht anyway. The Hallams stood in the shadows, according to Fleming Jr., with their revolvers drawn. Spracklin found no booze, and even more troubling, he admitted during the proceedings that "… he intercepted every boat that came along, whether or not he suspected it had liquor on board."

Chief Justice R.M. Meredith flatly and candidly condemned Spracklin's behaviour during the proceedings (published in the March 10, 1921, *Toronto Star*), saying simply, "He showed unwisdom." Later, Meredith questioned Spracklin's very appointment as a license inspector by asking, "Why did he take a position for which he was not fitted?" The

Anti-liquor crusader Rev. J.O.L. Spracklin, who shot the owner of a Sandwich speakeasy, as he appeared at the time of his trial.

Photo courtesy of the *Windsor Star*.

lawsuit drove the point home: extreme measures like arming the fanatical pastor were no solution to the bootlegging problem.

Middle Island's Blind Pig

News of J.O.L. Spracklin's demise would have been music to the ears of men like Joe Roscoe. Described by none other than FBI director J. Edgar Hoover as "the reputed gambling king of Toledo," Roscoe had a rap sheet that stretched back more than thirty years before the FBI finally caught up with him in January 1937. Like the stereotypical Hollywood gangster, Roscoe was also fond of aliases, and went under several, among them Vedo, Joseph Rosso, and Joseph Cole.

Dark rumours always seemed to surround Roscoe, whom the January 28, 1937, *Toledo Blade* baldly referred to as a "mysterious underworld character." Most of them circulated around the gambling houses in Toledo. The *Blade* asserted that Roscoe held a 25 percent interest in one such house, which "has been raided rather less frequently than some of its competitors."

But much of the public's interest in Roscoe surrounded a certain Lake Erie island he was reported to be involved with. There, just inside Canadian waters, Roscoe was said to be involved in all sorts of illegal activity, from tax evasion to gambling and bootlegging. It was also there, perhaps, that the answer to how Roscoe managed to keep the police off his back in Toledo might be found. According to the January 28, 1937, *Toledo Blade*: "The gossips today named some police department members who are said to have availed themselves of Mr. Roscoe's generous invitations to relax in pleasant company far from prying eyes and lifted eyebrows." The police officials were never named, though the same edition of the *Blade* also made note of the "certain amount of restlessness … evident in some quarters today as developments in the Roscoe case moved toward a climax in the searching limelight of a federal court."

The island in question was Middle Island, located just three kilometres south of Pelee Island, mere metres from American waters. Only a little more than eighteen hectares, Middle Island is the southernmost point of land in Canada, and its questionable past, earned during the Prohibition years, continues to mystify to this day.

Much of what actually happened on Middle Island remains shrouded in mystery, but what is certain is that its convenient location made it irresistible to men like Roscoe. And he was far from the biggest fish to set foot on Middle's sandy shores. The Purple Gang of Detroit, who rose from practically nothing to dominate the illegal liquor market in a city that at the time was the booming front line of liquor smuggling, were also rumoured to have a stake in the speakeasy that operated there. Even the king of all bootleggers himself, Al Capone, was thought to have paid at least a few visits. For many years, a rumour even circulated that Capone had hidden a large fortune in the walls of the club at Middle Island. But since the building now stands in ruins, and no bills have ever been found there, it's probably safe to consign this to yet another in a long line of Capone myths.

During the 1920s, a club, complete with an airstrip, was opened on Middle, and rum-runners, in their modified speedboats, would often load up with whiskey before speeding off to deliver their spoils to the nearby Bass Islands, Kelleys Island, or even directly to the Ohio mainland — and collect their handsome profits. But this was no easy task, as the Coast Guard had by this time begun to arm their boats, and they weren't shy about firing on suspected lawbreakers. On top of that, there was the risk of being hijacked by other rum-runners (the Purple Gang were pioneers of this brutal tactic on the Detroit River), and, like all other mariners, rum-runners always had to be wary of Lake Erie's tricky weather, be it vicious storms or even ice, which is practically invisible in the dark during the winter and spring.

All of this contributed to what was fast becoming a wild game of cat and mouse between the Coast Guard and the rum-runners in the waters surrounding the Lake Erie islands that was rivaled perhaps only by the goings-on just to the north on the Detroit River. In his rare 1939 memoir about visiting his uncle on Pelee Island during the 1920s, simply titled *Uncle Lawrence*, British author Oliver Warner, who would later go on to write a biography of legendary naval commander Horatio Nelson, writes of a run to the Bass Islands with his uncle on a friend's boat. They had just left the safety of Canadian waters when an American Coast Guard vessel set upon them. Instinctively, they began to throw the hooch over the side, when, at the last moment, their pursuer fixed his attention on another suspected rum-runner deemed to be a more valuable target. Warner writes:

> We watched the chase into the distance, proceeding unmolested. "They'll never catch Bill Ince," said young Thompson [one of Warner's companions that day], "unless he breaks down. *The Mary Bella* is the fastest boat on Erie. And if they do, he won't have any stuff on board, not he. Just out for his health and a little fishing."

But it wasn't all about smuggling. Men like Roscoe were as keen as anyone to have a good time, and the Middle Island Club certainly reflected this. There was a full casino operating in the basement, complete with poker tables, a chuck-a-luck wheel, and even slot machines. And if the guests had a little too much fun and couldn't find their way back to their boats, it was no problem — they could stay over in one of seven luxury rooms, each of which offered beautiful views of Lake Erie — and continue their little vacation from "dry" America the next day.

The federal case that put an end to Roscoe's run of luck stemmed from the helping hand he gave to gangsters Alvin Karpis and Harry Campbell, following their 1936 robbery of a mail train in Garrettsville, Ohio. Early in 1937, the FBI hauled Roscoe in and accused him of allowing the pair to hide out in his Adams Street apartment in Toledo. He pleaded guilty and was sentenced to seven and a half years in prison for his role in the heist.

Still, Roscoe lived to a ripe old age of seventy-five. When his obituary appeared in the November 22, 1965, *Toledo Blade*, it pulled surprisingly few punches about his past:

> During the middle 1930s, Mr. Roscoe owned Middle Island in Canadian waters, which was used as a base of operation in smuggling premium beers and liquors into this country ... to avoid alcoholic beverage taxes.

Today, there is little evidence on Middle Island of its shady history. After the repeal of the Eighteenth Amendment in 1933 (Ontario had already given up on Prohibition in 1927), the club was never as profitable as it was during its heyday, when the OTA and the Eighteenth Amendment conspired to make it a bootlegger's dream. It soon fell into disrepair, and in the decades that followed, Middle Island remained largely uninhabited and was rarely visited, except by the odd curious boater.

Things remained this way until 1999, when the island was finally put on the auction block by its Cincinnati-based owners, and was successfully snapped up by the Nature Conservancy of Canada for a final price tag of US$1.3 million. With that, Canada's southernmost point was returned to Canadian hands after nearly a century of American ownership. But even this wasn't done without some behind-the-scenes intrigue. The federal government quietly donated CAD$300,000 to the Conservancy's bid, which was enough to clinch the deal. It was necessary to keep the contribution quiet, however, so as to not tip off the other five bidders, all of whom were American, that the Canadian federal government had thrown its considerable financial might behind the Conservancy's bid — thus driving up the price even further.

After it had won the day, the Nature Conservancy promptly turned Middle Island and its over thirty-five rare and endangered species over to the care of Point Pelee National Park, where it will remain protected for generations to come.

Notwithstanding its reputation as the black sheep of the Lake Erie island chain, most Canadians were happy to hear that this remote southern outpost had finally come home.

The Whiskey Ship

Like most professional rum-runners of the day, John Sylvester McQueen knew a thing or two about exploiting the loopholes in the Ontario Temperance Act. Born in Amherstburg, Ontario, the sixty-five-year-old McQueen was also quite familiar with the many risks of sailing on Lake Erie, particularly in October and November, when the weather is generally at its worst. By 1922, he'd been hauling cargo on the Great Lakes for years, and his boat, the thirty-eight-metre wooden steamer *City of Dresden*, had already had a lengthy career by the time he bought it in 1914. Launched in Walkerville, near Windsor (and, ironically, home of the Hiram Walker Distillery) in 1872, the old *Dresden* had ferried passengers and cargo between Windsor, Leamington, and Pelee Island, among other Lake Erie ports, in her early years before being sold to Post & Company of Sandusky, which used her to haul fish and various other types of cargo around the lake's western basin.

Not long after she was launched, the *Dresden* suffered a mishap that ended up looking a lot like the one that would end up being her ultimate fate. On the afternoon of October 13, 1873, the *Dresden* was picking her way across the Detroit River on her way to Windsor when the steam barge *Jenness*, misjudging the *Dresden*'s course and speed, barreled headlong into her. For a short time, it looked as though the *Jenness* would doom the poor *Dresden* before she ever got her chance at Prohibition-era infamy. The October 15, 1873, *Detroit Free Press* tells the story:

> Between 7 and 8 p.m. Monday evening as the prop. *City of Dresden* was crossing to the Canada side, the steam barge *Jenness* came down the river at full speed, and mistaking

Photo courtesy of Parks Canada Agency — Fort Malden NHSC

The City of Dresden *in her younger days, before she fell victim to the sandbars of Long Point.*

the position of the propeller [the *Dresden*], struck her head on a little abaft [or behind] of midship. The shock of the collision keeled the propeller over on her beam ends, and the barge went tearing along her side for 30 or 40 ft., crushing deck beams, smashing planks and completely tearing off the bulwarks for 30 ft.

In the confused moments that followed, it was thought that both boats would surely sink, but the *Dresden* displayed the toughness for which she would later become renowned. Even though, according to the *Free Press*, "some of the planks were splintered almost as fine as matches," she was shortly repaired and was back in service by early the following year. Miraculously, no one on either boat was hurt.

After more than forty years of this type of punishment, then, it's not hard to imagine what shape the *City of Dresden* was in when she found her way into the hands of the resourceful McQueen in 1914. (The *Simcoe Reformer* would later describe the boat as "condemned" when McQueen bought it, but it is not clear that things were quite that bad.) Still,

McQueen managed to keep the old steamer in service, reinforcing her tattered hull and repairing her with all the spare parts his limited budget would allow. In the end, the *Dresden* wound up a bit of a mishmash, particularly in the engine room, where McQueen had installed a plethora of other refurbished and repurposed odds and ends, including a boiler and an engine from two different tugs. The end result was a serviceable vessel, stable enough to continue hauling cargo on the Great Lakes, though seriously underpowered.

A Clandestine Sailing

One day in mid-November, 1922, McQueen looked on as the *City of Dresden* was loaded with one of her more lucrative cargoes: 1,000 cases and 500 kegs of Corby's Special Select whiskey and Old Crow bourbon — CAD$65,000 worth in all. As she lay docked at Belleville, Ontario, the hooch was stowed in the hold and, when that was full, in just about any corner of the boat where space could be found. Finally, forty-two cases were lashed topside, to the *Dresden*'s main deck. Belleville, located on Lake Ontario's Bay of Quinte, not far from the Corby distillery, was at the time a central transit point for illicit liquor on its way to the "dry" United States.

When the cargo was finally secured into what was now a near-bursting *Dresden*, McQueen would likely have glanced over his clearance papers, with their final destination listed as "Mexico," and chuckled to himself. This was, of course, the OTA's Achilles heel. For even though liquor was effectively banned from being sold in Ontario, nothing in the law prevented distillers from making the spirits and selling them "to persons in other provinces or in foreign lands." With no mandate to scrutinize the destinations of shipments leaving the country, Canadian customs officials were forced to look the other way when small motorboats and even rowboats laden with booze set off for exotic destinations like "Mexico," only to return empty mere hours later. "Mexico," in the *Dresden*'s case, was Port Huron, Michigan, at the northern end of the St. Clair River.

But as the *Dresden* emerged onto Lake Erie from the Welland Canal early on Friday, November 17, it was starting to become clear to her captain and her five-man crew that this would not be just another routine rum-run. Dark clouds filled the sky and the rising north wind began to buffet the old steamer. Up in the wheelhouse, McQueen felt its pull on the ship's wheel as the *Dresden*, her engines already working at full steam, began to lose speed.

But McQueen, who was no stranger to this run, was reluctant to turn back; he had an appointment to keep, and he was eager to get the *Dresden*'s cargo, worth so much to him and his crew, into the hands of its thirsty buyers and get his boat safely back into Canadian waters as quickly as possible.

At best, it was an ill-conceived decision. McQueen had put in enough years on Lake Erie to know that he was choosing an unnecessarily risky course. But if he gave any thought to the perils that loomed before him, he showed no sign of it. Like many a captain who had been wrecked on Lake Erie before him, he was confident in his skills as a mariner, the abilities of his crew, and in his boat, which, of course, he had rebuilt with his own two hands.

By the time the *Dresden* began to round Long Point later that afternoon, the weather had worsened so much that the waves were now crashing over the deck, and the *Dresden*, with her antiquated engines, was barely able to make any headway. Worse, the old steamer was entering an area long known for its sandbars, many of which lurked just below the surface of the water. McQueen and his men now had a full-blown crisis on their hands.

The old captain was not a man who easily changed his mind, but by this point he had seen enough. In the hope of riding out the storm, he decided to anchor the *Dresden* four kilometres to the west of the Long Point lighthouse on the Point's south shore. There, the crew, which included McQueen's twenty-one-year-old son, Peregrine, put in a horrible night as the whiskey-laden vessel strained heavily on her anchor chains under the full fury of the wind. The men must have dreaded that at any moment the *Dresden* would slip its chains and they would all be pitched into the raging, freezing water. No one got much sleep that night, but the men did what they could in what had become an impossible situation, and, as day broke, the *Dresden* continued to hold firm, though just barely.

It was late in the morning when McQueen accepted the inevitable — the storm was not abating, and he had to move the *Dresden* to a less vulnerable spot or risk losing everything, including the lives of his crew. Tentatively, he ordered the men to haul up the anchor and, as soon as the *Dresden* floated free, McQueen gently coaxed her back toward what he hoped was safety on the north side of the point. But it was not to be — the *Dresden* rolled deeply and made little forward progress. McQueen was in a state of disbelief; he looked at the small fortune in whiskey strapped to his deck and knew that there was no other choice — if the *Dresden* was to survive the day, the booze, the sheer weight of which was literally driving the old steamer to a watery grave, had to go. Through gritted teeth, McQueen gave the fateful order.

When confronted with saving either their cargo or their own skins, the men showed no hesitation; the result was certainly one of the more peculiar scenes in Lake Erie's history as, one by one, forty-two cases of whiskey flew over the *Dresden's* deck railing and splashed into the frothing water below.

For a moment, it looked as though this just might be enough to save the rapidly foundering vessel. Ever so slowly, she came to heel and for the moment managed to hold her own in the face of the blistering wind. But this was simply not McQueen's day, for no sooner had he managed to coax the *Dresden* around the tip of the point than the unbelievable happened. The wind, which had been blowing out of the north, shifted suddenly. Now howling out of the southwest, it shoved the *Dresden* back toward the beach. On top of this, in the words of the November 22, 1922, Simcoe *British Canadian*, the boat "sprung a leak, and the water poured in so fast that all hope of reaching Port Burwell was abandoned, and Captain McQueen headed the vessel for shore." The *Dresden's* engineer, Ray Sawyer, did what he could, but this was no trickle — the very seams of the ship were actually beginning to split apart under the enormous strain of the wind and the heavy cargo. With the hull now compromised, water surged into the hold and soon overwhelmed the pumps. The *Dresden* was entering her final moments.

At 4:30 in the afternoon, about ten kilometres to the west of Port Rowan, the *Dresden* hit a sandbar, lurched over onto her side, and almost immediately began to break apart. All the while, McQueen yanked as hard as he could on the steam whistle, hoping against hope that rescue might find its way to him. But in such a sea, he must have known how hopeless his situation was.

Then, unbelievably, things found a way to get even worse for McQueen and his besieged rum-runners. As the men were attempting to lower one of the *Dresden's* two lifeboats, the tiny craft was flipped over by a large wave, leaving them with only one boat. But as the crew scrambled aboard, disaster struck yet again; Peregrine McQueen, who had been trying to help a crewman who was hobbled by a wooden leg, was suddenly swept over the side. In desperation, his father reached out, but was seconds too late to grab hold of Peregrine as he was swept away by the frigid current — although he did manage to pull the disabled crewman back into the lifeboat. Even worse, the men discovered that the lifeboat's oars were no longer aboard as it parted ways with the sinking *Dresden*.

As the crew did their best to keep the little craft upright in the howling gale, safe from the shipwreck, but still adrift and very much in danger, their minds would have been focused entirely on their own survival. But they would also likely have caught at least a glimpse of the crowd that was beginning to gather on the beach, a mere three hundred metres away and, knowing how interesting they would find the wrecked steamer's cargo, had an inkling of the chaos that was about to begin.

A Prohibition Beach Party

According to local legend, the first local to profit from the whiskey wave that was about to wash over Long Point was a crew member from the point's lifesaving station, who had been walking along the tip of Long Point that day, watching carefully as the *Dresden* finally made her turn around the peninsula. When he looked out into the waves breaking over the shore, something else caught his eye — a lone case of whiskey bobbing in the surf. Quickly forgetting about the struggling mariners (he would be far from the first to do so that day), he rounded up as many cases as washed ashore and buried them in the sand, using the telephone poles leading out to the Long Point lighthouse as markers. Once the dust settled, he is rumoured to have sold the cases — over forty in all — to local bootleggers for a very tidy profit.

Meanwhile, the residents of Port Rowan and the surrounding country-side were making their way to the beach, drawn by the wail of the *Dresden's* steam whistle. Among them were two women from a nearby farm: Pearl Rockefeller and her niece, Viola Blackenbury.

The wreck, it seemed, made a good Saturday evening show for those with time on their hands. They watched as the first lifeboat capsized and was swept away by the storm, followed by the second, successful launch that killed Peregrine McQueen. As the men of Port Rowan gathered on the shore, rumours of the boat's business in the area began to spread. When one old farmer was heard to utter that the boat could indeed be carrying whiskey, the crowd erupted in a frenzy, and from that moment on, both the best and the worst in human nature was put on display. As Pearl Rockefeller and her niece kept an eye on the struggling sailors in the lifeboat, the crowd's suspicions about the *Dresden's* illicit cargo were confirmed. Under the heading "Woman Saves Crew, Men Salvage Liquor," the *British Canadian* reported:

> As case after case came crashing to the shore, while hundreds of bottles from broken cases were bobbing about in the surf, willing farmers eagerly gathered the welcome spoils. Farmers fetched their wagons and trucks, others came

with bags, and the liquor was quickly gathered up. The harvest of the storm was nearly all gathered when License Inspector Edmonds, Provincial Constable Lawrence and County Constable Alway arrived on the scene and upon arrival there was little left for the officers to seize.

Some of the men were so happy for the chance to have a drink after so many dry years under the OTA, they simply guzzled much of the blessed cargo right then and there, often while standing knee-deep in the surf. But for those with more long-term plans, there were logistical concerns to think about. Not wanting to lose a single bottle, they hauled away as much as they could, and buried the rest in the sand to retrieve later. Again, according to the *British Canadian*:

> All Sunday afternoon it was reported that a number of those who had benefited by their salvage operations were busily engaged in driving backward and forward to the beach and in various directions along the roads, making it impossible for the officers who were attempting to trace down the liquor to follow tracks into the various farmyards.

The remaining crewmembers of the *Dresden* were able to guide their lifeboat to shore, with no small thanks being owed to Mrs. Rockefeller, who, in a twentieth-century impression of Abigail Becker (see Chapter 5), waded out into the frigid water to grab hold of a rope that the crew tossed to her. The *British Canadian* showed no restraint in praising her efforts, declaring: "Alone she ventured out into the surf and by dint of daring and great efforts managed to drag the helpless and exhausted men to the shore." In all likelihood, Rockefeller had at least some help with her rescue effort, but her care for the men, and her subsequent feeding and tending to them at the Rockefeller farm, is a part of the *Dresden* story that is often, unfortunately, overlooked.

Peregrine McQueen's body washed up the following day, just as the looters were claiming the last few bottles of whiskey from the beach. His father, suffering from exhaustion and exposure, was, according to the November 23, 1922, *Simcoe Reformer*, in a state of "shock from which the aged mariner may never recover." McQueen, with the help of his brother, who had hurried to the scene from Belleville, claimed his son's body and took it back to the family home in Amherstburg.

A Lasting Legend

The police, led by Inspector "Dickey" Edmonds, didn't respond to the accident until Sunday evening. The delayed response, along with the confused initial police reports of the *Dresden* sinking, including a November 24 *Toronto Star* article that reported that "the officers state that the liquor is at the bottom of the lake," were likely caused, at least in part, by a loss of communication with the nearby town of Simcoe, where the authorities were based. The farmers had a friendly saboteur, it seemed, who cut the phone line, thus keeping the police at bay a little longer while they hid their haul. Regardless, according to the *Reformer*, the police "were too late to discover anything except empty cases and strewn labels."

Still, enough suspicion had been raised about the *Dresden* and her fishy cargo that the Simcoe crown attorney, W.E. Kelly, was ordered to make his way to Port Rowan to find out what he could about the legality of the shipment, while, on the spot, the police were doing all they could to round up suspects. The investigation began to resemble something of a witch hunt, with Edmonds and his men conducting surprise spot searches in hopes of catching guilty scavengers red-handed. And the farmers went to great lengths to try to outsmart him. One was rumoured to have lined the eavestroughs of his barn with bottles, laid end to end, and was surely relieved when Edmonds and his men searched his property and came up empty. Others simply hid bottles in false ceilings, dropped them down wells, laid them in feed troughs, or covered them with canvas and old feed bags in their barns.

But any real evidence continued to elude Edmonds. The farmers, and everyone else in town for that matter, were no help, either. When six of them were finally charged with stealing from the wreck, Kelly had a hard time building any kind of a case against them, mainly due to a lack of witnesses willing to testify. This frustrated things so much that the magistrate ordered the proceedings delayed for a week so Kelly could find some bodies to fill the witness chair. The December 7, 1922, *Simcoe Reformer* said that a clearly frustrated Kelly had "indicated" that his predicament was "a serious reflection on the manhood of the community." And those who did come forward had little new to offer, and in many cases simply added to Kelly's anguish. In the words of an article in the December 28, 1922, *Reformer*:

> Mr. Brewster, K.C., of Brantford, and Mr. H.P. Innes,
> K.C., for the defence, had a quiet afternoon, while Crown

Attorney Kelly, K.C., tried every resort to bring out new and incriminating evidence. The majority of the witnesses, however, were at the scene of the wreck within hours of the catastrophe, but remembered little of what took place.

But the authorities weren't ready to give up just yet — especially Inspector Edmonds. He vowed to keep searching for another month, despite the high seas that flooded the wreck site and the frigid temperatures, which plummeted even further as winter approached. Still, despite all the tough talk, the investigation continued to sputter. In the case of Delbert Rockefeller, who was one of the accused, the December 21, 1922, *Simcoe Reformer* reported: "... officers testified that ring marks of ten kegs were found in his wagon on the Monday following the wreck, and also that his horses were rarin' in the stables with harness on." This was hardly the stuff of a solid prosecution.

In the end three farmers, including Rockefeller, probably hoping the whole mess would just go away, turned up at court and pleaded guilty to drinking in a public place. They were fined $100 each, which was the sum total of the charges that were levelled in the *City of Dresden* incident. The vast majority of the steamer's massive liquor cargo was never accounted for, although bottles continued to be found along the beach long after the fact.

As for the *Dresden* herself, the storm did to her what collision and hard labour could not, permanently ending her career on the Great Lakes and scattering her wreckage along the Long Point shoreline. The only thing of any real value that McQueen was able to recover was her engine, which he had installed himself after he had bought the old steamer back in 1914. Returning to the wreck site a year after the tragedy, he and Ray Sawyer somehow managed to pry it loose from Lake Erie's sandy bottom and haul it away. But even though the *City of Dresden* is no more, the rumours, tall tales, and intrigue that she spawned remain, and will likely last for generations to come.

Acknowledgements

This book has been many years in the making. Unofficially, I can trace its roots back to the early 1980s when my late father, Brad Fraser, introduced me to Lake Erie in the only way fathers of the time knew how — by nudging me into its warm waters one summer afternoon at the government dock in Kingsville, Ontario. While I have long since forgiven him, I have never forgotten his message: love the lake, and treasure the time you spend on her. But always respect her.

As a kid, I would visit my grandparents, Ken and Margaret Fraser, at their cottage on Pelee Island. Pelee has always intrigued me, and I particularly remember the tall tales that were told around the fireplace that kept that old cottage toasty on chilly late-summer nights. Members of my family have fished the waters of Erie's western basin for many years, and fishing and boating yarns were the main fare, but every now and then someone would offer up something unexpected, like the legend of Huldah, a Native woman who, in the throes of despair over a lost British lover, threw herself off a high rock on the island's west side.

These were the stories that fired my imagination, and I knew there had to be more out there, just waiting to be uncovered. Over the years since, I have, both consciously and unconsciously, been looking for more evidence of the people who have shaped Lake Erie — and been shaped by her. This book is the result of those explorations.

As with any project of this scope, there is no way it could have come together without the help of a huge group of talented and generous people. Tony Hawke, my editor at Dundurn Press, believed in the idea from the start, and his encouragement and enthusiasm inspired me to keep digging into Lake Erie's intriguing past. My colleague Stephen Bishop selflessly dedicated countless hours to reading draft chapters, and was quick to point out historical inaccuracies.

My wife, Amy Harkness, played a critical role, keeping my spirits up while I spent hours writing and researching. My mother, Linda Fraser, and my stepfather and good friend, Jim Klym, provided boundless moral support in the way only those closest to you can. Shannon Whibbs, also of Dundurn, did a masterful job of editing the final text.

On Pelee Island, Ronald Tiessen kindly donated a good deal of time, and threw open the doors of his impressive Pelee Island Heritage Centre. The Centre's publications, many of which are listed in the bibliography of this book, were of particular help in uncovering Pelee's mysteries, especially the story of its lighthouse and the Battle of Pelee Island during the Upper Canadian Rebellion of 1837.

Gayle Struska, Louise Eidsmoe, Robert R. Eidsmoe, and Edward Bertsch shared crucial information relating to their countryman and ancestor, Amund Eidsmoe, and his terrifying night aboard the steamer *Atlantic*. James Donahue provided some much-needed direction on the *Clarion* incident.

At Put-in-Bay, Susie Cooper of the Lake Erie Islands Historical Society graciously offered me access to her files, which unleashed a wealth of information on the Battle of Lake Erie and the rather obscure story of the Green Island lighthouse. Michael Gora of Middle Bass Island was especially patient with my many questions, and deserves special praise for reprinting and significantly adding to Lydia Ryall's 1913 *Sketches and Stories of the Lake Erie Islands*, a rare and little-known chronicle of the early history of the islands, which was of immeasurable value to my research.

Staff at the Great Lakes Historical Society in Vermilion, Ohio, were also helpful and, in my opinion, the Society's quarterly journal, *Inland Seas*, should be on the "must-read" list of anyone interested in the colourful past of the Great Lakes. The Johnson's Island Preservation Society staff recommended a number of sources that were vital to understanding day-to-day life at the island's Civil War prison camp.

In Amherstburg, I benefited from the assistance of John MacLeod at the Fort Malden National Historic Site, who recommended some excellent secondary sources and allowed me access to the fort's files, which provided useful background on the Battle of Lake Erie and the Battle of Pelee Island. Kerry Wamsley and Debbie Reid allowed me the run of the Port Dover Harbour Museum, which does a wonderful job of showcasing Lake Erie art and shipping memorabilia, including the rich history of the area's fishing industry and priceless artifacts from the *Atlantic*.

In Toronto, staff at the Ontario Archives and the Toronto Reference Library were a great help. Both the Archives and the Reference Library are underrated services that contain a wealth of newspapers, original documents, letters, reports, and much more relating to the recent history and early exploration of Lake Erie. Special thanks also go to the Ontario Arts Council for supporting this project through the Writers' Reserve program.

Undoubtedly I am forgetting people, and I apologize for this. But those of you who provided support and encouragement know who you are, and I am forever grateful. And, of course, I alone am responsible for the errors and omissions that will inevitably crop up over time.

Associated Sites

Fort Malden National Historic Site
P.O. Box 38, 100 Laird Avenue,
Amherstburg, Ontario, Canada N9V 2Z2
Tel.: (519) 736-5416
Web: http://www.pc.gc.ca/lhn-nhs/on/malden/index_E.asp

Fort Malden, in Amherstburg, Ontario, was built in 1796 and once served as one of Canada's bulwarks against American expansion into the Midwest. During the War of 1812, it housed the colony's Indian Department and was the home port of the British fleet on Lake Erie, which was lost to the Americans in the Battle of Lake Erie in 1813. Today, the fort's earthworks are still plainly visible, and the museum is rich with artifacts from the area's days of early settlement and warfare. Special attention is paid to Fort Malden's role in defending the colony against William Lyon Mackenzie's loyalists during the Upper Canadian Rebellion of 1837.

Great Lakes Historical Society
480 Main Street
Vermilion, Ohio, USA 44089
Tel.: (440) 967-3467 or (800) 893-1485
Web: http://www.inlandseas.org

Located in picturesque Vermilion, Ohio, the Great Lakes Historical Society's Inland Seas Maritime Museum focuses heavily on the history of shipping and navigation on the Great Lakes (fittingly, as Vermilion was once known as a town of freighter captains). Highlights include interactive exhibits on navigation and seamanship, art, and artifacts, the most notable of which being the reconstructed wheelhouse of the ore/car carrier *Canopus*, from which you can enjoy a stunning view of Lake Erie. The Society's research library is widely known for its wealth of documents pertaining to Great Lakes ships and shipwrecks.

Lake Erie Islands Historical Society
P.O. Box 25, 25 Town Hall Place
Put-in-Bay, Ohio, USA 43456
Tel.: (419) 285-2804
Web: http://www.leihs.org

Located in the resort town of Put-in-Bay on South Bass Island, the Lake Erie Islands Historical Society is a treasure trove of artifacts and information on the settlement of the American Lake Erie islands, each of which has a unique character all its own. Significant space is devoted to Oliver Hazard Perry's victory over the British fleet in the Battle of Lake Erie during the War of 1812.

Long Point Provincial Park
Box 99
Rowan, Ontario, Canada N0E 1M0
Tel: (519) 586-2133
Web: http://www.ontarioparks.com/english/long.html

Recognized as a United Nations World Biosphere Reserve, Long Point boasts some of the best fishing and finest beaches on Lake Erie. It is also rife with history; the site of the Old Cut, a natural shipping channel that was filled in by a vicious storm in 1906, is just outside the gates to the park.

In the mid-nineteenth century, local heroine Abigail Becker lived in a small cabin among Long Point's many sand dunes before she made headlines by rescuing the crew of the stranded schooner *Conductor* from a terrible fate in November 1854. Because of its great length (nearly forty kilometres), Long Point spans nearly half of Lake Erie, which made it a rum-running hotspot during the Prohibition years (and a magnet for shipwrecks).

Marblehead Lighthouse State Park
110 Lighthouse Drive
Marblehead, Ohio, USA 43440
Contact: East Harbor State Park
1169 North Buck Road
Lakeside-Marblehead, Ohio, USA 43440
Tel: (419) 734-4424
Web: http://www.dnr.state.oh.us/tabid/763/Default.aspx

A great place for a picnic, the Marblehead Lighthouse State Park is a peaceful spot to sit and watch Lake Erie's waves crash over the park's rocky shoreline. The lighthouse, in immaculate condition and long since automated, is one of the oldest on the Great Lakes and is still needed to guide vessels into the shallows of Sandusky Bay and through the sometimes ornery South Passage. A museum occupies the former keeper's dwelling.

Pelee Island Heritage Centre
West Dock Place
Pelee Island, Ontario, Canada N0R 1M0
Tel.: (519) 724-2291
Web: http://www.peleeislandmuseum.ca

Thoughtfully curated by Pelee resident Ronald Tiessen, the Pelee Island Heritage Centre contains a number of displays and a great deal of information about the history of Canada's southernmost community, from its early settlement by William McCormick and his family to the environmental challenges the island faces today. Upstairs, an exhibit on uninhabited Middle Island, which lies to Pelee's south, explores Middle's role as a gambling and rum-running haven during Prohibition and its long-defunct lighthouse.

Perry's Victory and International Peace Memorial
P.O. Box 549
Put-in-Bay, Ohio, USA 43456
Tel.: (419) 285-2184
Web: http://www.nps.gov/pevi

Built to mark the centenary of Oliver Hazard Perry's victory over the British fleet in the Battle of Lake Erie in 1813, Perry's Monument, as it's locally known, towers over the village of Put-in-Bay on South Bass Island. The view of the Lake Erie island chain from the observation deck is breathtaking, and on a clear day the Canadian mainland is visible to the north. The monument is dedicated to the peace that has existed between the two nations since the War of 1812 and, fittingly, the remains of six officers from the Battle of Lake Erie — three American and three British — lie in a communal grave that is marked by a plaque on the main floor at the monument's base.

Point Abino Lighthouse Tours
Tel.: (905) 871-1600, ext. 2431
Web: http://www.town.forterie.ca (Select "Infrastructure Services" from the "Town Departments" menu, then navigate to "Parks & Leisure," and "Point Abino lighthouse.")

The Point Abino lighthouse can only be accessed via a private road leading to the point's tip. As such, public visitation is restricted, but guided tours are available during the summer. Trips feature a trolley ride to the lighthouse and a look inside this unique heritage building. The Point Abino lighthouse succeeded the ill-fated Lightship *No. 82*, which used to mark the tricky rock shelf that juts out from here until the vessel was lost in the Great Storm of 1913. It is recognized as the worst to ever hit the Great Lakes. Call or check the web site for tour dates.

Point Pelee National Park
407 Monarch Lane, R.R. 1
Leamington, Ontario, Canada N8H 3V4
Tel.: (519) 322-2365 or (888) 773-8888
Web: http://www.pc.gc.ca/pn-np/on/pelee/index_E.asp

Canada's southernmost mainland point is a haven for birdwatchers and its rich marshes, gentle trails, and sandy beaches have been attracting more and more paddlers and ecotourists in recent years. Its shifting tip is off-limits to swimming and the treacherous shoals that lurk between here and Pelee Island, Canada's southernmost community, have been the final resting place of an enormous number of vessels over the years.

Port Dover Harbour Museum
44 Harbour Street
Port Dover, Ontario, Canada N0A 1N0
Tel.: (519) 583-2660
Web: http://www.norfolktourism.ca (Click on "Things to Do" and navigate to "Museums & Historic sites" to locate the link to museum.)

The Port Dover Harbour Museum inhabits part of an old fishing net shanty on the waterfront of this cozy port town. This is no coincidence; the museum is devoted mainly to shipping, including commercial fishing, which is still a key driver of the local economy. Of particular interest are artifacts from the passenger steamer *Atlantic*, which took over 200 souls to the bottom of Lake Erie on the evening of August 19, 1852. Inhabiting the net shanty is a wide variety of fishing artifacts, from nets and early gear to models showing the evolution of fishing vessels over the past two hundred years. The wintering place of Sulpician missionaries François Dollier de Casson and René de Bréhant de Galinée, the first Europeans to spend a winter on Lake Erie, is located nearby, at the mouth of the Lynn River.

S.S. Meteor Whaleback Museum
300 Marina Drive
Superior, Wisconsin, USA 54880
Tel.: (715) 394-5712
Web: http://www.superiorpublicmuseums.org/ssmeteor
NewMETEORMAIN.htm

Now high and dry on Barker's Island in Superior Wisconsin, the *Meteor* was first launched in 1896. One of Captain Alexander McDougall's innovative "whaleback" designs (of which the *James B. Colgate*, lost on Lake Erie in the "Black Friday" storm of October 1916, was one), she carried all manner of cargo, and was even converted into an oil tanker before being brought back to Superior, where she was originally built, and turned into a museum. Visitors can tour the inside of the ship and even see her original steam engine.

> U.S. Brig Niagara
> 150 East Front Street
> Erie, Pennsylvania, USA 16507
> Tel.: (814) 452-2744
> Web: http://www.brigniagara.org

Moored at the Erie Maritime Museum in Erie, Pennsylvania, the *Niagara* is a reconstruction of the brig that Oliver Hazard Perry used to deliver the final blows to the British fleet in the Battle of Lake Erie during the War of 1812. As one would expect, the museum pays a great deal of attention to the battle. Aside from the *Niagara*, it features a reconstruction of the midsection of the *Lawrence*, Perry's first flagship on that bloody day. Perry later transferred his flag to the *Niagara* when the *Lawrence*, demolished by the relentless British barrage, became too damaged to carry on.

Additional Resources

About the Great Lakes: http://www.aboutthegreatlakes.com

Buffalo Light: *Guardian of the Harbor*: http://www.buffalohistoryworks. com/light/introduction.htm
Another account of the sinking of Lightship *No. 82* can be found here.

Dictionary of Canadian Biography Online: http://www.biographi.ca/EN

Great Lakes and Seaway Shipping: http://boatnerd.com
Boatnerd, as it is commonly known, contains a wealth of information for the Great Lakes history enthusiast, with a focus on vessels employed in the shipping trade and lighthouses.

The Great Lakes Atlas: http://www.epa.gov/glnpo/atlas/intro.html
Jointly maintained by Environment Canada and the U.S. Environmental Protection Agency, The Great Lakes Atlas is a comprehensive guide to the environment, people, and development issues surrounding the Great Lakes region.

Great Lakes Information Network: http://www.great-lakes.net
A plethora of facts and figures on the development, population, and environment of the Great Lakes.

Johnson's Island Preservation Society: www.johnsonsisland.org

Library and Archives Canada: http://www.collectionscanada.gc.ca

Lighthouse Digest: http://www.lhdigest.com

Maritime History of the Great Lakes: http://www.hhpl.on.ca/GreatLakes
This site, maintained by Great Lakes historian Walter Lewis, contains a wealth of documents and images relating to the Great Lakes, particularly the shipping trade. It is a valuable archive, particularly of newspaper coverage of Great Lakes shipwrecks. Some of these articles have been referenced in this book.

Middle Bass Island: *Middle Bass on the Web*: http://www.middlebass.org
Middle Bass Island resident Michael Gora maintains this site, which is an authoritative source of information pertaining not only to the history of Middle Bass, but to the entire Lake Erie island chain.

National Park Service: *History & Culture*: http://www.nps.gov/history

Norway Heritage: *Hands Across the Sea*: http://www.norwayheritage.com
Norwegian immigrant Amund Eidsmoe's firsthand account of the sinking of the *Atlantic* can be found here.

Parks Canada: *National Historic Sites of Canada*: http://www.pc.gc.ca/progs/lhn-nhs/index_E.asp

U.S. Brig Niagara: http://www.brigniagara.org

Virtual Museum of New France: http://www.civilization.ca/vmnf/vmnfe.asp
A thorough, user-friendly resource outlining many aspects of life in New France, from the social organization of the colony to explorers like La Salle.

Bibliography

Books

Antal, Sandy. *A Wampum Denied: Procter's War of 1812*. Ottawa: Carleton University Press, 1997.

Atkins, Kenneth S. "Le Griffon: A New View." *Inland Seas* 46, no. 3 (1990): 162–169.

Baird, David. *Northern Lights: Lighthouses of Canada*. Toronto: Lynx Images, 1999.

Barcus, Frank. *Freshwater Fury: Yarns and Reminiscences of the Greatest Storm in Inland Navigation*. Detroit: Wayne State University Press, 1960.

Barrett, Harry B. *Lore & Legends of Long Point*. Don Mills, Ont.: Burns & MacEachern, 1977.

Bourrie, Mark. *Many a Midnight Ship: True Stories of Great Lakes Shipwrecks.* Toronto: Key Porter Books, 2005.

Bourrie, Mark. *True Canadian Stories of the Great Lakes.* Toronto: Key Porter Books, 2004.

Bowen, Dana Thomas. *Lore of the Lakes.* Cleveland: Freshwater Press, 1940.

Bown, Stephen R. *Scurvy: How a Surgeon, a Mariner, and a Gentleman Solved the Greatest Medical Mystery of the Age of Sail.* Toronto: Thomas Allen Publishers, 2003.

Boyer, Dwight. *Ships and Men of the Great Lakes.* New York: Dodd, Mead & Company, 1977.

Boyer, Dwight. *True Tales of the Great Lakes.* New York: Dodd, Mead & Company, 1971.

Burns, Noel M. *Erie: The Lake that Survived.* Totowa, NJ: Rowman & Allanheld Publishers, 1985.

Butts, Edward. *Outlaws of the Lakes: Bootlegging & Smuggling from Colonial Times to Prohibition.* Toronto: Lynx Images, 2004.

Calnan, Joe. "Moise Hillaret: The First Shipwright on the Great Lakes." *Inland Seas* 58, no. 3 (2002): 190–207.

Calvert, R. *The Story of Abigail Becker, the heroine of Long Point as told by her step-daughter, Mrs. Henry Wheeler.* Toronto: William Briggs, 1899.

Campeau, Lucien. "The Discovery of Lake Erie." *Inland Seas* 31, no. 2 (1975): 238–252.

Campeau, Lucien. "The Discovery of Lake Erie." *Inland Seas* 31, no. 2 (1975): 238–252.

Chesnel, Paul. *History of the Cavelier de la Salle.* Translated by Andrée Chesnel Meany. New York: G.P. Putnam's Sons, 1932.

Dale, Ronald J. *The Fall of New France: How the French Lost a North American Empire.* Toronto: James Lorimer & Company, 2004.

Dale, Ronald J. *The Invasion of Canada.* Toronto: James Lorimer & Company, 2001.

De Casson Dollier, François, and René De Bréhant de Galinée. *Exploration of the Great Lakes 1669–1670: Galinee's Narrative and Map.* Translated and edited by James H. Coyne. Toronto: Ontario Historical Society, 1903.

Delafield, Joseph. *The Unfortified Boundary: A Diary of the First Survey of the Canadian Boundary Line from St. Regis to Lake of the Woods.* Edited by Robert McElroy and Thomas Riggs. New York: n.p., 1943.

Dickson, Kenneth R. "The Amazing Life History of a Small Island." *Inland Seas* 49, no. 2 (1993): 88–92.

Dobbins, W.W. *History of the Battle of Lake Erie (September 10, 1813) and the Reminiscences of the Flagship "Lawrence."* Erie, Penn., 1875.

Donahue, James L. *Terrifying Steamboat Stories: True Tales of Shipwreck, Death, and Disaster on the Great Lakes.* Michigan: Thunder Bay Press, 1997.

Douglas, Henry Kyd. *I Rode With Stonewall.* 1949. Reprint, Marietta, Ga: Mockingbird Books, 1979.

Dowling, Rev. Edward J. "The Story of the Whaleback Vessels and of Their Inventor, Alexander McDougall." *Inland Seas* 13, no. 3 (1957): 172–183.

Dunphy, W.P. "Whalebacks." *Mariner's Mirror* 65, no. 4 (1979): 351–355.

Ermatinger, Charles Oakes. *The Talbot Regime or the First Half Century of the Talbot Settlement.* St. Thomas, Ont.: Municipal World, 1904.

Ferris, Theodore N. "The *Griffon* Tercentenary." *Inland Seas* 35, no. 3 (1979): 192–195.

FitzGibbon, Mike. "Captain Alexander McDougall." *Inland Seas* 49, no. 3 (1993): 161–183.

Fleming, Roy F. "Abigail Becker, Heroine of Long Point, Lake Erie." *Inland Seas* 2, no. 4 (1946): 219–223.

Foster, Sir George Eulas. *The Canada Temperance Manual and Prohibitionist's Handbook.* Toronto: The Ontario Branch of the Alliance for the Total Suppression of the Liquor Traffic, 1881.

Francis, David W. "Johnson's Island: A History of the Resort Era." *Inland Seas* 33, no. 3 (1980): 156–164.

Frohman, Charles E. *Rebels on Lake Erie.* Columbus: The Ohio Historical Society, 1965.

Frohman, Charles E. *Sandusky's Yesterdays.* Columbus: The Ohio Historical Society, 1968.

Gaither, Frances. *Fatal River: The Life and Death of La Salle.* New York: Henry Holt and Company, 1931.

Gardiner, Robert, ed. *The Naval War of 1812.* Annapolis, Md: Naval Institute Press, 1998.

Garno, Noah. *The Story of Pelee.* n.p., ca. 1954.

Geographic Board of Canada. *Handbook of Indians of Canada: Published as an Appendix to the Tenth Report of the Geographic Board of Canada.* 1913. Facsimile reprint, Toronto: Coles Publishing Company, 1971.

Gervais, C.H. *The Rumrunners: A Prohibition Primer.* Scarborough, Ont.: Firefly Books, 1984.

Gora, Michael, ed. *Lake Erie Islands: Sketches and Stories of the First Century After the Battle of Lake Erie.* Victoria, B.C.: Trafford Publishing, 2004.

Graham, J. Robertson. *Where Canada Begins: A Visitor's Guide to Point Pelee National Park.* n.p., n.d.

Graves, Donald E. *Guns Across the River: The Battle of the Windmill, 1838.* Prescott, Ont.: The Friends of Windmill Point, 2001.

Guillet, Edwin C. *The Lives and Times of the Patriots.* 2nd ed. Toronto: University of Toronto Press, 1968.

Gutsche, Andrea and Cindy Bisaillon. *Mysterious Islands: Forgotten Tales of the Great Lakes.* Toronto: Lynx Images, 1999.

Hallowell, Gerald A. *Prohibition in Ontario, 1919–1923.* Ottawa: Ontario Historical Society, 1972.

Harrison, Tim, and Ray Jones. *Endangered Lighthouses.* Guilford, Ct: Globe Pequot Press, 2001.

Harrison, Tim, and Ray Jones. *Lost Lighthouses: Stories and Images of America's Vanished Lighthouses.* Guilford, Ct: Globe Pequot Press, 2000.

Hatcher, Harlan. *Lake Erie.* New York: The Bobbs-Merrill Company, 1945.

Havighurst, Walter. *The Long Ships Passing.* New York: The Macmillan Company, 1942.

Hazen, Sharon, ed. *Down by the Bay: A History of Long Point and Port Rowan 1799–1999.* Erin, Ont.: Boston Mills Press, 2000.

Hennepin, Louis. *A new discovery of a vast country in America.* 1698. Reprint (Introduction, notes and index by Reuben Gold Thwaites), Toronto: Coles Publishing Company, ca. 1974.

Hitsman, J. Mackay. *The Incredible War of 1812: A Military History.* Toronto: University of Toronto Press, 1965. Reprint (updated by Donald E. Graves with foreword by Sir Christopher Prevost), Toronto: Robin Brass Studio, 2004.

Holland, F. Ross. *America's Lighthouses.* Brattleboro, Vt: Greene Press, 1972.

Hooper, Marion McCormick. *Pelee Island, Then and Now.* [Ontario?], ca. 1967.

Hoxie, Frederick E., ed. *Encyclopedia of North American Indians.* New York: Houghton Mifflin Company, 1996.

Hunt, C.W. *Booze, Boats and Billions: Smuggling Liquid Gold!* Toronto: McClelland and Stewart, 1988.

Inkster, Tom H. "McDougall's Whalebacks." *American Neptune* 25, no. 3 (1965): 168–175.

Irving, Lukin Homfray. *Officers of the British Forces in Canada during the War of 1812.* Welland, Ont.: Welland Tribune Print, 1908.

Jackson, Matt. "Dangerous Waters." *The Beaver* 84, no. 3 (June/July 2004): 36–39.

Jones, Ray. *The Lighthouse Encyclopedia: The Complete Reference.* Guilford, Ct: *Lighthouse Digest* and the American Lighthouse Foundation, 2004.

Joutel, Henri. *A Journal of the Last Voyage Perform'd by Monsr. de la Sale, to the Gulph of Mexico, to Find Out the Mouth of the Missisipi River.* London, 1714. Online facsimile edition at www.americanjourneys. org/aj-121/ (accessed November 15, 2006).

Jury, Elsie McLeod. *The Neutral Indians of South-Western Ontario.* London, Ont.: The Museum of Indian Archaeology, The University of Western Ontario, 1974.

Killen, William. *The 1864 Prison Diary of Lt. William E. Killen, 45th Georgia Infantry.* [Ohio?], n.d.

Kyvig, David E. *Repealing National Prohibition.* Chicago: University of Chicago Press, 1979.

La Salle, Robert Cavelier de. *Relation of the Discoveries and Voyages of Cavelier de La Salle from 1679 to 1681: The Official Narrative.* Translated by Melville B. Anderson. Chicago: The Caxton Club, 1901. Online facsimile edition at www.americanjourneys.org/aj-122/ (accessed October 24, 2006).

Lesstrang, Jacques. *Lake Carriers: The Saga of the Great Lakes Fleet: North America's Fresh Water Merchant Marine.* Salisbury, Wa: Salisbury Press, 1977.

Ligibel, Ted, and Richard Wright. *Island Heritage: A Guided Tour to Lake Erie's Bass Islands.* Columbus: Ohio State University Press, 1987.

Lindsey, Charles. *The Life and Times of William Lyon Mackenzie.* Toronto: P.R. Randall, 1862.

Long, Roger. "Johnson's Island Prison." *Blue & Gray Magazine* (March 1987): 6–31.

Lossing, Benson John. *The Pictorial Field-Book of the War of 1812.* New York: Harper, 1869. Reprint, Glendale, NY: Benchmark Publishing, 1970.

Lowe, Eileen. *Notes from the North Shore: Excerpts from the Personal Journals of Eileen Lowe.* Transcribed by Barra Gotts. n.p., n.d.

Lucas, Daniel Bedinger. *Memoir of John Yates Beall: his life; trial; correspondence; diary and private manuscript found among his papers, including his own account of the raid on Lake Erie.* Montreal: John Lovell, 1865.

Maitland, John. "Report of the Battle of Pellee Island." Amherstburg: March, 1838.

Malcolmson, Robert, and Thomas Malcolmson. *HMS Detroit: The Battle for Lake Erie.* St. Catherines, Ont.: Vanwell Publishing, 1990.

Malcolmson, Robert. *Warships of the Great Lakes.* Great Britain: Chatham Publishing, 2001.

Marsh, Robert. *Seven Years of My Life or A Narrative of Patriot Exile.* Buffalo: Faxon & Stevens, 1848.

Marshall, O.H. "The Building and Voyage of the Griffon in 1679." Paper read before the Buffalo Historical Society, February 3, 1863, and revised by the author in 1879. Reprint, Ottawa: Canadian Institute for Historical Microreproductions, 1987.

Martin, J.P. "The Patriot Invasion of Pelee Island." *Ontario History* 56, no. 3 (September 1964): 153–165.

Martin, Jessie A. *The Beginnings and Tales of the Lake Erie Islands.* [Ohio?], 1990.

Mayers, Adam. *Dixie & the Dominion: Canada, the Confederacy, and the War for the Union.* Toronto: The Dundurn Group, 2003.

McCormick, William S., ed. *The William McCormick Papers: 1784–1840.* Produced for private distribution by William S. McCormick. Detroit: 1947.

McCullough, A.B. *The Commercial Fishery of the Canadian Great Lakes.* Ottawa: Ministry of the Environment, 1989.

McDougall, Alexander. "The Autobiography of Captain Alexander McDougall." *Inland Seas* 23, no. 2 (1967): 91–103.

McDougall, Alexander. "The Autobiography of Captain Alexander McDougall." *Inland Seas* 23, no. 3 (1967): 199–216.

McDougall, Alexander. "The Autobiography of Captain Alexander McDougall." *Inland Seas* 23, no. 4 (1967): 282–301.

McDougall, Alexander. "The Autobiography of Captain Alexander McDougall." *Inland Seas* 24, no. 1 (1968): 16–33.

McDougall, Alexander. "The Autobiography of Captain Alexander McDougall." *Inland Seas* 24, no. 2 (1968): 138–147

McNeilledge, Alexander. *Sailing Directions and Remarks Accompanied with a Nautical Chart of the North Shore of Lake Erie.* Buffalo: Steam Press of Jewett, Thomas & Co., 1848.

Miller, Al. "McDougall's White Swan: The First Voyages of the *Christopher Columbus*." *Inland Seas* 49, no. 3 (1993): 180–184.

Mills, Norman E. *A History of Kelleys Island, Ohio.* 1925. Reprint, Kelleys Island Historical Society, 1982.

Milner, Bruce. *Lakelore: A History of the Fishing Industry Along the North Shore of Lake Erie.* Simcoe, Ont.: Norfolk School of Agriculture, 1973.

Muhlstein, Anka. *La Salle: Explorer of the North American Frontier.* New York: Arcade Publishing, 1994.

Murphy, Patrick. "The Loss of Lightship *No. 82.*" *Inland Seas* 31, no. 1 (1975): 28–33.

Mutrie, R. Robert. *The Long Point Settlers.* Ridgeway, Ont.: Log Cabin Publishing, 1992.

Nation, Carry A. *The Use and the Need of the Life of Carry A. Nation.* Topeka, Ks: F.M. Steves and Sons, 1905. Online facsimile edition at http://etext.virginia.edu (accessed August 19, 2007).

Neidecker, John F. "Robert E. Lee Visits the Great Lakes Country." *Inland Seas* 30, no. 2 (1974): 125–127.

Niedecker, Betty. *The Marblehead Lighthouse: Lake Erie's Eternal Flame.* n.p., 1995.

"Notable Rescues on Lake Vessels." *Marine Review* (January 1910): 29–32.

Ontario Historical Society. *1837 Rebellion Remembered: Papers Presented at the 1837 Rebellion Remembered Conference of The Ontario Historical Society at Black Creek Pioneer Village, 28 September to 3 October, 1987.* Meaford, Ont.: The Ontario Historical Society, 1988.

Orford, McLeod. "Early Exploration of Lake Erie and Lake Huron." *Inland Seas* 24, no. 4 (1968): 267–278.

Owen, Egbert Americus. *Pioneer Sketches of Long Point Settlement.* 1898. Reprint (new introduction by Edward Phelps), Belleville, Ont.: Mika Silk Screening, 1972.

Parkman, Francis. *La Salle and the Discovery of the Great West.* 1897. Reprint, Williamstown, Mass: Corner House Publishers, 1968.

Parsons, Usher. "Brief Sketches of the Officers who were in the Battle of Lake Erie." *New England Historical and Genealogical Register* (January 1863).

Parsons, Usher. *Battle of Lake Erie: A discourse delivered before the Rhode Island Historical Society on the evening of Monday, February 16, 1852.* Providence: B.T. Albro, 1854.

Patenaude, J.O. *The Lake Erie Cross, Port Dover, Ontario.* Ottawa: Canadian National Parks Historic Sites Division, 1934.

Patterson, Edmund DeWitt. *The Civil War Journal of Edmund DeWitt Patterson.* Chapel Hill: University of North Carolina Press, 1966.

Payne, Michael. *The Fur Trade in Canada: An Illustrated History.* Toronto: James Lorimer & Company, 2004.

Perry, Oliver Hazard. *Documents in relation to the differences between the late Commodore O.H. Perry and Captain J.D. Elliott.* Washington, 1821.

Porter, Peter A. *How Lake Commerce Began: La Salle's Visits to the Niagara.* Niagara Falls, NY, 1914.

Prothero, Frank, and Nancy Prothero. *Tales from the North Shore.* Port Stanley, Ont.: Nan-Sea Publications, 1987.

Ratigan, William. *Great Lakes Shipwrecks & Survivals.* Grand Rapids, Mi: Eerdmans, 1977.

Rauh, Lou. "Heroes of the *Clarion,* the *Monroe* and the *Hanna.*" *Inland Seas* 54, no. 4 (1998): 254–256.

Roosevelt, Theodore. *The Naval War of 1812.* Annapolis, Md: Naval Institute Press, 1987.

Rose-Holden, Mary E. *The Neutral Nations: The Eries.* n.p., ca. 1900.

Ryall, Lydia. *Sketches and Stories of the Lake Erie Islands*. Norwalk, Oh: The American Publishers Company, 1913.

Schmitt, Paul J. "The Great Storm of 1913 Remembered." *Inland Seas* 44, no. 4 (1988): 154–169.

Sewell, John. *Mackenzie: A Political Biography of William Lyon Mackenzie*. Toronto: James Lorimer & Company, 2002.

Skaggs, David Curtis. *A Signal Victory: The Lake Erie Campaign*, 1812–1813. Annapolis, Md: Naval Institute Press, 1997.

Smith, Thaddeus. *Point au Pelee Island: An Historical Sketch of and an Account of the McCormick Family, who were the First White Owners of the Island*. 1899. Reprint, Pelee Island: Pelee Island Heritage Centre, 1993.

Sobol, Julie Macfie, and Ken Sobol. *Lake Erie: A Pictorial History*. Erin, Ont.: Boston Mills Press, 2004.

Steinke, Gord. *Mobsters & Rumrunners of Canada: Crossing the Line*. Edmonton: Folklore Publishing, 2003.

Stone, Dave. *Long Point: Last Port of Call*. Erin, Ont.: Boston Mills Press, 1988.

Strobridge, Truman R. "Early Coast Guard Lightships on the Great Lakes." *Inland Seas* 29, no. 1 (1973): 16–26.

Tennyson, Brian Douglas. "Sir William Hearst and the Ontario Temperance Act." *Ontario History* 55 no. 4 (1963): 233–245.

Terrell, John Upton. *La Salle: The Life and Times of an Explorer*. New York: Weybright and Talley, 1968.

Theller, E.A. *Canada in 1837–38, showing, by historical facts, the causes of the late attempted revolution and of its failure; the present condition of the people, and their future prospects, together with the personal adventures of the author, and others who were connected with the revolution*. New York: J & H.G. Langley, 1841.

Thomas, Emory M. *Robert E. Lee: A Biography*. London: W.W. Norton & Company, 1997.

Thomas, Thomas J. "On the Shoals." *World Wide Magazine* (April, 1911). Online edition at http://www.hhpl.on.ca/GreatLakes/Wrecks/details.asp?ID=18815 (accessed March, 2007).

Thompson, David. "David Thompson's Journal of the International Boundary Survey 1817–1827 Western Lake Erie." Edited by Clarke E. Leverette. *Inland Seas* 44, no. 3 (1988): 32–45.

Thwaites, Reuben Gold. *The Jesuit relations and allied documents travels and explorations of the Jesuit missionaries in New France, 1610–1791: the original French, Latin, and Italian texts, with translations and notes*. Cleveland, Burrows, 1899. Online facsimile edition at http://www.collectionscanada.ca/jesuit-relations (accessed October 29, 2007).

Tiessen, Ronald, and Irena Knezevic. *A Brief History of the Pelee Island Lighthouse*. Pelee Island: Pelee Island Heritage Centre, 1999.

Tiessen, Ronald. *A Bicycle Guide to Pelee Island*. 2nd ed. Pelee Island: Pelee Island Heritage Centre, 1992.

Tiessen, Ronald. *The Vinedressers: A History of Grape Farming & Wineries on Pelee Island*. Pelee Island: Pelee Island Heritage Centre, 1996.

Tonty, Henri de. *Relation of Henri de Tonty Concerning the Explorations of La Salle from 1678 to 1683*. Translated by Melville B. Anderson. Original French reprinted from Pierre Margry's "Origines Françaises des pays d'Outre-Mer" (Paris, 1879). Chicago: The Claxton Club, 1898.

Townsend, Robert B. *Captain John Williams: Master Mariner*. Carrying Place, Ont.: Odyssey Publishing, 2002.

Warner, Oliver. *Uncle Lawrence*. London: Chatto & Windus, 1939.

Warnes, Kathleen. "Confederate Prisoners of War on Lake Erie." *Inland Seas* 52, no. 4 (1996): 302–310.

Warnes, Kathleen. "Rumrunning on the Detroit River." *Inland Seas* 53, no. 3 (1997): 170–177.

Warnes, Kathy. "Elizabeth Turner McCormick Woman Voyageur." *Inland Seas* 55, no. 3 (1999): 187–191.

Weaver, Bruce. "Forgotten Shipwreck, Recovered Memory." *Budstikken* 36, no. 1 (May 2006): 5–7.

Weisenburger, Francis Phelps. "Lake Erie: The Ohio Shore a Century Ago." *Inland Seas* 55, no. 4 (1999): 266–269.

Wilds of Pelee Island. *Pelee Island: Human and Natural History; Guide to a Unique Island Community.* Pelee Island: Wilds of Pelee Island, 2003.

Winks, Robin W. *Canada and the United States: The Civil War Years.* Montreal: Harvest House, 1971.

Wolcott, Merlin D. "Marblehead Lifesaving Station." *Inland Seas* 22, no. 4 (1966): 295–300.

Wolcott, Merlin D. "Marblehead Lighthouse Supplement." *Inland Seas* 37, no. 2 (1981): 84–89.

Wolcott, Merlin D. "Marblehead Lighthouse." *Inland Seas* 10, no. 4 (1954): 274–277.

Wood, William, ed. *Select British Documents of the Canadian War of 1812.* Toronto: Champlain Society, 1920.

Wright, Patricia and Larry Wright. *Bonfires & Beacons: Great Lakes Lighthouses.* Erin, Ont.: Boston Mills Press, 1996.

Newspapers

American
Buffalo Daily Courier, Buffalo, New York
Buffalo Daily Republic, Buffalo, New York
Cleveland Herald, Cleveland, Ohio
The Cleveland Leader, Cleveland, Ohio
Detroit Free Press, Detroit, Michigan
Marine Record, Cleveland, Ohio
News Herald, Port Clinton, Ohio
New York Times, New York, New York
Sandusky Register, Sandusky, Ohio
Toledo Blade, Toledo, Ohio

Canadian
The Border Cities Star (presently the *Windsor Star*)
The British Canadian, Simcoe, Ontario
The British Colonist, Toronto, Ontario
Evening Record, Windsor, Ontario (presently the *Windsor Star*)
Kitchener-Waterloo Record, Kitchener, Ontario
The Review, Niagara Falls, Ontario
Simcoe Reformer, Simcoe, Ontario
The Globe, Toronto, Ontario (presently *The Globe and Mail*)
Toronto Patriot, Toronto, Ontario
Toronto Star, Toronto, Ontario
Windsor Star, Windsor, Ontario